Lab Manual for
CompTIA® Network+
Guide to Networks,
Seventh Edition

Todd Verge

CENGAGE
Learning®

Australia • Brazil • Mexico • Singapore • United Kingdom • United States

CENGAGE
Learning®

**Lab Manual for CompTIA® Network+
Guide to Networks, Seventh Edition**
Todd Verge

SVP, GM Skills & Global Product
Management: Dawn Gerrain

Product Director: Kathleen McMahon

Product Team Manager: Kristin McNary

Senior Director, Development:
Marah Bellegarde

Product Development Manager:
Leigh Hefferon

Senior Content Developer:
Michelle Ruelos Cannistraci

Product Assistant: Abigail Pufpaff

Vice President, Marketing Services:
Jennifer Ann Baker

Senior Marketing Manager: Eric LaScola

Senior Production Director: Wendy Troeger

Production Director: Patty Stephan

Senior Content Project Manager:
Brooke Greenhouse

Senior Art Director: Jack Pendleton

Cover image(s): © vovan/Shutterstock.com

> For product information and technology assistance, contact us at
> **Cengage Learning Customer & Sales Support, 1-800-354-9706**
> For permission to use material from this text or product,
> submit all requests online at **www.cengage.com/permissions.**
> Further permissions questions can be e-mailed to
> **permissionrequest@cengage.com**

Library of Congress Control Number: 2015936128

ISBN: 978-1-305-09309-6

Cengage Learning
20 Channel Center Street
Boston, MA 02210
USA

Cengage Learning is a leading provider of customized learning solutions
with employees residing in nearly 40 different countries and sales in more
than 125 countries around the world. Find your local representative at
www.cengage.com.

Cengage Learning products are represented in Canada by
Nelson Education, Ltd.

To learn more about Cengage Learning, visit **www.cengage.com**

Purchase any of our products at your local college store or at our preferred
online store **www.cengagebrain.com**

Notice to the Reader

Publisher does not warrant or guarantee any of the products described herein or perform any independent analysis in connection with any of
the product information contained herein. Publisher does not assume, and expressly disclaims, any obligation to obtain and include information
other than that provided to it by the manufacturer. The reader is expressly warned to consider and adopt all safety precautions that might
be indicated by the activities described herein and to avoid all potential hazards. By following the instructions contained herein, the reader
willingly assumes all risks in connection with such instructions. The publisher makes no representations or warranties of any kind, including
but not limited to, the warranties of fitness for particular purpose or merchantability, nor are any such representations implied with respect to
the material set forth herein, and the publisher takes no responsibility with respect to such material. The publisher shall not be liable for any
special, consequential, or exemplary damages resulting, in whole or part, from the readers' use of, or reliance upon, this material.

Printed in the United States of America
Print Number: 01   Print Year: 2015

TABLE OF CONTENTS

PREFACE

Hands-on learning is the best way to master the networking skills necessary for both CompTIA's Network+ exam and a networking career. This book contains over 70 hands-on exercises that apply fundamental networking concepts as they would be applied in the real world. Many labs can be completed from home using a single computer with an Internet connection. In addition, each lab includes multiple review questions to reinforce your mastery of networking topics covered in this lab manual as well as the core book, *CompTIA Network+ Guide to Networks, Seventh Edition*.

This book follows the same organization as Cengage Learning's *CompTIA Network+ Guide to Networks, Seventh Edition*. Using the two together will provide an effective learning experience. This book is suitable for a beginning or intermediate networking course. As a prerequisite, students should have at least six months of computer experience and should be familiar with some basic networking components, such as NICs and patch cables. Passing CompTIA's A+ certification exam would suffice in lieu of this experience.

FEATURES

To ensure a successful experience for instructors and students alike, this book includes the following features:

- **Network+ Certification Objectives**—Each chapter lists the relevant objectives from CompTIA's Network+ N10-006 exam.

- **Lab Objectives**—Every lab has a brief description and list of learning objectives.

- **Materials Required**—Every lab includes information on network access privileges, hardware, software, and other materials you will need to complete the lab.

- **Virtual Labs**—Labs that can be completed at home with a single computer using virtualization software are highlighted with a Virtual Lab icon.

- **Completion Times**—Every lab has an estimated completion time, so that you can plan your activities more accurately.

- **Step-by-Step Instructions**—Logical and precise step-by-step instructions guide you through the hands-on activities in each lab.

- **Review Questions**—Questions help reinforce concepts presented in the lab and in the core book, *CompTIA Network+ Guide to Networks, Seventh Edition*.

Note for instructors: Answers to review questions are available on the Instructor Companion Site at http://login.cengage.com.

New to This Edition

- All labs updated to Windows 8.1 and Server 2012 R2, with additional steps for Windows 7
- New and expanded labs on topics such as:
  - Client and server virtualization
  - Network troubleshooting
  - Windows Firewall
  - Network baselines and inventory
  - Router configuration
- Updated to the newest versions of equipment and software
- Suggestions for online and distance students
- Updated for CompTIA's new Network+ N10-006 certification
  - Updated mapping to exam objectives
  - Updated practice questions

Hardware Requirements

The following is a list of hardware required to complete all the labs in the book. The hardware requirements for many of the individual labs are less extensive, and in the cases where you do not meet the requirements, alternative activities are often possible.

Note that most of the labs can be performed on a single physical computer using virtualization software such as VMware or VirtualBox. Multiple virtual operating systems can be run at the same time and can communicate with each other through a virtual network. The installation of virtualization software is covered both in the textbook and in Lab 1.2.

The minimum requirements for a single virtual host are as follows:

- Pentium or compatible processor running at 2 GHz or higher running Windows 8.1 or Windows 7
- 1 GB of RAM minimum (2 GB Recommended)
- At least 40 GB of available storage
- A CD or DVD-ROM drive
- Internet Access (cable, DSL, or faster preferred)

If you choose to install each operating system on a separate physical machine, the other computers have the same minimum requirements. In addition, each computer must have compatible hardware with the operating system being installed.

- Hardware compatibility with Windows 8.1, Windows 7, and Server 2012 R2 can be found at *www.microsoft.com/whdc/hcl/default.mspx*

Other hardware required for various labs include the following:

- One wireless router that can function as a DHCP server and a compatible wireless NIC
- A second PCI or USB Ethernet network interface card
- Category 5 (or better) UTP cabling for making cables
- At least six straight-through Category 5 (or better) UTP patch cables
- At least three crossover Category 5 (or better) UTP patch cables
- RJ-45 connectors
- A computer professional's toolkit that includes a Phillips screwdriver, a ground strap, and a ground mat
- A networking professional's kit that includes a cable tester, crimper, wire stripper, and a wire cutting tool
- One network printer
- Four 100Base-T (or better) Ethernet switches
- Two switches with fiber uplink ports and a compatible fiber cable
- Two modems and a dial-up Internet account
- Access to two analog outside phone lines (or two digital lines and two digital-to-analog converters)

SOFTWARE/SETUP REQUIREMENTS

The following is a list of software required to complete all the labs in the book:

- At least two copies of Windows Server 2012 R2
- At least two copies of Windows 8.1 or Windows 7
- At least one copy of a current Linux distribution such as Fedora Linux or Ubuntu (note that a single copy can be used for all installations)

Note: Many of the labs written for Server 2012 R2 can also be done in Server 2008 or Windows 7 with only minor changes.

NOTES ON THE LABS

The following is a list of tips that will assist readers working through the labs:

- Unless otherwise stated, at the beginning of each lab it is assumed that the student has turned on each computer but has not yet logged on.
- On Windows computers, Control Panel should be set to Category View, which is the default; the default Start menu should also be used.

- Windows firewall may interfere with several of the labs. To disable the firewall, click the **Start** button, click **Control Panel**, click **System and Security**, click **Windows Firewall**, click **Turn Windows Firewall on or off**, select the **Turn off Windows Firewall** radio button, and click **OK**.

- Although these labs were designed using Fedora, most popular distributions are quite similar at the command line and could easily be substituted.

- It's a good idea to save all of your work. However you should take special care to save following labs, because they are used throughout the lab manual:
  - Lab 1.2 Installing a Virtual Client Image
  - Lab 1.3 Building a Simple Peer-to-Peer Network
  - Lab 1.4 Building a Simple Client-Server Network
  - Lab 2.6 Using FTP
  - Lab 3.5 Using the Traceroute Utility to Troubleshoot a TCP/IP Network
  - Lab 4.4 Creating a Multi-Homed Computer by Installing Two NICs
  - Lab 6.3 Installing a Wireless Router
  - Lab 8.1 Auditing

DISTANCE LEARNING STUDENTS

Some students may not have access to all of the suggested equipment. In most cases, some simple equipment substitutions can be made, although the reader may need to consult the Internet to find the correct steps. In any event, students will still find it useful to read through all of the labs. The following is a list of tips for students who are attempting a lab without all of the required resources:

- For labs requiring Server 2012 R2, Server 2012 can be substituted with only minor differences. In some cases, it's possible to substitute Server 2012 R2 with Windows 8.1 or Windows 7.

- Readers with only one computer can attempt many of the labs by installing multiple operating systems in a virtual environment such as VMware, Virtual Box, or Virtual PC. Details of these programs can easily be found on the Internet and have been covered both in this lab manual and in the core book, *CompTIA Network+ Guide to Networks, Seventh Edition*.

- In labs where the ping or tracert utility is used to test a network connection, an ISP's home router can be substituted for a second computer on the network.

ABOUT THE AUTHOR

Todd Verge has worked as a technologist and teacher for over 20 years and is the author of several Cengage Learning titles on information technology and mathematics. He graduated with a Bachelor of Science in Physics from Dalhousie University, a Masters Degree in Philosophy from Carleton University, and a Diploma in Adult Education from the Nova Scotia Community College.

ACKNOWLEDGMENTS

Thank you to the many helpful people on the Cengage Learning staff who made the seventh edition a reality. My sincere appreciation goes out to: Kristin McNary, Product Team Manager; Michelle Ruelos Cannistraci, Senior Content Developer; Brooke Baker, Senior Content Product Manager. Thanks also to Ann Shaffer, Developmental Editor at Shaffer Technical Editing, LLC, for her guidance and encouragement throughout the editorial process. For their amazing attention to detail, I am grateful to our Technical Editors for Manuscript Quality Assurance: Serge Palladino and Nicole Spoto. Many warm thanks to Aravinda Kulasekar Doss of Lumina Datamatics, who oversaw the production process, and to our very helpful copy editor, Karen Annett. A huge thank you goes to the following instructors, who faithfully reviewed every chapter and made numerous helpful suggestions and corrections: Jane Perschbach, Central Texas College; Gregg Tennefoss, Tidewater Community College; and Richard Smolenski, Westwood College.

Screenshots of software programs and operating systems included in the text are courtesy of the following companies: Microsoft, Fedora Linux, Ubuntu Linux, Wireshark, PuTTY, and VMware.

Finally, I'd like to thank my friends and colleagues at the Nova Scotia Community College for inspiring me with their love of learning.

INTRODUCTION TO NETWORKING

Labs included in this chapter

- Lab 1.1 Understanding Elements of a Network
- Lab 1.2 Installing a Virtual Client Image
- Lab 1.3 Building a Simple Peer-to-Peer Network
- Lab 1.4 Building a Simple Client-Server Network
- Lab 1.5 Troubleshooting Client Logon Problems
- Lab 1.6 Sharing a Network Printer

CompTIA Network+ Exam Objectives

Objective	Lab
1.1 Explain the functions and applications of various network devices	1.1
1.4 Explain the characteristics and benefits of various WAN technologies	1.1
1.6 Differentiate between common network topologies	1.1, 1.3, 1.4, 1.5
1.11 Compare and contrast technologies that support cloud and virtualization	1.2
1.12 Given a set of requirements, implement a basic network	1.3, 1.4, 1.6
3.2 Compare and contrast common network vulnerabilities and threats	1.1
4.1 Given a scenario, implement the following network troubleshooting methodology	1.5

Lab 1.1 Understanding Elements of a Network

Objectives

When first learning about network components, it is often helpful to observe a live network and talk with experienced networking professionals. The concept of segments, connectivity devices, or structured wiring techniques, for example, can be more easily demonstrated on a real network than in a textbook. The goal of this lab is to explore some real-life examples of basic networking concepts. To complete this lab, you will be required to tour your school's computer laboratory or a local business and identify various networking components at that site.

After completing this lab, you will be able to:

- Identify and sketch an organization's network topology
- Identify the nodes on a real-life network
- Identify a network's client and network operating systems
- Identify protocols used by a network

Materials Required

This lab will require the following:

- A network professional or instructor willing to give you a tour of your school's computer laboratory or data center, or a network professional willing to give you a tour of a network at a business or other site
- Pencil and paper
- Access to software that can be used for creating network diagrams such as Microsoft Visio (optional)

> Estimated completion time: **1–3 hours**

Activity

1. If you cannot tour your school's computer laboratory or data center, contact a business, school, or other organization and ask to interview the person in charge of the network. Explain that your purpose is purely educational and that you desire to learn more about networking. Also, explain that you will need to take notes. Because revealing information about a network might pose a security risk, some network professionals might be unwilling to share this information. If this is the case, you might need to ask your instructor to create a fictitious or virtual network and play the role of the network administrator. Alternatively, you can view a prerecorded tour on YouTube by searching "Data Center Tour" and choosing one that interests you.

2. Make the visit and, with the guidance of the network administrator, observe the organization's network. Remember to ask for details about the network's transmission media, physical topology, hardware, operating systems, services, and protocols.

3. On a separate piece of paper, draw the site's network topology, using boxes to represent the network components such as computers and printers. Draw lines to connect the

components. The scope of this diagram will depend on the size of the network. If you're working with a small network, you can probably label every computer. If you're viewing a large data center, you may need to group components together in a more abstract diagram. You might also use network-diagramming software such as Microsoft Visio to diagram the network.

4. On your diagram, label the end devices such as servers, workstations, and printers. Also label the intermediate devices used to connect other devices together, such as switches and routers. If you are unsure about a network component, label the box with a "?".

5. Ask your tour guide for specifics about the network operating system (NOS) running on the server(s) as well as the operating system(s) running on the workstations. Record this information.

6. Ask for information on the physical media connecting the network components. Record the details of any wires, connectors, and network interface cards (NICs). Are the workstation NICs integrated or are they removable? Note how many different types of NICs this network uses.

7. Ask your tour guide if any wireless LANs are used on this network. Record information about any wireless devices used.

8. How is software installed on the workstations? Does it need to be installed individually or should a software imaging and distribution product be used?

9. Ask your tour guide what sorts of measures the organization takes to make the network secure. Ask about the possible effects of an intrusion or loss of data. Record this information.

10. Thank your tour guide. If you toured an outside organization's network, follow up later with a letter of thanks.

Certification Objectives

Objectives for the CompTIA Network+ Exam:

- 1.1 Explain the functions and applications of various network devices
- 1.4 Explain the characteristics and benefits of various WAN technologies
- 1.6 Differentiate between common network topologies
- 3.2 Compare and contrast common network vulnerabilities and threats

Review Questions

1. Which of the following best describes a network's physical topology?

   a. The method by which multiple nodes transmit signals over a shared communications channel

   b. The physical layout of a network

   c. The distance spanned by a network's cable and wireless infrastructure

   d. The software used to ensure reliable connections between nodes on a network

2. Which of the following is the most popular type of modern network architecture for business?

   a. Client-server

   b. Terminal/mainframe

   c. Peer-to-peer

   d. Mainframe/dial-up

3. Which of the following elements is *not* required for a client to connect to a server on a client-server LAN?

   a. Protocols

   b. Media

   c. Email account

   d. Client software

4. Which of the following are capable of acting as a network server? (Choose all that apply.)

   a. Windows XP

   b. Windows Server 2012 R2

   c. Windows 7

   d. Linux/UNIX

5. Network protocols are used to do which of the following? (Choose all that apply.)

   a. To ensure reliable delivery of data

   b. To determine the nearest printer for a print job

   c. To interpret keyboard commands

   d. To indicate the source and destination addresses for data packets

6. True or False? On a client-server network, clients may have only one protocol installed at any time.

7. A significant difference between the peer-to-peer and client-server network types is that a peer-to-peer network:

   a. Is more difficult to set up

   b. Does not allow for resource sharing between workstations

   c. Does not usually provide centralized management for shared resources

   d. Is more secure

8. Why is it necessary for each client on a client-server network to have a unique address?

Lab 1.2 Installing a Virtual Client Image

Objectives

Virtualization is a common term in the field of information technology. It refers to the process of using a single physical computer to create multiple software environments. A single machine running virtualization software, for example, can replace many physical servers with corresponding savings in space and costs. Many products are available for virtualizing both servers and desktop workstations.

Many of the labs in this manual can be completed in a virtual environment running on a single computer. The first chapter of the textbook covers setting up a virtual machine using Hyper-V and VirtualBox. In this lab, you will be installing Microsoft Windows 8.1 or Windows 7 in a virtual environment using VMware Workstation 10. You can use the virtual environment of your choice to complete most of the upcoming labs virtually if you only have access to a single computer.

After completing this lab, you will be able to:

- Install a virtual Windows client image in VMware
- Clone a client image to create a second virtual machine

Materials Required

This lab will require the following:

- A computer running Windows 8.1 or Windows 7 with at least 4 GB of RAM
- VMware Workstation 10 installed
- A Windows 8.1 or Windows 7 installation DVD or ISO file
- Appropriate Windows licenses for two installations of Windows

Estimated completion time: **45 minutes**

Activity

1. Log on to your physical machines as an administrator and launch VMware Workstation 10.
2. Click the **Create a New Virtual Machine** icon. The New Virtual Machine Wizard opens.
3. Select **Custom (advanced)** and click **Next**.
4. Click **Next** to accept the default hardware compatibility.
5. Select the location of your Windows installation CD or ISO file and click **Next**.
6. Enter the Windows product key and change the Full name to **WORKSTATION1**.

7. Enter a password, record it so you don't forget it later, and click **Next**.

8. Change the Virtual machine name to Workstation1.

9. Record the location of the virtual machine and click **Next**.

10. Accept the default Processor Configuration unless your instructor suggests otherwise, and then click **Next**.

11. If your physical machine has 8 GB of RAM or more, allocate 2 GB of RAM to the virtual machine. Otherwise, set the memory for the virtual machine to 1 GB. Click **Next**.

12. Accept Network Address Translation as the network type and click **Next**.

13. Continue to click **Next** to accept the default selections for I/O controller types, disk type, and disk selection.

14. Accept the default maximum disk size and click **Next**.

15. Click **Next** again to use the default disk filename.

16. Review your virtual machine selections and click **Finish**. VMware Workstation will take a few minutes to create the virtual machine, power it on, and begin installing Windows.

17. Windows Setup will handle most of the installation process and may restart the virtual machine several times.

18. Once the virtual machine is running, open Internet Explorer to test your Internet connection.

19. Shut down your virtual machine. VMware Workstation shows the details of the virtual machine, which is now powered off, as shown in Figure 1-1.

20. If you need additional copies of a virtual image, VMware Workstation allows you to clone an existing image rather than reinstalling from a CD or ISO file.

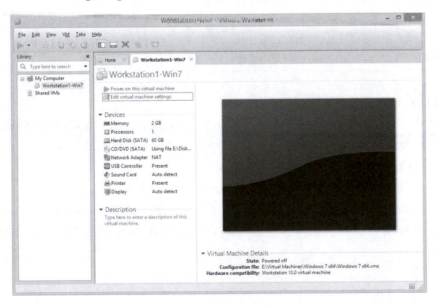

Figure 1-1   VMware Workstation

21. In the pull-down menu, select **VM**, select **Manage**, and then click **Clone**.

22. The Clone Virtual Machine Wizard opens. Click **Next**.

23. Click **Next** again to accept the default choice, cloning from the current state of the original virtual machine.

24. Select **Create a full clone** and click **Next**.

25. Name the new virtual machine **Workstation2** and click **Finish**.

26. After the cloning is complete, change the Full name of the new image to **WORKSTATION2** and click **Close**.

27. VMware Workstation now has a tab for each virtual workstation.

28. Shut down both virtual machines and log off your physical computer.

Certification Objectives

Objectives for the CompTIA Network+ Exam:

- 1.11 Compare and contrast technologies that support cloud and virtualization

Review Questions

1. Which of the following is *not* a network type option for virtual computers in VMware Workstation 10?

   a. Bridged

   b. NAT

   c. Structured

   d. Host-only

2. Which virtual disk types are available in VMware Workstation 10? (Choose all that apply.)

   a. MFM

   b. IDE

   c. SCSI

   d. SATA

3. One disk file is created for every _____ of virtual disk capacity.

   a. 2 MB

   b. 2 GB

   c. 20 MB

   d. 20 GB

4. What is the primary difference between bridged and NAT as a network type?

5. True or False? Three 2-GB virtual machines could all run simultaneously on a physical machine with 4 GB of RAM.

Lab 1.3 Building a Simple Peer-to-Peer Network

Objectives

Peer-to-peer networks are commonly found in offices where only a handful of users have access to networked computers, as they do not scale well and do not provide much security. However, peer-to-peer networks are an excellent choice in a few situations because they are simple and inexpensive to configure. A home office with three to five computers and only a couple of users, for example, would make a good candidate for peer-to-peer networking. Even in client-server networks, users might find it convenient to allow other users to access files on their computers. This is often a security risk, however, as a user might share files without sufficient security or even without security.

The goal of this lab is to become familiar with the methods for establishing a simple peer-to-peer network. During this lab, you will be introduced to the hardware and software required to connect two workstations so that they can share each other's resources.

After completing this lab, you will be able to:

- Build a simple peer-to-peer network

Materials Required

If you are doing this lab physically, you will require the following:

- Administrative access to two computers running Windows 8.1 or Windows 7, with NICs installed
- Neither computer configured as a member of a domain
- Two straight-through Category 5 (or better) UTP cables with RJ-45 connectors and a switch or home router compatible with the Ethernet port or NICs on both computers

Most of the steps in this lab can also be completed in a virtual environment using virtualization software such as VMware.

If you are doing this lab virtually on a single computer, you will require the following:

- A virtualization product such as VMware, Hyper-V, or VirtualBox installed on your PC
- Two virtual images running Windows 8.1 or Windows 7
- Neither image configured as a member of a domain

Estimated completion time: **45 minutes**

Activity

1. If you are doing this lab physically, plug one end of one of the cables into the NIC in one machine and the other end into the switch or home router. Repeat with the second cable and the second computer. A link light on both NICs illuminates, indicating that each NIC has successfully connected.

2. On each machine, if necessary, press **CTRL+ALT+Del**. The Log On to Windows dialog box opens.

3. Log on to both machines as an administrator. The Windows desktop appears.

4. In this activity, the machine you are accessing will be referred to as *WORKSTATION1*, and the other will be referred to as *WORKSTATION2*.

If you are using Windows 8.1, follow these steps:

1. On *WORKSTATION1*, right-click the **Start** button, and then click **Control Panel**.

2. Click **System and Security**, and then click **System**.

3. Click **Change settings**. The System Properties dialog box opens.

4. Click the **Change** button. Type **WORKSTATION1** in the Computer name text box.

5. For Member of section, if necessary, select **Workgroup** and type **NETPLUS** in the Workgroup name text box. Click **OK**.

6. Click **OK,** close any open windows, and restart the computer when prompted.

7. Log on with an administrative account. Right-click the **Start** button, and then click **File Explorer**. The This PC window opens.

8. Right-click the icon for the C: drive, move your mouse pointer over **Share with**, and select **Advanced sharing**. The Properties dialog box opens, with the Sharing tab displayed.

9. Click the **Advanced Sharing** button. The Advanced Sharing dialog box opens.

10. Check the **Share this folder** check box. Type **Shared Drive** in the **Share name** text box.

11. Click **OK**. The Advanced Sharing dialog box closes. Click **Close** to close the Properties dialog box.

12. Repeat Steps 1 through 6 on *WORKSTATION2*, using **WORKSTATION2** as the name of the computer in Step 4.

13. On *WORKSTATION2*, right-click the **Start** button, click **File Explorer,** and click **Network** in the left pane. If prompted, switch on **Network Discovery**. The Network window opens.

14. Double-click the icon for **WORKSTATION1** to open it. If the Connect to WORKSTATION1 dialog box opens, type **Administrator** in the User name text box, type the password for *WORKSTATION1* in the Password text box, and then click **OK**.

15. Right-click the icon for the Shared Drive drive on *WORKSTATION1* and click **Open**. The files on *WORKSTATION1* are listed.

16. Close the shared drive and log off both computers.

If you are using Windows 7, follow these steps:

1. On *WORKSTATION1*, click the **Start** button, and then click **Control Panel**.

2. Click **System and Security** and then click **System**.

3. Click **Change settings**. The System Properties dialog box opens.

4. Click the **Change** button. Type **WORKSTATION1** in the Computer name text box.

5. In the Member of section, if necessary, select **Workgroup** and type **NETPLUS** in the Workgroup name text box. Click **OK**.

6. Click **OK,** close any open windows, and restart the computer when prompted.

7. Log on with an administrative account. Click the **Start** button, and then click **Computer**. The Computer window opens.

8. Right-click the icon for the C: drive, move your mouse pointer over **Share with,** and select **Advanced sharing**. The Properties dialog box opens, with the Sharing tab displayed.

9. Click the **Advanced Sharing** button. The Advanced Sharing dialog box opens, as shown in Figure 1-2.

10. Check the **Share this folder** check box and click **Add**. Enter **Shared Drive** in the Share name text box and click **OK**.

11. Click **OK**. The Advanced Sharing dialog box closes. Click **Close** to close the Properties dialog box.

12. Repeat Steps 1 through 6 on *WORKSTATION2*, using **WORKSTATION2** as the name of the computer in Step 4.

13. On *WORKSTATION2*, click the **Start** button, and then click **Computer**. The Computer window opens.

14. Double-click the icon for **WORKSTATION1** to open it. If the Connect to WORKSTATION1 dialog box opens, type **Administrator** in the User name text box, type the password for *WORKSTATION1* in the Password text box, and then click **OK**.

15. Right-click the icon for the shared drive on *WORKSTATION1* and click **Open**. The files on *WORKSTATION1* are listed.

16. Close the shared drive and log off both computers.

Figure 1-2 Sharing a drive

Certification Objectives

Objectives for the CompTIA Network+ Exam:

- 1.6 Differentiate between common network topologies
- 1.12 Given a set of requirements, implement a basic network

Review Questions

1. What physical topology would you use to create your peer-to-peer network where all the workstations are connected to a single switch?

   a. Bus

   b. Tree

   c. Star

   d. Cube

2. Which of the following operating systems will allow you to create a peer-to-peer network from a group of workstations? (Choose all that apply.)

   a. MS-DOS

   b. Windows 8.1

   c. Linux

   d. Windows 7

3. Which of the following components are *not* necessary to create a peer-to-peer network from a group of workstations? (Choose all that apply.)

   a. Client operating system

   b. NIC or motherboard with onboard NIC

   c. Network media

   d. Web browser

   e. Network operating system

4. What is the primary difference between peer-to-peer and client-server architectures?

5. True or False? On a peer-to-peer network consisting of four Windows 7 or 8.1 workstations, each user can individually control which of her local data files she wants to share with other users.

Lab 1.4 Building a Simple Client-Server Network

Objectives

Client-server networks are found in all but the smallest organizations. Although client-server networks are more difficult to configure than a peer-to-peer network, they are more scalable and can grow larger than peer-to-peer networks can. With more than a handful of computers, a peer-to-peer network quickly becomes unwieldy. In a client-server network, however, you can manage user accounts and network resources such as printers from a single machine. For instance, to change the printer used by all users on a peer-to-peer network, you would need to go to each machine and configure the new printer. Imagine having to do this on 500 machines! In a client-server network, however, you can typically change this setting on the server for all users.

The goal of this lab is to become familiar with the methods for establishing a simple client-server network. During this lab, you will be introduced to the hardware and software required to connect one or more workstations to a server. As part of the setup for this lab, both the server and the workstation need to be configured with an IP address. Computers and other network devices use the IP address to find other computers. You will learn about addressing beginning in Chapter 2.

After completing this lab, you will be able to:

- Build a simple client-server network
- Add a Windows 8.1 or 7 client computer to a Windows Server 2012 R2 domain

Materials Required

This lab will require the following:

- One computer named *SERVER1* running Windows Server 2012 R2, or an equivalent virtual image, with an Ethernet port or NIC, configured with an IP address of 192.168.54.1
- *SERVER1* configured as the domain controller for the netpluslab.net domain
- A user account named *netplus* in the Users group in the netpluslab.net domain on *SERVER1*
- A second computer named *WORKSTATION1* running Windows 8.1 or Windows 7, or an equivalent virtual image, with an Ethernet port or NIC, configured with an IP address of 192.168.54.2; this computer should not be configured as a member of a domain
- Access to *WORKSTATION1* as a regular user
- Both computers should be connected either virtually or through a switch or home router like the network in Lab 1.3

Most of the steps in this lab can also be completed in a virtual environment using virtualization software such as VMware.

Estimated completion time: **60 minutes**

Activity

1. If you are building this network physically, plug one end of one of the cables into the switch. Plug the other end of the cable into one of the computers. The link light on both the hub and on the NIC in the back of the computer should illuminate.

2. Repeat Step 1 to connect the other computer to the switch.

3. On *SERVER1* (the Windows Server 2012 R2 computer), press **CTRL+ALT+Del** to sign in.

4. Select **Administrator,** and type the password for this account in the Password text box and click the **Submit** button arrow. The Server Manager window opens.

5. Click the File Explorer icon on the task bar or right-click the **Start** button, and then click **File Explorer**.

6. Right-click the icon for the Local Disk (C:), point to **Share with** in the shortcut menu, and click **Advanced Sharing**.

7. Click the **Advanced Sharing** button and then click the **Share this folder** option button. Record the name that appears in the Share name text box. This is the name by which the shared drive will be identified on the other computer. Click **OK** and then click **Close**.

8. Log on as an administrator on WORKSTATION1. The Windows desktop appears.

9. Open Control Panel, and then click **System and Security**.

10. Click **System**. The System window opens.

11. In the lower-right corner, click **Change settings**. You see the System Properties dialog box shown in Figure 1-3.

Figure 1-3   System Properties dialog box

12. Click **Network ID**.

13. If necessary, select the **This computer is part of a business network; I use it to connect to other computers at work** option button. Click **Next**.

14. If necessary, click the **My company uses a network with a domain** option button. Click **Next**.

15. Click **Next**.

16. Type **netplus** in the User name text box. Type the password for the netplus account in the Password text box. Type **NETPLUSLAB.NET** in the Domain name text box. Click **Next**. If a dialog box appears asking if you would like to use an existing domain, select **No**.

17. Now you will enter information about the computer itself. In the Computer name text box, type **WORKSTATION1**. In the Computer domain text box, type **NETPLUSLAB.NET**. Click **Next**. The Domain User Name and Password dialog box opens.

18. In the User name text box, type **Administrator**. Type the password for this account in the Password text box. Type **NETPLUSLAB.NET** in the Domain text box. Click **OK**.

19. The wizard asks you to add a user account to this computer. The **Add the following user account** option button is selected by default. Also, by default, **netplus** appears in the User name text box, and **NETPLUSLAB.NET** appears in the User domain text box. If that is not the case on your computer, select these settings now, and then click **Next**.

20. The wizard asks you what sort of access the netplus user should have to this computer. Make sure the **Standard account** option button is selected, and then click **Next**.

21. Click **Finish** and click **OK** in the System Properties dialog box. A window opens, informing you that you must restart the computer for the changes to take effect.

22. Click **Restart Now** to reboot the computer.

23. When the computer has rebooted, if necessary, enter **netplus** in the User name text box. In the Password text box, enter the password for this account. In Windows 7, select **NETPLUSLAB** from the Log on to drop-down menu. Click **OK**.

24. Right-click the **Start** button (click the **Start** button in Windows 7), and then click **Network**. If an information bar appears at the top of the window indicating that network discovery and file sharing are turned off, click the information bar, then click **Turn on network discovery and file sharing**, and enter your credentials when prompted.

25. Double-click the **SERVER1** icon. A list of all the folders shared on *SERVER1* appears.

26. Right-click the folder name you recorded for the shared drive on the server. Click **Open** in the shortcut menu (or Explore in Windows 7). You see a list of the contents of the shared drive.

27. Close the shared drive and log off both computers.

Certification Objectives

Objectives for the CompTIA Network+ Exam:

- 1.6 Differentiate between common network topologies
- 1.12 Given a set of requirements, implement a basic network

Review Questions

1. Which of the following could be shared as resources across a network? (Choose all that apply.)

   a. Microsoft Word and other Office applications

   b. Printers

   c. Documents

   d. Network interface cards

2. True or False? In a client-server network, it is possible to share documents between individual users' computers as you can in a peer-to-peer network.

3. You are the network administrator for a small company. When users take vacations, they would like to allow other users to update the files stored on their computers. Additionally, several users have complained that they have accidentally deleted important files on their local computer, and would like some way to recover them. How would you recommend that they store their files?

   a. Make multiple copies on their local hard drive.

   b. Store the files on the server, which is backed up nightly.

   c. Make copies of the file on a USB thumb drive.

   d. Burn the files onto a CD.

4. A very large organization might have thousands of servers. Do the benefits of client-server networks still apply to such an organization?

   a. No, because managing so many servers is difficult.

   b. No, because the organization can rely on a large peer-to-peer network to share files instead.

   c. Yes, because it is easier to manage thousands of servers than it is to manage the hundreds of thousands of workstations that such an organization might have.

   d. Yes, because managing thousands of servers is no more difficult than managing a few servers.

5. In this lab, what kind of network service did you configure on your client-server network?

   a. Management service

   b. Mail service

   c. Internet service

   d. File service

6. Which two of the following issues make peer-to-peer networks less scalable than client-server networks?

    a. Each time a new user is added, the peer-to-peer network cabling must be reinstalled between nodes.

    b. Adding nodes to a peer-to-peer network results in diminished overall network performance.

    c. Adding nodes to a peer-to-peer network increases the risk that an intruder can compromise a shared data folder.

    d. Adding new resource-sharing locations and ensuring that all authorized users have access to new resources becomes less manageable as the peer-to-peer network grows.

Lab 1.5 Troubleshooting Client Logon Problems

Objectives

In this lab, you will troubleshoot a scenario in which a user cannot log on to the server. From a user's perspective, when they cannot log on to the server, the network is unavailable, no matter what the reason. However, the ultimate cause of the problem might be anything from a hardware failure on the server to an expired password.

When troubleshooting problems, you should attempt to be as methodical as possible. You can start by determining the scope of the problem. Is only one user affected, or are all users affected? Then determine if the user's computer (or the users' computers, if multiple users are affected) and the server have physical connectivity. Do all the NICs seem to be working properly? Is the switch functioning and is the network cabled properly? After establishing that physical connectivity is not the problem, determine whether the user's computer has network connectivity. Can you ping the server from the user's computer? After you have determined that network connectivity is not the problem, try to determine if the application is functioning properly.

Keep in mind that being able to log on to a computer does not necessarily indicate that the network is functioning properly. Windows computers cache passwords for usernames, so that a user can still log on to a computer during a network outage.

In this lab, you will first verify that the network, the client computers, and the server are all functioning properly by logging on to two client computers. Then your instructor or another set of lab partners will do something to prevent at least one of the computers from logging on to the server. Your assignment will be to identify and solve the problem.

After completing this lab, you will be able to:

- Follow a logical troubleshooting methodology to determine the nature of client connectivity problems

- Identify a network problem by interpreting the results of diagnostic utilities such as Ping and Ipconfig

Materials Required

This lab will require the following:

- A computer named *SERVER1* running Windows Server 2012 R2, configured as a domain controller for the netpluslab.net domain, with an IP address of 192.168.54.1 and a subnet mask of 255.255.255.0

- The DHCP server running on *SERVER1* and configured to assign DHCP addresses in the range from 192.168.54.50 to 192.168.54.100, with a subnet mask of 255.255.255.0

- Access as the Administrator to the netpluslab.net domain and user accounts named *client1* and *client2* in the Domain Users group

- A shared folder named NETPLUS on *SERVER1*, configured so that the users in the Domain Users group have full control over the shared folder on the network

- Two computers running Windows 8.1 or Windows 7 named *WORKSTATION1* and *WORKSTATION2*, each configured to receive DHCP addresses

- Both *WORKSTATION1* and *WORKSTATION2* configured as members of the netpluslab.net domain

- All three computers configured to use *SERVER1* as their DNS server

- No network protocols besides TCP/IP configured on any of the computers

- Each computer connected to a switch with straight-through Cat 5 (or better) UTP cables, as shown in Figure 1-4

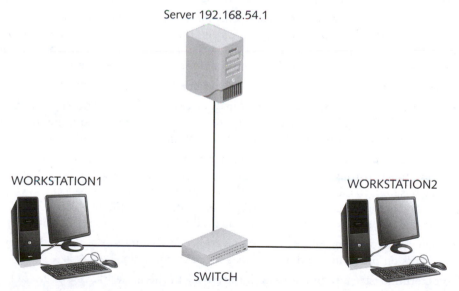

Figure 1-4 Network layout of Lab 1.5

- A faulty straight-through cable that is the same color of at least one of the working Cat 5 (or better) cables; a crossover cable may be substituted

- An instructor or classmate assigned to cause a problem in the network; if you are working alone, you can play both roles

Most of the steps in this lab can also be completed in a virtual environment using virtualization software such as VMware.

Estimated completion time: **60–90 minutes**

Activity

1. Log on to *WORKSTATION1* as client1. The Windows desktop appears.

2. Open File Explorer (in Windows 8.1) or the Computer window (in Windows 7).

3. Click **Map network drive** on the toolbar. The Map Network Drive dialog box opens.

4. Accept the default setting for the Drive drop-down menu, Z:. In the Folder text box, type **\\SERVER1\netplus** and click **Finish**. The computer maps the NETPLUS shared folder.

5. Return to This PC (Computer in Windows 7). The netplus (\\server1) icon appears in the Network locations section.

6. Repeat Steps 1 through 5 on *WORKSTATION2*, logging on as the client2 user. You have now verified that you can connect to *SERVER1* with both client computers.

7. Leave the room while your instructor or classmate causes a network problem by performing one of the actions listed in Table 1 1. If you are working in a virtual environment, you may not have the option to disconnect the virtual network cables. After performing one of the actions, your instructor or classmate should log off all three computers.

8. When you return to the room, reboot both client computers.

9. Attempt to repeat Steps 1 through 5 on *WORKSTATION1*. You should be unable to browse to the NETPLUS folder. Attempt to solve the problem using the following steps. If you identify the problem before completing all the steps, proceed to Step 16.

10. Begin to determine the scope of the problem by attempting to log on to *WORKSTATION2*. Repeat Steps 1 through 5. If you are able to log on and browse the NETPLUS folder, the problem is local to the *WORKSTATION1* computer and you may concentrate on potential problems that affect only *WORKSTATION1*. Otherwise, the problem is common to all clients and you should concentrate on potential problems that affect all clients.

11. To determine the state of physical connectivity in the network, check the status of the link lights on the switch and in the NICs for each computer.

12. To determine the state of network connectivity in the network, on *WORKSTATION1*, open a Command Prompt window. Type **ping 127.0.0.1** and then press **Enter**. Success indicates that the TCP/IP stack on *WORKSTATION1* is working. Depending on the scope of the problem, repeat this step for *WORKSTATION2*.

Table 1-1 Possible actions to be performed by a classmate or instructor

Action	Instruction
Install faulty cable on *WORKSTATION1*	Replace the network cable connecting *WORKSTATION1* to the switch with the faulty network cable.
Install faulty cable on server	Replace the network cable connecting the Windows Server to the switch with the faulty network cable.
Disrupt cable connection	Pull the cable far enough out of *WORKSTATION1*'s NIC so that the link light turns off, but not so far that it falls completely out of the NIC.
Reconfigure the IP address on *WORKSTATION1*	a. Log off *WORKSTATION1*, and then log back on as an administrator. The Windows desktop appears. b. Open the Network Connections window. c. Right-click **Local Area Connection** (Ethernet0 - Windows 8.1) and click **Properties**. The Local Area Connection (Ethernet0) Properties window opens. d. Double-click **Internet Protocol Version 4 (TCP/IPv4)**. The Internet Protocol Version 4 (TCP/IPv4) Properties window opens. e. Click the **Use the following IP address** option button, if necessary. In the IP address text box, type **192.168.154.50**. In the Subnet mask text box, type **255.255.255.0**. f. Click **OK** twice, and then close all open dialog boxes.
Disable network adapter on *WORKSTATION1*	Open Device Manager, right-click the **Network adapter** and click **Disable**.
Reconfigure the IP address on *SERVER1*	a. Log on as an administrator. The Server Manager appears. b. In Server Manager, click the IP address next to the Ethernet connection. c. Right-click Ethernet and click **Properties**. The Ethernet Properties window opens. d. Double-click **Internet Protocol Version 4 (TCP/IPv4)**. The Internet Protocol Version 4 (TCP/IPv4) Properties window opens. e. Click the **Use the following IP address** option button. In the IP address text box, type **192.168.54.11**. In the Subnet mask text box, type **255.255.255.0**. f. Click **OK** twice, and then close all open dialog boxes or windows.
Reconfigure the IP address on *WORKSTATION2*	a. Log off *WORKSTATION2*, and then log back on as an administrator. The Windows desktop appears. b. Open the Network Connections window. c. Right-click **Local Area Connection** (Ethernet0) and click **Properties**. The Local Area Connection (Ethernet0) Properties window opens. d. Double-click **Internet Protocol Version 4 (TCP/IPv4)**. The Internet Protocol Version 4 (TCP/IPv4) Properties window opens. e. Click the **Use the following IP address** option button, if necessary. In the IP address text box, type **192.168.154.50**. In the Subnet mask text box, type **255.255.255.248**. f. Click **OK** twice (or click **OK**, and then click **Close**), and then close all open dialog boxes.

13. At the command prompt on *WORKSTATION1*, type `ping 192.168.54.1` and then press **Enter**. If the output indicates success, network connectivity exists between *WORKSTATION1* and the server. Depending on the scope of the problem, repeat this step for *WORKSTATION2*.

14. If there is no network connectivity, at the command prompt on *WORKSTATION1*, type `ipconfig` and then press **Enter**. IP addressing information displays on the computer. If this is correct, there might be a problem with the network configuration on the server. Depending on the scope of the problem, repeat for *WORKSTATION2*.

15. On *SERVER1*, repeat Steps 12 through 14. However, in Step 13, ping the IP addresses of the client computers.

16. By this time, you should have identified the problem. Fix it and repeat Steps 7 through 15, asking your instructor or classmate to perform another action listed in Table 1-1.

Certification Objectives

Objectives for the CompTIA Network+ Exam:

- 1.6 Differentiate between common network topologies
- 4.1 Given a scenario, implement the following network troubleshooting methodology

Review Questions

1. Which of the following comes first in the series of steps recommended for a logical approach to network troubleshooting?

   a. Establish what has changed on the network.

   b. Implement a solution.

   c. Establish the symptoms.

   d. Identify the affected area.

2. If a client workstation has been assigned the wrong IP address, which of the following will be true?

   a. The client will be able to connect to other nodes on the LAN, but will not be able to connect through its default gateway to the Internet.

   b. The client will be able to ping the loopback address successfully, but will not be able to connect to other nodes on the LAN.

   c. The client will not be able to ping the loopback address successfully, nor will it be able to connect to other nodes on the LAN.

   d. The client will be able to connect to other nodes on its LAN segment, but will not be able to connect to nodes on other segments.

3. Which of the following commands will reveal TCP/IP addressing information on a Windows Server 2012 R2 computer?

   a. `ipconfig`

   b. `winipcfg`

   c. `ifconfig`

   d. `netipcfg`

4. If the LED on a workstation's NIC is blinking green, which of the following is true?

   a. The workstation is connected to the network and successfully exchanging data over its connection.

   b. The workstation is connected to the network, but is not currently exchanging data over its connection.

   c. The workstation is connected to the network, but is experiencing errors when attempting to exchange data over the network.

   d. The workstation is not successfully connected to the network.

5. Of the following troubleshooting actions, which one would come first in a logical troubleshooting methodology?

   a. Replace a faulty memory chip on a server.

   b. Determine whether a problem is limited to a segment or affects the whole network.

   c. Summarize your solution in a troubleshooting database.

   d. Determine whether your solution will result in any other problems.

Lab 1.6 Installing a Network Printer

Objectives

The ability to access resources among all the users in an organization is an important reason why networks are so widely used. To print a document without a network, a user would need a printer directly attached to her computer, or she would need to copy the document to a form of portable media such as a CD-R or USB drive and then find a computer with an attached printer. In an organization with even a few employees, this can be both expensive and time consuming. In an organization with thousands of employees, this can waste an enormous amount of time and cost a great deal of money.

In this lab, you will set up a network printer so that users can access it. Depending on the make and model of the printer, the steps required to install printer drivers might vary from the steps provided here.

After completing this lab, you will be able to:

- Set up a printer in a peer-to-peer network

Materials Required

This lab will require the following:

- Administrative access to a computer running Windows 8.1 or Windows 7

- A network printer with an RJ-45 port that is compatible with your version of Windows

- Drivers for the printer that are compatible with your version of Windows; these drivers should be available either among the default drivers installed with Windows or in a known location on a CD

- A home router running DHCP

- Both the computer and the printer should be attached to the home router with straight-through Cat 5 (or better) UTP cables

Estimated completion time: **20 minutes**

Activity

1. Ensure that both WORKSTATION1 and the printer are attached to the home router and powered on.

2. Determine the assigned IP address of the printer by printing a network configuration page. If you're not sure how to do this, consult your printer's documentation. Record the IP address of the printer.

In Windows 8.1:

1. On WORKSTATION1, right-click the **Start** button and select **Network Connections**.

2. Double-click the Ethernet card's icon and click **Properties**.

3. Select **Internet Protocol Version 4 (TCP/IPv4)** and click **Properties**.

4. Ensure that the **Obtain an IP address automatically** option button is selected and click **OK**.

5. Click **Close** to close the Ethernet0 Properties window.

6. Click **Close** to close the Ethernet0 Status window.

7. Click the **Start** button and type **Devices and Printers** in the search box.

8. Click **Devices and Printers**. The Devices and Printers window opens.

9. Click **Add a printer**. If Windows automatically detects your printer, follow your printer's installation instructions. Otherwise, click **Next**.

10. The Add Printer dialog box appears, as shown in Figure 1-5.

11. Select **Add a printer using a TCP/IP address or hostname** and click **Next**.

12. In Device type, select **TCP/IP Device**.

Select this option ⟶

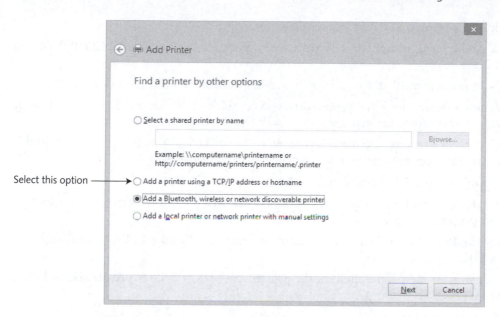

Figure 1-5   Add Printer dialog box

13. In Hostname or IP address, enter the IP address of your printer and click **Next**.

14. If Windows doesn't have the proper drivers, you can get them from a known location or download them from the manufacturer's Web site.

15. If necessary, select **Share this printer so that others on your network can find and use it** and click **Next**.

16. Click **Print a test page** and click **Finish**.

In Windows 7:

1. On *WORKSTATION1*, click the **Start** button, and then click **Control Panel**. The Control Panel window opens.

2. Select **Network and Internet**, **Network and Sharing Center**, and **Local Area Connection** to open the Local Area Connection Status window.

3. Click **Properties** and click **Yes** if prompted by the User Account Control window.

4. Select **Internet Protocol Version 4 (TCP/IPv4)** and click **Properties**.

5. Ensure that the **Obtain an IP address automatically** option button is selected and click **OK**.

6. Click **Close** to close the Local Area Connections Properties window.

7. Click **Close** to close the Local Area Connection Status window.

8. Now click the **Start** button, and then click **Devices and Printers**. The Devices and Printers window opens.

9. Click **Add a printer**. The Add Printer dialog box opens.

10. Click **Add a local printer**, select **Create a new port**, choose **Standard TCP/IP Port**, and click **Next**.

11. In the Hostname or IP address dialog box, enter the printer's IP and click **Next**.

12. If Windows doesn't have the proper drivers, you can get them from a known location or download them from the manufacturer's Web site.

13. Don't click **Print a test page** yet. Depending on the printer, you may have to first disable bidirectional support to prevent a never-ending series of pages.

14. Click **Finish** in the Add Printer dialog box.

15. In the Devices and Printers window, right-click the newly installed printer and select the **Printer properties** page.

16. Select the **Ports** tab, select your printer, and unselect **Enable bidirectional support**. Click **OK**.

17. To test your printer, right-click on the printer icon, select **Printer properties**, and click **Print Test Page**.

18. Log off your computer.

Certification Objectives

Objectives for the CompTIA Network+ Exam:

- 1.12 Given a set of requirements, implement a basic network

Review Questions

1. Most printers come with network cards so that they do not need to be attached to a computer. How would the process of sharing such a printer differ from sharing a printer attached to a computer? (Choose all that apply.)

   a. The printer would need a network address so that other computers can find it.

   b. The process would not differ.

   c. You would have to add the printer to the domain.

   d. You would not need to connect the printer to another computer via a cable.

2. Users may share printers in a peer-to-peer network. What are the potential disadvantages of this? (Choose all that apply.)

   a. A user could easily misconfigure or turn off her workstation, preventing all other users from accessing the attached printer.

   b. No one will be able to use the printer if the network is down.

   c. The printer will not be backed up.

   d. The printer will not be under centralized control.

3. In this lab, how does the printer obtain an IP address?

    a. Management service

    b. Printer service

    c. DHCP

    d. Static assignment

4. File and Print Services operate on which level of the OSI model?

    a. Data Link layer

    b. Physical layer

    c. Application layer

    d. Network layer

5. How can you tell whether a printer is shared in Windows 7 or 8.1?

    a. The word *shared* is written on the Printer icon.

    b. There is no way to tell.

    c. A small sharing icon appears in the Devices and Printers window next to "State."

    d. Each shared printer appears in the Shared Printers folder.

CHAPTER TWO

HOW COMPUTERS FIND EACH OTHER ON NETWORKS

Labs included in this chapter

- Lab 2.1 IP Address Assignments
- Lab 2.2 Configuring TCP/IP for a Windows Computer
- Lab 2.3 Configuring IP Addresses and Subnet Masks
- Lab 2.4 Automatically Assigning IP Addresses with DHCP
- Lab 2.5 Configuring Domain Name System (DNS) Properties
- Lab 2.6 Using FTP
- Lab 2.7 Understanding Port Numbers

CompTIA Network+ Exam Objectives

Objective	Lab
1.3 Install and configure the following networking services/applications	2.2, 2.3, 2.4, 2.5
1.8 Given a scenario, implement and configure the appropriate addressing schema	2.2, 2.3
4.2 Given a scenario, analyze and interpret the output of troubleshooting tools	2.1, 2.2, 2.3, 2.5
4.6 Given a scenario, troubleshoot and resolve common network issues	2.4, 2.5
5.9 Compare and contrast the following ports and protocols	2.7
5.10 Given a scenario, configure and apply the appropriate ports and protocols	2.4, 2.5, 2.6

Lab 2.1 IP Address Assignments

Objectives

A Regional Internet Registry (RIR) is an organization that assigns IP addresses to public and private organizations. There are five RIRs: the American Registry for Internet Numbers (ARIN), the Asia-Pacific Network Information Centre (APNIC), the Latin America and Caribbean Network Information Centre (LACNIC), the Réseaux IP Européens (RIPE), and the African Network Information Centre (AfriNIC). Each RIR assigns IP addresses in a different area.

As a network administrator, you might sometimes find that you need to track down the owner of a particular IP address. For instance, you might discover that a host at an IP address outside of your network is generating excessive amounts of traffic to your Web server, sending your mail server unsolicited commercial email, or otherwise abusing your network. To ask whoever owns this host to stop, you must be able to contact the owner. You can use the Web site of an RIR to find this information. All of the RIRs maintain a Web site and a WHOIS database, which tracks IP assignments. You can find the Web sites for each organization at *arin.net*, *apnic.net*, *lacnic.net*, *ripe.net*, and *afrinic.net*. Often, IP address assignments are divided further. An Internet service provider (ISP), for instance, will usually delegate some of its IP addresses to its customers.

In this lab, you will use the `nslookup` command to find the IP address of a site. Then you will look up that IP address on the ARIN site.

Note that the steps in this lab were correct at the time this book was published. If ARIN changes its Web site significantly, the steps might not work exactly as written. However, you should still be able to go to *arin.net* and follow the links for WHOIS.

After completing this lab, you will be able to:

- Describe the function of an RIR
- Track down the organization owning an IP address

Materials Required

This lab will require the following:

- A computer running Windows 8.1 or Windows 7 with a connection to the Internet (and instructions on how to access it, if necessary)
- Access to the Internet
- A Web site address (such as *google.com*) whose IP address was assigned by ARIN; your instructor should tell you which Web site to use

Estimated completion time: **20–25 minutes**

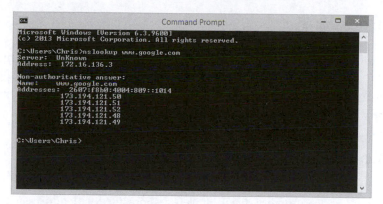

Figure 2-1   Typical output from the `nslookup` command

Activity

1. Log on to the Windows computer. The desktop appears. If necessary, perform whatever steps are needed to access the Internet.

2. Open a Command Prompt window.

3. In the Command Prompt window, type **nslookup** followed by a space and then the name of the Web site assigned to you by your instructor. (For instance, if you were assigned *www.google.com*, you would type **nslookup www.google.com**.) Press **Enter**. The output of this command should look similar to Figure 2-1.

4. You should see the IP address of the Web site directly under the name of the Web site. In Figure 2-1, for instance, the IP address of *www.google.com* is 173.194.121.49. Record the IP address you found. Some Web sites might have multiple IP addresses. If this is the case, record the last IP address found.

5. Open Internet Explorer.

6. In the address box, type **www.arin.net/whois/** and then press **Enter**. The ARIN WHOIS Database Search page opens.

7. In the Search WhoisRWS text box, type the IP address you recorded in Step 4 and press **Enter**. The query results appear.

8. Record the name of the organization to which the IP address belongs. In some cases, more than one organization might be listed. For instance, an organization and its ISP might be listed.

9. What happens if you enter this IP address in the address box of Internet Explorer?

10. Close any open windows and log off the computer.

Certification Objectives

Objectives for the CompTIA Network+ Exam:

- 4.2 Given a scenario, analyze and interpret the output of troubleshooting tools

Review Questions

1. A host has been overloading your Web server with a flood of requests and you want to investigate whether this is some kind of network attack. You look up the IP address on *arin.net* to determine its owner, but ARIN's Web site tells you that LACNIC owns the IP address. What should you do?

   a. Complain to the owner of the *lacnic.net* Web site.

   b. Look up LACNIC in the Regional Internet Registry.

   c. Look up the owner of the IP address on the LACNIC Web site.

   d. Look up the owner of the IP address on the APNIC Web site.

2. What might happen if no organization were responsible for IP addressing on the Internet? (Choose all that apply.)

   a. Organizations might try to use the same ranges of IP addresses.

   b. Anyone could host their own Web server.

   c. Nothing would happen.

   d. The Internet would use another protocol besides IP.

3. You look up an IP address on *arin.net* and two organizations are listed. What does this mean?

   a. The two organizations share the IP address assignment.

   b. That IP address is currently involved in a network attack.

   c. The RIR made a mistake.

   d. One organization delegated the IP address to the second.

4. What is a Regional Internet Registry responsible for?

   a. Maintaining Internet connectivity

   b. Replacing IP with TCP

   c. Assigning IP addresses

   d. Signing up users with ISP accounts

5. In which of the following situations would it be useful to contact the owner of an IP address? (Choose all that apply.)

   a. A host outside your network has been attempting to log on to your servers without your permission.

   b. A host inside your network has been attempting to log on to your servers without your permission.

   c. A host outside your network has been attempting to send large amounts of unsolicited commercial email or spam.

   d. A host outside your network has been accessing your Web site once an hour.

Lab 2.2 Configuring TCP/IP for a Windows Computer

Objectives

An IP address is a logical address, which means it is assigned to a computer and may be changed. For two computers to communicate directly using TCP/IP, they must have separate IP addresses that are on the same network. An IPv4 address consists of four numbers with values between 0 and 255 separated by dots. For instance, 10.172.255.93 is a valid IP address. When written in binary, an IPv4 address is 32 bits long. Each section can be expressed as an 8-bit binary number called an octet.

A subnet mask is used to determine the network address. The subnet mask also consists of four octets separated by dots. However, only certain values are allowed. When written in binary, a valid subnet mask looks like a series of ones followed by a series of zeroes. A host with an improperly configured subnet mask might not be able to communicate with some or any hosts. You can use the `ipconfig` command to display a computer's IP configuration, including IP address and subnet mask.

In this lab, you will configure an IP address and subnet mask on a computer so that it can communicate with other computers on a network. You will then use the ping (Packet Internet Groper) utility to verify that two hosts can communicate with each other at the Network layer in a TCP/IP network. The `ping` command sends one or more packets using the Internet Control Message Protocol (ICMP) to a remote computer. If the remote computer receives these packets, it sends a reply. If the sender receives the replies, the `ping` command was successful.

After completing this lab, you will be able to:

- Configure an IP address on a Windows computer

Materials Required

This lab will require the following:

- Two computers running Windows 8.1 or Windows 7 named *WORKSTATION1* and *WORKSTATION2*
- The Windows Firewall disabled on both machines
- Both computers connected to a hub or switch with a straight-through Category 5 (or better) cable
- Administrator access to both computers

Most of the steps in this lab can also be completed using virtualization software such as VMware.

Estimated completion time: **20 minutes**

Activity

1. On *WORKSTATION1*, log on as an administrator. The Windows desktop appears.

2. Open **Control Panel**, click **Network and Internet**, click **Network and Sharing Center**, and click **Change adapter settings**. The Network Connections window opens.

3. Right-click the **Ethernet0** or **Local Area Connection** icon, then click **Properties** in the shortcut menu.

4. Double-click **Internet Protocol Version 4 (TCP/IPv4)**. The Internet Protocol Version 4 (TCP/IPv4) Properties dialog box opens.

5. Click the **Use the following IP address** option button.

6. Enter **192.168.54.1** in the IP address text box.

7. Enter **255.255.255.0** in the Subnet mask text box.

8. Enter **192.168.54.1** in the Default gateway text box.

9. Click the **Use the following DNS server addresses** option button.

10. In the Preferred DNS server text box, enter **192.168.54.1**. At this point, your Internet Protocol Version 4 (TCP/IPv4) Properties dialog box should match the one shown in Figure 2-2.

11. Click **OK** to close the Internet Protocol Version 4 (TCP/IPv4) Properties dialog box.

12. Click **OK** to close the Ethernet0 Properties window.

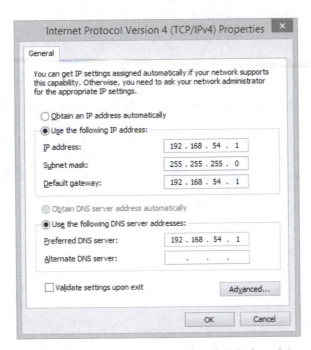

Figure 2-2   Configuring an IP address in Windows 8.1

13. On WORKSTATION2, set the IP address to **192.168.54.2** using the same method used in Steps 2 through 12.

14. Now you will verify that you have successfully configured an IP address for the Windows computer. On WORKSTATION1, open a Command Prompt window.

15. Type `ping 192.168.54.2` and press **Enter**. The Windows computer sends four ICMP packets to 192.168.54.1, and indicates that it has received four replies from the remote computer.

16. Type `ipconfig` and press **Enter**. The computer displays its IP address, subnet mask, and default gateway. Does this match the information you entered in the Internet Protocol Version 4 (TCP/IPv4) Properties dialog box in Steps 6, 7, and 8?

17. Log off.

Certification Objectives

Objectives for the CompTIA Network+ Exam:

- 1.3 Install and configure the following networking services/applications
- 1.8 Given a scenario, implement and configure the appropriate addressing schema
- 4.2 Given a scenario, analyze and interpret the output of troubleshooting tools

Review Questions

1. Which of the following information is included in the results of the `ping` command? (Choose all that apply.)
   a. The operating system used by the remote computer
   b. The IP address or name of the remote computer
   c. The number of packets that were lost
   d. The time it took for the reply to be received

2. Which of the following commands can you use to print information about a computer's Network layer configuration?
   a. `netstat`
   b. `ipconfig`
   c. `arp`
   d. `ping`

3. How can you verify that two hosts are connected and communicating properly?
   a. From one host, run the `ping` command to the other host.
   b. From a third host, run the `ping` command to both hosts.
   c. Run the `arp` command on both hosts.
   d. Run the `ipconfig` command on both hosts.

4. What protocol does the `ping` command use?

  a. TCP/IP

  b. UDP

  c. ICMP

  d. ARP

5. A Dynamic Host Configuration Protocol (DHCP) server can be used to assign IP addresses automatically. Why might this be useful to a network administrator?

6. On many networks, DHCP is used to assign workstations their IP addresses. However, DHCP is rarely used to assign addresses for servers. Why?

  a. DHCP is too expensive.

  b. DHCP is not scalable enough.

  c. Servers don't have the option to use DHCP.

  d. It would be more difficult for a client to find a server if its IP address changes.

Lab 2.3 Configuring IP Addresses and Subnet Masks

Objectives

To address a TCP/IP host properly, you need both an IP address and a subnet mask. The subnet mask is used to further divide a network. This allows a network administrator to control access or traffic between two subnetworks (or subnets). A router or Layer 3 switch is required to route network traffic between the two subnets. For instance, you might want to prevent users from directly accessing a Web server. If you put the users and the Web server on different subnets, you can then use a router to control user access to the Web server.

An IP address consists of four numbers separated by dots. Each individual number in the address is called an octet. For instance, in the IP address 10.172.11.145, the first octet is 10, the second octet is 172, and so on. IP addresses have traditionally been divided into classes based on the first octet. The first octet of Class A addresses is between 1 and 126, the first octet of Class B addresses is between 128 and 191, and the first octet of Class C addresses is between 192 and 223. Class D addresses, whose first octet ranges from 224 to 239, are reserved for multicast. Class E addresses, whose first octet ranges from 239 to 254, are reserved for experimental purposes. Finally, addresses whose first octet is 255 are reserved for broadcasts.

Subnet masks can be used to conserve IP addresses. The size of a subnet mask determines the number of hosts that can be placed on a network. Using subnet masks, you can allocate IP address blocks that fit the number of hosts you have. The default subnet mask of a Class B network is 255.255.0.0, and it can have up to 65,534 hosts. A Class A network has a default subnet mask of 255.0.0.0, and it can have up to 16,777,214 hosts. Without subnetting, you would be unable to divide these very large networks into smaller networks. With subnetting, you can carve a larger network into many smaller networks. For instance, suppose you were assigned a Class B network. If you subdivided this network into smaller networks with subnet masks of 255.255.255.0 (the default subnet mask for Class C networks), you would be able to divide the Class B network into 256 smaller networks.

After completing this lab, you will be able to:

- Configure IP addresses and subnet masks in Windows 8.1 or Windows 7
- Discuss the purpose of subnet masks

Materials Required

This lab will require the following:

- Two computers running Microsoft Windows 8.1 or Windows 7, both configured as members of the NETPLUS workgroup
- Access to each computer as an administrator
- Both computers connected to a hub or switch with Category 5 (or better) UTP cables

Most of the steps in this lab can also be completed using virtualization software such as VMware.

Estimated completion time: **20 minutes**

Activity

1. Log on to both computers as an administrator.

2. On one computer, open **Control Panel**, click **Network and Internet**, click **Network and Sharing Center**, and click **Change adapter settings**. The Network Connections window opens.

3. In the Network Connections window, right-click **Ethernet0** or **Local Area Connection** icon and then select **Properties** from the shortcut menu. The Ethernet0 or Local Area Connection Properties window opens.

4. Double-click **Internet Protocol Version 4 (TCP/IPv4)**. The Internet Protocol Version 4 (TCP/IPv4) Properties dialog box opens.

5. Click the **Use the following IP address** option button.

6. Enter **172.20.1.1** in the IP address text box.

7. Enter **255.255.255.0** in the Subnet mask text box. If necessary, clear the Default gateway and DNS server fields.

8. Click **OK** and then click **Close**. The Local Area Connection or Ethernet0 Properties window closes.

Table 2-1   IP address and subnet mask assignments in different networks

Computer	IP address	Subnet mask
First computer	172.20.1.1	255.255.255.0
Second computer	172.20.2.1	255.255.255.0

9. Now you will configure the second computer in a different network. Repeat Steps 2 through 8 on the second computer, using 172.20.2.1 as the IP address and 255.255.255.0 as the subnet mask. Table 2-1 shows the IP addresses and subnet masks on each computer.

10. You have configured the two computers on two different subnets. To demonstrate this, open the Command Prompt window.

11. In the Command Prompt window, type **ping 172.20.1.1** and press **Enter**. You see a timeout message indicating that the remote computer is unreachable. The message appears on the screen four times, as shown in Figure 2-3.

12. Repeat Steps 10 and 11 on the first computer, attempting to ping 172.20.2.1.

13. Now you will change the subnet mask so that both computers are on the same network. Repeat Steps 3 through 8 on the first computer, keeping the IP address the same but changing the subnet mask to 255.255.0.0.

14. Repeat Steps 3 through 8 on the second computer, keeping the IP address the same but changing the subnet mask to 255.255.0.0. Table 2-2 summarizes the new IP address assignments for the network.

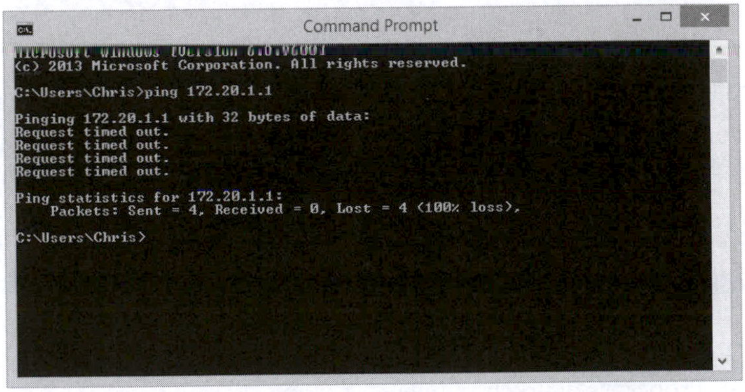

Figure 2-3   An unsuccessful attempt to ping another computer

Table 2-2   New IP address assignments in the same network

Computer	IP address	Subnet mask
First computer	172.20.1.1	255.255.0.0
Second computer	172.20.2.1	255.255.0.0

15. Repeat Step 11 on the second computer, attempting to ping 172.20.1.1. The computer receives four replies, indicating that there is network connectivity between the two computers.

16. Repeat Step 11 on the first computer, attempting to ping 172.20.2.1.

17. Log off both computers.

Certification Objectives

Objectives for the CompTIA Network+ Exam:

- 1.3 Install and configure the following networking services/applications
- 1.8 Given a scenario, implement and configure the appropriate addressing schema
- 4.2 Given a scenario, analyze and interpret the output of troubleshooting tools

Review Questions

1. What is the class of network that you configured in this activity?

    a. Class A

    b. Class B

    c. Class C

    d. Class D

2. What is the purpose of a subnet mask?

    a. To indicate which protocols a particular network uses

    b. To further subdivide a network

    c. To mask, or prevent access to the whole network

    d. To limit the protocols used in a particular network

3. A network has a subnet mask of 255.255.255.0. How many usable IP addresses are available for network hosts?

    a. 65,535

    b. 65,534

    c. 256

    d. 254

4. Assuming that it has the default subnet mask, why can't you assign the IP address 192.168.54.255 to a host?

    a. This address is reserved for multicast.

    b. This address is reserved for experimental uses.

    c. This address describes the network.

    d. This address is the broadcast address.

5. Which of the following commands can you use in Windows to display information about the subnet mask configured for a particular NIC?

a. `ipconfig`

b. `ping`

c. `cmd`

d. `netstat`

Lab 2.4 Automatically Assigning IP Addresses with DHCP

Objectives

In this lab, you will allow a Dynamic Host Configuration Protocol (DHCP) server to assign IP addresses to client workstations automatically. DHCP assigns IP addresses from a central location, making it unnecessary to configure each workstation individually. In all but the smallest networks, this will save you time. You can also let DHCP configure additional information, such as the default gateway and any DNS or WINS servers to be used.

DHCP works by assigning a pool of IP addresses to a network. When a workstation requests an IP address, the DHCP server assigns one of the available addresses from the pool. Most network administrators do not use DHCP to address their servers, routers, or other network devices like printers. You might find it useful to set aside a range of IP addresses on each network for devices with static IP addresses. Servers and most network devices typically have static IP addresses, and are not often moved. However, you can use DHCP to assign static addresses based on a device's MAC address.

If a Windows computer configured to use DHCP is unable to obtain IP address information from a DHCP server, it will use Automatic Private IP Addressing (APIPA) to assign itself an IP address. However, the DHCP client will periodically attempt to reach the DHCP server until it can obtain an IP address. APIPA addresses are in the range 169.254.0.0 to 169.254.255.255 and have a subnet mask of 255.255.0.0. The APIPA address pool is a Class B address set aside by the Internet Assigned Numbers Authority (IANA) so that network administrators will not use it for any other purpose. Although APIPA can simplify address assignment on simple networks, it does not work well in networks with more than one subnet or in networks that need to connect to the Internet.

To configure the Windows DHCP server, you create a DHCP scope, which is a range of IP addresses to be assigned. You also need to specify the addresses to be excluded from the scope, as well as other information to be assigned to clients. Multiple DHCP scopes are typically used when a DHCP server needs to assign addresses for multiple subnets.

After completing this lab, you will be able to:

- Configure the DHCP server on Windows Server
- Understand DHCP and dynamic addressing

Materials Required

This lab will require the following:

- A computer named *SERVER1* running Windows Server 2012 R2, configured as a DNS server and a domain controller for the netpluslab.net domain, with an IP address of 192.168.54.1 and a subnet mask of 255.255.255.0

- DHCP installed on *SERVER1* but not configured

- A computer named *WORKSTATION1* running Windows 8.1 or 7 in the netpluslab.net domain, without a specified IP address

- Administrative access to both computers

- Both computers connected to a hub or switch with straight-through Category 5 (or better) UTP cables

Most of the steps in this lab can also be completed using virtualization software such as VMware.

Estimated completion time: **30 minutes**

Activity

1. Log on to *SERVER1* as the administrator. Windows Server Manager opens.

2. Select **Tools,** and then click **DHCP.** The DHCP window opens.

3. Click **server1.netpluslab.net** in the left pane of the window. Right-click **IPv4** and click **New Scope.** The New Scope Wizard opens.

4. Click **Next.**

5. Enter **Net Plus Lab** in the Name text box. Enter **Test** in the Description text box. Click **Next.**

6. Now you will configure the DHCP server to assign IP addresses to clients, with the addresses ranging from 192.168.54.10 to 192.168.54.200. This range allows for servers and network devices with static IP addresses from 192.168.54.1 to 192.168.54.9 and 192.168.54.201 to 192.168.54.254. In the Start IP address text box, enter **192.168.54.10.** In the End IP address text box, enter **192.168.54.200.** In the Subnet mask text box, enter **255.255.255.0,** if necessary. Figure 2-4 shows the New Scope Wizard. Click **Next.**

7. Now you will exclude the IP address 192.168.54.100 from the DHCP scope. In the Start IP address text box, enter **192.168.54.100.** This allows you to reserve this static IP address for the existing server in the middle of the range of IP addresses to be used for the DHCP scope. Click **Add.** The computer excludes the address from the DHCP scope. Click **Next.**

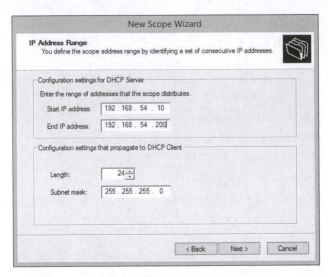

Figure 2-4 IP Address Range window of the New Scope Wizard

8. Now you can specify the amount of time that a client can use an IP address assigned to it from the DHCP server before it needs to renew the address. Enter **10** in the Days text box. Click **Next**.

9. Now you have the opportunity to configure further options. Click the **Yes, I want to configure these options now** option button, if necessary. Click **Next**.

10. Now you can specify the default gateway used by clients. Click **Next**, as this network has no default gateway.

11. Now you can specify information about domain name resolution for clients. In the Parent domain text box, enter **netpluslab.net**. In the IP address text box, enter **192.168.54.1** and click **Add**. Clients will now use this server as their DNS server. Click **Next**.

12. In this window, you can specify WINS servers. Click **Next**.

13. Now you must activate the DHCP scope. Make sure that the **Yes, I want to activate this scope now** option button is selected, click **Next**, and then click **Finish**.

14. If the IPv4 icon is a white circle with a red arrow in the center, right-click **server1. netpluslab.net** in the left pane, and select **Authorize** from the shortcut menu. Wait a few seconds and press **F5**. If the server1.netpluslab.net icon in the left pane is not a green circle with a white check mark in the center, press **F5** every few seconds until it is. A white green circle with a white check mark indicates that the scope is active, whereas a red arrow indicates that it is not. The DHCP server is now authorized to assign IP addresses in the netpluslab.net domain.

15. Log on to the *WORKSTATION1* as an administrator. The Windows desktop appears.

16. Right-click the network icon in the system tray, then click **Open Network and Sharing Center**. Click **Change adapter settings** in the left panel. The Network Connections window opens.

17. Right-click the **Ethernet0** or **Local Area Connection** icon and select **Properties** from the shortcut menu. The Ethernet0 or Local Area Connection window opens.

18. Double-click **Internet Protocol Version 4 (TCP/IPv4)**. The Internet Protocol Version 4 (TCP/IPv4) Properties dialog box opens.

19. Click the **Obtain an IP address automatically** and **Obtain DNS server address automatically** option buttons. Click **OK**, and then click **Close** to close the Ethernet0 or Local Area Connection Properties window.

20. Open a Command Prompt window.

21. Type **ipconfig** and press **Enter**. What is the current IP address of this computer?

22. Type **ipconfig/release** and press **Enter**. The computer releases any current address assigned by DHCP.

23. Type **ipconfig/renew** and press **Enter**. The computer obtains an IP address from the DHCP server and displays it on the screen. What is the new IP address?

24. Type **ipconfig/all** and press **Enter**. Record the name or address of the DNS server, the DHCP server, and the time the DHCP lease expires.

25. Now you will examine what happens when a computer running Windows fails to get an IP address through DHCP. Disconnect the cable connecting *SERVER1* to the hub or switch. (Do not disconnect *WORKSTATION1* from the hub or switch.)

26. In the Command Prompt window, type **ipconfig/release** and press **Enter**. The computer prints information for the NIC indicating that the IP address and subnet mask are both 0.0.0.0.

27. Type **ipconfig/renew** and press **Enter**. After a couple of minutes, the computer indicates that it was unable to contact the DHCP server.

28. Type **ipconfig/all** and press **Enter**. The computer prints the new IP address and subnet mask for the computer. What are the IP address and subnet mask now? What DNS server and domain name are now configured for the server?

29. Connect *SERVER1* to the hub again. Wait a couple of minutes and type **ipconfig** in the Command Prompt window. Repeat this step until the computer is able to obtain an IP address from the DHCP server.

30. Log off both computers.

Certification Objectives

Objectives for the CompTIA Network+ Exam:

- 1.3 Install and configure the following networking services/applications
- 4.6 Given a scenario, troubleshoot and resolve common network issues
- 5.10 Given a scenario, configure and apply the appropriate ports and protocols

Review Questions

1. What was the IP address the Windows computer obtained in Step 23?

2. When does the DHCP lease you obtained in this lab expire?

3. Which of the following are valid methods of assigning IP addresses to workstations, servers, and network devices? (Choose all that apply.)

   a. Manual configuration

   b. DHCP

   c. BOOTP

   d. POST

4. You would like to assign a WINS server to each workstation. Can you accomplish this via DHCP?

5. Your colleague placed a second DHCP server on the network by mistake. What might happen as a result? (Choose all that apply.)

   a. The second DHCP server might lease duplicate addresses to some hosts.

   b. The second DHCP server might give out incorrect settings to its clients.

   c. DHCP might stop working on the first DHCP server.

   d. You might need to configure IP addresses on some hosts manually.

6. Which of the following information could not be given out by a DHCP server?

   a. WINS server address

   b. DNS server address

   c. Default gateway

   d. Additional network protocols to be used

7. All of the following configuration information can be supplied by a DHCP server. Which of the following cannot be supplied by APIPA? (Choose all that apply.)

   a. IP address

   b. Subnet mask

   c. DNS servers

   d. Default gateway

Lab 2.5 Configuring Domain Name System (DNS) Properties

Objectives

The Domain Name System (DNS) is a method of associating an IP address with a host name. It is an alternative to the hosts file, and is much easier to manage and maintain over many servers. For that reason, DNS is used throughout the Internet. When you open a Web browser and attempt to connect to *comptia.org*, for example, the Web browser first queries a DNS server to find the IP address of the Web site. If the DNS server your computer is configured to use does not know the IP address associated with *comptia.org*, it queries the authoritative name server for the comptia.com domain (or zone). The authoritative name server is the DNS server with the definitive DNS information for that domain. When the authoritative DNS server responds with the IP address to your DNS server, your DNS server sends that information to your computer. The Web browser on your computer then uses that IP address to connect to the Web site.

In addition to finding the IP address belonging to a particular host name (a process known as a forward DNS lookup), DNS is also used to find the host name belonging to a particular IP address. This process is known as a reverse DNS lookup. A computer can use a reverse DNS lookup to determine the name of a computer attempting to access its network resources. However, reverse DNS lookups are not a reliable way of determining this information.

One tool you can use to find DNS information directly is the `nslookup` command. This command allows you to find the IP address associated with a particular host name and other information.

Keep in mind that beginning with Windows 2000 Server, DNS has become tightly integrated with Active Directory. Before Windows 2000 Server, making a mistake when configuring DNS might prevent you from accessing a server by name. Now, making a mistake configuring DNS can prevent Active Directory from working properly. Keeping DNS working properly is very important in networks that use Windows Server.

After completing this lab, you will be able to:

- Add a DNS server to DNS
- Add a DNS zone
- Add a DNS host
- Configure a computer to refer to the DNS server
- Access a computer using its DNS name

Materials Required

This lab will require the following:

- A computer named *SERVER1* running Windows Server 2012 R2 configured with an IP address of 192.168.54.1 and a subnet mask of 255.255.255.0

- *SERVER1* configured as a domain controller for the netpluslab.net domain with the DNS server role installed

- A reverse lookup zone configured for the 192.168.54.x subnet

- A computer running Windows 8.1 or Windows 7 named *WORKSTATION1* configured with an IP address of 192.168.54.3 and a subnet mask of 255.255.255.0, but without a DNS server configured

- A second computer running Windows 8.1 or Windows 7 named *WORKSTATION2* configured with an IP address of 192.168.54.5 and a subnet mask of 255.255.255.0, but without a DNS server configured

- Each computer connected to a hub or switch with straight-through Cat 5 (or better) UTP cables

Most of the steps in this lab can also be completed using virtualization software such as VMware.

Estimated completion time: **30 minutes**

Activity

1. Log on to *SERVER1* as the administrator. Windows Server Manager opens.

2. Click **Tools**, and then click **DNS**. The DNS Manager window opens.

3. Double-click the server name to expand the tree underneath it. Right-click the name of the server. Click **New Zone**. The New Zone Wizard opens.

4. Click **Next**. The next window in the wizard asks you to select the type of zone you want to configure.

5. Make sure that the **Primary zone** option button is selected and click **Next**. The next window in the wizard asks you to choose whether you want to create a forward or reverse lookup zone.

6. Make sure that the **Forward lookup zone** option is selected and click **Next**. The wizard now asks you to choose a name for the zone.

7. In the Zone name text box, type **otherorg.net**, and then click **Next**. The next window asks if you want to create a new zone file or use an existing one.

8. Make sure the **Create a new file with this file name** option button is selected, and then click **Next**. The next window in the wizard asks you to select the type of DNS updates to be used.

9. Click **Next** to select the default option. The next window in the wizard summarizes the options that you have chosen and indicates that you have finished.

10. Click **Finish**. The New Zone Wizard closes.

11. In the left pane of the DNS Manager window, click the **right-facing arrow** next to the Forward Lookup Zones folder. The tree expands, showing a list of domains for which this DNS server is authoritative, including the new otherorg.net domain.

12. In the left pane, click the **otherorg.net** folder to select it. Right-click the **otherorg.net** folder, and click **New Host (A or AAAA)** from the shortcut menu. The New Host dialog box opens.

13. In the Name text box, type **workstation1**. In the IP address text box, type **192.168.54.3**. Place a check in the **Create associated pointer (PTR) record** check box. Figure 2-5 shows the DNS Manager window and the New Host dialog box.

14. Click the **Add Host** button. The DNS dialog box opens, indicating that the host record workstation1.otherorg.net was successfully created.

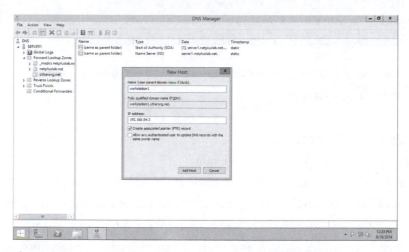

Figure 2-5   The DNS Manager window and New Host dialog box

15. Click **OK**. The DNS dialog box closes.

16. Click **Done**. The New Host dialog box closes.

17. Click the **netpluslab.net** folder to select it, right-click the **netpluslab.net** folder, and then click **New Host (A or AAAA)** from the shortcut menu. The New Host dialog box opens.

18. In the New Host dialog box, repeat Steps 13 through 15, creating the domain name **workstation2.netpluslab.net** with an IP address of **192.168.54.5**.

19. Click **Done**.

20. Log on to *WORKSTATION1* as an administrator. The Windows desktop appears.

21. Right-click the network icon in the system tray. Click **Open Network and Sharing Center**. Click **Change adapter settings**. The Network Connections window opens.

22. Right-click the **Ethernet0** or **Local Area Connection** icon and then click **Properties** in the shortcut menu. The Ethernet0 or Local Area Connection Properties window opens.

23. Double-click **Internet Protocol Version 4 (TCP/IPv4)**. The Internet Protocol Version 4 (TCP/IPv4) Properties window opens.

24. Click the **Use the following DNS server addresses** option button, if necessary. In the Preferred DNS server text box, type **192.168.54.1**.

25. Click **OK** twice to exit the Ethernet0 Properties window.

26. Open a Command Prompt window.

27. In the Command Prompt window, type `nslookup workstation2.netpluslab.net` and press **Enter**. The computer displays the name *workstation2.netpluslab.net* and its IP address, as well as the IP address of the DNS server answering the request.

28. Type **ping workstation2.netpluslab.net** and press **Enter**. The computer indicates that it has received four replies from the remote computer, and displays its IP address.

29. Repeat Steps 27 and 28, pinging **workstation1.otherorg.net**.

30. Log off all three computers.

Certification Objectives

Objectives for the CompTIA Network+ Exam:

- 1.3 Install and configure the following networking services/applications
- 4.2 Given a scenario, analyze and interpret the output of troubleshooting tools
- 4.6 Given a scenario, troubleshoot and resolve common network issues
- 5.10 Given a scenario, configure and apply the appropriate ports and protocols

Review Questions

1. What is the purpose of a name server?

   a. To maintain the MAC address database for an entire zone

   b. To supply clients with IP address resolution for requested hosts

   c. To track and record all TCP/IP host name information for a network

   d. To track and record all NetBIOS naming information for a network

2. What is the term for the group of devices that a name server manages?

   a. Hierarchy

   b. Tree

   c. Zone

   d. Directory

3. Which of the following are examples of top-level domains? (Choose all that apply.)

   a. .net

   b. .com

   c. .uk

   d. .aut

4. When a DNS server retrieves the host name associated with an IP address, what type of lookup is it accomplishing?

   a. Forward

   b. Adjacent

   c. Backward

   d. Reverse

5. What is one advantage of using DNS instead of hosts files?

   a. DNS does not require manual updating of files on multiple networked nodes.

   b. DNS is more compatible with Linux systems.

   c. DNS will map both NetBIOS and TCP/IP host names to IP addresses, whereas hosts files will map only TCP/IP host names to IP addresses.

   d. Using DNS is more secure than using hosts files.

Lab 2.6 Using FTP

Objectives

In this lab, you will connect to a File Transfer Protocol (FTP) server on a remote host. FTP is used throughout the Internet to make files available for downloading. If a network administrator would like to make files available to the general public, she can create an anonymous FTP server. Users can log on to an anonymous FTP server by using a special account named *anonymous* without knowing the password.

FTP servers are available on nearly all platforms. If you run an anonymous FTP server, you should be careful when allowing anonymous users to upload files (that is, transfer files to the server) because malicious users could fill up your server's disk drive with their files. Another potential problem with FTP is that it sends passwords in unencrypted text, so they could be captured by a malicious user. In a later lab, you will explore some of the security limitations of using an unsecure FTP.

A variety of FTP clients are available for almost all modern operating systems. Command-line FTP clients are built into most modern operating systems, including Linux and Windows, but various GUI clients are also available. A GUI client will automate the FTP process for you, and might include additional features such as the ability to resume interrupted downloads.

After completing this lab, you will be able to:

- Log on to an FTP site
- Download files from an FTP site
- Copy files to an FTP site
- Define security policies for an FTP site

Materials Required

This lab will require the following:

- A computer named *SERVER1* running Windows Server 2012 R2 configured with an IP address of 192.168.54.1 and a subnet mask of 255.255.255.0
- Internet Information Services (IIS) version 8.5 installed and running on *SERVER1* with the FTP service installed, with a root of C:\Inetpub\ftproot for the FTP service and with the default configuration and sample files in place
- The folder C:\Inetpub\ftproot configured so that users in the Domain Users group have Read, Write, and Execute permissions

- *SERVER1* firewall configured to allow FTP traffic
- Access to *SERVER1* as the administrator
- A user account named *netplus* in the Domain Users group in the netpluslab.net domain
- A computer running Windows 8.1 or Windows 7 named *WORKSTATION1*, configured with an IP address of 192.168.54.3 and a subnet mask of 255.255.255.0
- Both computers connected to a hub with Cat 5 (or better) UTP cables

Most of the steps in this lab can also be completed using virtualization software such as VMware.

Estimated completion time: **35 minutes**

Activity

1. Log on to *SERVER1* as the administrator. Windows Server Manager opens.

2. Right-click the **Start** button and then click **Command Prompt**. A Command Prompt window opens.

3. In the Command Prompt window, type **echo** *your name* **> C:\Inetpub\ftproot\netplus.txt** (substituting your name for *your name*) and then press **Enter**. This creates a file named *netplus.txt* containing your name in the C:\Inetpub\ftproot directory.

4. At the command prompt, type **copy C:\Inetpub\wwwroot\iis-85.png C:\Inetpub\ftproot** and press Enter. The computer copies the file from one directory to the other. This image file now will be available on the FTP site configured on this computer.

5. Log on to *WORKSTATION1* as the netplus user. The Windows desktop appears.

6. Click the **Start** button, type **cmd**, and then press **Enter**. A Command Prompt window opens.

7. In the Command Prompt window, type **ftp 192.168.54.1** and press **Enter**. The computer indicates that you have connected to 192.168.54.1, and that the remote computer is running the Microsoft FTP service. The prompt changes to User (192.168.54.1:(none)):.

8. At the User (192.168.54.1:(none)): prompt, type **anonymous** and press **Enter**. The computer indicates that anonymous access is allowed and asks you to type an email address or other form of identity as a password. The Password prompt also appears. At the Password prompt, type an email address or a brief phrase, and then press **Enter**. Note that the letters you type do not echo to the screen. The computer indicates that you have logged on successfully, and the prompt changes to ftp>. Figure 2-6 shows a user logging on to an FTP server.

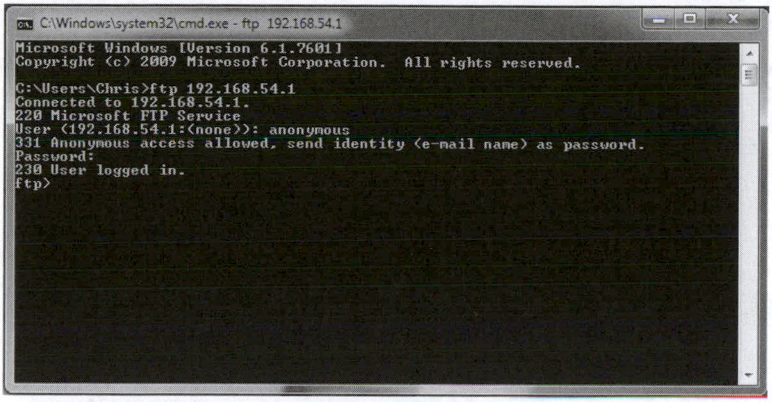

Figure 2-6   Logging on to an FTP server

9. Type **dir** and press **Enter**. A list of the files found on the remote computer, including iis-85.png and netplus.txt, is displayed.

10. At the prompt, type **get netplus.txt** and press **Enter**. The default file transfer type is ASCII mode data connection. ASCII mode allows FTP to transfer plaintext files more quickly and ensures that a plaintext file is readable by the computer that downloads it. An ASCII mode transfer will corrupt files that are not in plaintext, such as image or program files. It will also corrupt many word processor files, such as Microsoft Word documents, because these are not stored as plaintext files by the word processor.

11. To transfer the image file, type **binary** at the prompt, and then press **Enter**. The computer will now transfer files using binary mode. In a binary mode transfer, an exact copy of the file is transferred from the server.

12. Type **get iis-85.png** at the prompt, and then press **Enter**. The computer indicates that the file is being transferred in binary mode. The ftp> prompt returns when the transfer is complete.

13. Type **!copy netplus.txt upload.txt** and press **Enter**. The computer displays the message "1 file(s) copied." The exclamation mark (!) tells the FTP program that you want to run a command on *WORKSTATION1* that copies the file netplus.txt to upload.txt in the directory you are working in on *WORKSTATION1*.

14. To try to upload a file to the remote server, type **put upload.txt** and press **Enter**. The computer indicates that access is denied.

15. Type **quit** and press **Enter** to exit the FTP site.

16. Log off both computers.

Certification Objectives

Objectives for the CompTIA Network+ Exam:

- 5.10 Given a scenario, configure and apply the appropriate ports and protocols

Review Questions

1. Which of the following commands would you type at the `ftp>` prompt to copy a file named *textfile.doc* from your C:\ directory to an FTP server?

   a. `copy "textfile.doc"`

   b. `put C:\textfile.doc`

   c. `get C:\textfile.doc`

   d. `move C:\textfile.doc`

2. On what Transport layer protocol does FTP rely?

   a. TCP

   b. UDP

   c. ICMP

   d. NTP

3. What is the term for an FTP site that allows any user to access its directories?

   a. Anonymous

   b. Restricted

   c. Private

   d. Unlimited

4. What command allows you to list the contents of a directory on an FTP server?

   a. `list`

   b. `lf`

   c. `ls`

   d. `la`

5. What would you type at the `ftp>` prompt to view a list of available FTP commands? (Choose all that apply.)

   a. `list`

   b. `?`

   c. `help`

   d. `commands`

6. What two file types can you specify when transferring files via FTP?

   a. ASCII and binary

   b. Alphabetical and numeric

   c. Program and data

   d. Dynamic and static

Lab 2.7 Understanding Port Numbers

Objectives

In TCP/IP, servers use port numbers to identify processes associated with different services. For instance, a server might run several different services over TCP, including HTTP and FTP. Based only on the IP address, there is no way to distinguish between the two services. However, requests from client computers can connect to different port numbers. The default port number for the HTTP service, for example, is 80, whereas the default port number for the FTP control service is 21.

Most client software is designed to look for the default port number when connecting to a service. For example, by default, Web browsers attempt to find Web servers at port 80. However, you can usually configure a service to run on another port and configure the client software to look for that service on the new port.

You can tell a Web browser to look for a Web server at a nondefault port by adding a colon and the port number after the Web site name or IP address in the URL. For instance, to go to the Microsoft Web site using the default port (80), you would use the URL *microsoft.com*. To look for a Web server at the same site on port 7777, you would use the URL http//:www.*microsoft.com:7777* instead. Port numbers in UDP work the same way as port numbers in TCP.

After completing this lab, you will be able to:

- Identify default port numbers for several services
- Modify a service's default port numbers
- Connect to a service using a nondefault port number

Materials Required

This lab will require the following:

- A computer named *SERVER1* running Windows Server 2012 R2, configured as a domain controller for the netpluslab.net domain, with an IP address of 192.168.54.1 and a subnet mask of 255.255.255.0
- Internet Information Services (IIS) installed and running on *SERVER1* with the default configuration; to ensure that the default configuration is enabled, you can remove and reinstall the software
- A text file in *SERVER1's* Web root (C:\Inetpub\wwwroot) named *default.htm* and containing the text "This is a test page."
- Access as the Administrator to *SERVER1*
- A computer running Windows 8.1 or Windows 7 named *WORKSTATION1*, configured with an IP address of 192.168.54.3 and a subnet mask of 255.255.255.0
- Access with an ordinary user account to the client computer
- Both computers connected to a hub or switch with straight-through Cat 5 (or better) UTP cables

Most of the steps in this lab can also be completed using virtualization software such as VMware.

Estimated completion time: **20 minutes**

Activity

1. Log on to *WORKSTATION1* with an ordinary user account. The Windows desktop appears.

2. Open Internet Explorer.

3. In the address box, type **http://192.168.54.1** and press **Enter**. A Web page opens containing the text "This is a test page."

4. If you are not already logged on to *SERVER1* as the Administrator, do so now.

5. In Server Manager, click **Tools,** and then click **Internet Information Services (IIS) Manager**. The Internet Information Services (IIS) Manager window opens.

6. Right-click the **Default Web Site** icon in the right pane of the window, and then click **Edit Bindings**. The Site Bindings dialog box opens.

7. Select http and click **Edit,** change the port number from 80 to **8880**. This tells IIS to run the Web server on port 8880 instead of on port 80. Click OK. Figure 2-7 shows the Site Bindings dialog box.

8. Click **Close** to close the Site Bindings dialog box, and then, in the right pane of the Internet Information Services (IIS) Manager window, click **Restart**.

9. Close the Internet Information Services (IIS) Manager window.

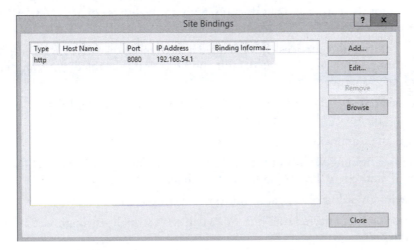

Figure 2-7 The Site Bindings dialog box

10. On *WORKSTATION1*, close Internet Explorer. This ensures that Internet Explorer does not use its disk cache of the Web page when you try to load the Web page again.

11. Now reopen Internet Explorer.

12. In the address box, type **http://192.168.54.1** and then press **Enter**. An error message appears indicating that the page cannot be displayed.

13. In the address box, type **http://192.168.54.1:8880** and then press **Enter**. A Web page displays the text "This is a test page."

14. Log off both computers.

Certification Objectives

Objectives for the CompTIA Network+ Exam:

- 5.9 Compare and contrast the following ports and protocols

Review Questions

1. What symbol is used to separate the computer name from the port number in a URL (assuming that IP version 4 is in use)?

   a. ;

   b. :

   c. #

   d. .

2. What is the default port number for the Telnet service?

   a. 20

   b. 21

   c. 22

   d. 23

3. What is the default port number for the HTTP service?

   a. 40

   b. 44

   c. 60

   d. 80

4. What range of port numbers comprises the well-known port numbers?

   a. 0 to 64

   b. 0 to 128

   c. 0 to 1023

   d. 0 to 8880

5. What is a socket?

   a. A virtual connector that associates a URL with its IP address

   b. A method of identifying the IP addresses belonging to clients as they connect to servers

   c. A logical address assigned to a specific process running on a computer

   d. A discrete unit of data

6. Which of the following addresses could represent the SMTP service using its default port on a mail server?

   a. 188.65.79.80:25

   b. 188.65.79.80...24

   c. 188.65.79.80$24

   d. 188.65.79.80;25

CHAPTER THREE

HOW DATA GETS TRANSPORTED OVER NETWORKS

Labs included in this chapter

- Lab 3.1 Finding the MAC Address of Another Computer
- Lab 3.2 Looking at Network Connections on a Windows Computer
- Lab 3.3 Examining Ethernet Frames in Wireshark
- Lab 3.4 Capturing Network Data in Wireshark
- Lab 3.5 Using the Ping Utility to Troubleshoot a TCP/IP Network
- Lab 3.6 Using the Traceroute Utility to Troubleshoot a TCP/IP Network
- Lab 3.7 Troubleshooting Web Client Problems

CompTIA Network+ Exam Objectives

Objective	Lab
1.8 Given a scenario, implement and configure the appropriate addressing schema	3.1
2.1 Given a scenario, use appropriate monitoring tools	3.3
3.2 Compare and contrast common network vulnerabilities and threats	3.4
4.1 Given a scenario, implement the following network troubleshooting methodology	3.5, 3.7
4.2 Given a scenario, analyze and interpret the output of troubleshooting tools	3.1, 3.2, 3.5, 3.6, 3.7
4.7 Given a scenario, troubleshoot and resolve common security issues	3.1, 3.4
5.1 Analyze a scenario and determine the corresponding OSI layer	3.1, 3.2

Lab 3.1 Finding the MAC Address of Another Computer

Objectives

The MAC address operates at the Media Access Control sublayer of the Data Link layer. It is a unique address assigned by the manufacturer when the NIC is built. In TCP/IP networks, the Address Resolution Protocol (ARP) allows a computer to associate another computer's MAC address at the Data Link layer with its IP address at the Network layer. A computer keeps track of these associations in its ARP cache. If a computer does not see packets from one of the computers whose MAC address is in its ARP cache for a certain period of time (called the ARP timeout), the computer removes that MAC address from its ARP cache.

A MAC address consists of two parts. The first part, known as the *block ID*, consists of six characters assigned to the vendor by the Institute of Electrical and Electronics Engineers (IEEE). The second part, known as the *device ID*, consists of six characters assigned by the vendor. Each MAC address should be unique. Each character in a MAC address is a hexadecimal number, consisting of numbers from 0 to 9 and letters from *a* to *f*. A MAC address is often represented with colons or dashes between every pair of characters, such as 00:60:97:7F:41:A1 or 00-60-97-7F-41-A1.

You can use the `arp` command to look at the entries in a computer's ARP cache and to find the MAC addresses of other computers it has communicated with on its local network segment. Incorrect ARP entries can prevent two computers from communicating. For instance, on very rare occasions, two computers will be found on the same network with identical MAC addresses (generally due to manufacturer error). These computers will have difficulty communicating with other computers on that network. More commonly, replacing a computer's NIC might prevent that computer from communicating with other computers on the network until their ARP cache entries time out.

In this lab, you will use the `arp` command to find the MAC address of another computer. After completing this lab, you will be able to:

- Use the `arp` command to find and set the MAC address of another computer

Materials Required

This lab will require the following:

- The network required in Lab 1.4, consisting of a computer named *SERVER1* running Windows Server 2012 R2 with an IP address of 192.168.54.1 and a computer named *WORKSTATION1* running Windows 8.1 or Windows 7 with an IP address of 192.168.54.2

- Administrative access to both computers

Most of the steps in this lab can also be completed using virtualization software such as VMware.

Estimated completion time: **20–30 minutes**

Figure 3-1 Typical output from the `ping` command

Activity

1. Log on to *WORKSTATION1* as an ordinary user. The Windows desktop appears.

2. Open the Command Prompt window.

3. You will now test network connectivity between *WORKSTATION1* and *SERVER1*. Type **ping 192.168.54.1** in the Command Prompt window and press **Enter**. The computer indicates that it has received four replies from 192.168.54.1. See Figure 3-1 for an example of the output produced. This indicates that the two computers can communicate with each other over the network. If they could not, the `ping` command would display an error message such as "Request timed out."

4. Repeat Steps 1 through 3 on *SERVER1*, logging on as an administrator. Use the IP address **192.168.54.2** in Step 3.

5. On *SERVER1*, type **arp -a** in the Command Prompt window and press **Enter**. The computer prints a list of IP addresses and the physical addresses, or MAC addresses, associated with each. Record the MAC address for 192.168.54.2, the *WORKSTATION1*.

6. Now you will replace the actual MAC address of *WORKSTATION1* with a bogus MAC address and see how it affects the ability of the two machines to communicate with each other. On *Server1*, open the Command Prompt window as an administrator, type **arp -s 192.168.54.2 00-11-22-33-44-55** and press **Enter**. The Windows Server computer replaces the MAC address for *WORKSTATION1* in its ARP cache with an incorrect one.

7. Type **arp -a** and press **Enter**. What is the MAC address for *WORKSTATION1* now?

8. On *WORKSTATION1*, repeat Step 3. Are you able to ping *SERVER1* successfully?

9. In the Command Prompt window, type **ipconfig /all**. The computer prints detailed information about its network configuration, including its MAC address. Does this MAC address match the one for *WORKSTATION1* that you found in Step 5?

10. Now you will delete the ARP entry you created for *WORKSTATION1*. On *SERVER1*, type **arp -d** and press **Enter**. All ARP entries are deleted. For your reference, Table 3-1 lists some options for the `arp` command in Windows.

Table 3-1   Options for the `arp` command in Windows

Command	Action
`arp -a`	Displays all the addresses in the ARP cache
`arp -s`	Adds a static, or permanent, entry to the ARP cache
`arp -d`	Deletes entries from the ARP cache

© 2016 Cengage Learning®

11. On *WORKSTATION1*, repeat Step 3. Are you able to communicate with *SERVER1* successfully now?

12. Log off both computers.

Certification Objectives

Objectives for the CompTIA Network+ Exam:

- 1.8 Given a scenario, implement and configure the appropriate addressing schema
- 4.2 Given a scenario, analyze and interpret the output of troubleshooting tools
- 4.7 Given a scenario, troubleshoot and resolve common security issues
- 5.1 Analyze a scenario and determine the corresponding OSI layer

Review Questions

1. What do the first six characters of a MAC address indicate?
   a. The device ID assigned by the vendor
   b. The block ID assigned by IEEE
   c. The logical address assigned by DHCP
   d. The logical address assigned by DNS

2. Which of the following is a valid MAC address?
   a. 01-ba-cd83-21
   b. 01-ba-cd-de-83-21-42
   c. 01-ba-cd-de-83-21-42-a0
   d. 01-ba-cd-de-83-21

3. Which of the following commands can you use to find a Windows computer's MAC address from a Command Prompt window on that computer?
   a. `ipconfig`
   b. `ipconfig /all`
   c. `arp -a`
   d. `netstat`

4. Which of the following commands can you use to find the MAC address of another computer on the same network?

   a. `ipconfig`

   b. `ipconfig /all`

   c. `arp -a`

   d. `netstat`

5. Under what circumstances is it possible for a computer to have more than one MAC address?

   a. Never

   b. If a computer has more than one NIC

   c. If a computer has more than one NIC, but only if it is acting as a router

   d. If a computer is a router

6. You have just replaced the NIC on a server, making no other changes. It can communicate with all the computers on its network but one. What is the most likely explanation for this?

   a. The new NIC is not working properly.

   b. Both computers have the same MAC address.

   c. The remote computer has the old MAC address entry in its ARP cache.

   d. The remote computer has a bad NIC.

7. Which of the following is a function of the Data Link layer?

   a. Arranging data in proper sequence at the destination

   b. Encrypting data prior to transmission

   c. Dividing data into distinct frames

   d. Issuing electrical signals onto a wire

8. What part of a data frame checks to make sure that the data arrived exactly as it was sent?

   a. CRC

   b. Start delimiter

   c. Payload

   d. Padding

Lab 3.2 Looking at Network Connections on a Windows Computer

Objectives

The Transport layer ensures that data travels from the source host to the destination host. Transport layer protocols might check for errors. They also might ensure that data arrives in the proper order. In the TCP/IP stack, TCP is the protocol operating at the Transport layer. Because TCP is a connection-oriented protocol, the computers on both ends of a TCP connection must keep track of the status of the connection.

You can use the `netstat` command on Windows, UNIX, and other operating systems to look at active connections. This command can show detailed information about active network connections, including their status, the number of bytes sent over the network, and other information. UDP, on the other hand, is a connectionless protocol and does not keep track of the connection. As a result, the `netstat` command provides much less information about UDP connections.

After completing this lab, you will be able to:

- Use the `netstat` command to view information about the Transport layer

Materials Required

This lab will require the following:

- The network required in Lab 1.4, consisting of a computer named *SERVER1* running Windows Server 2012 R2 with an IP address of 192.168.54.1 and a computer named *WORKSTATION1* running Windows 8.1 or Windows 7 with an IP address of 192.168.54.2

- Administrative access to both computers

- Terminal Services running on *SERVER1* and the computer configured to allow users to log on remotely

Most of the steps in this lab can also be completed using virtualization software such as VMware.

Estimated completion time: **20 minutes**

Activity

1. Log on to *WORKSTATION1* as an administrator. The Windows desktop appears.

2. Open the Command Prompt window.

3. Type **netstat** and press **Enter**. The computer displays information about all open connections on the computer, or returns to the prompt if there are none.

4. Now you will open a new TCP connection by using the Remote Desktop Connection. This program is used to log on to Windows machines remotely. In this lab, you will just use it to create a TCP connection. Click **Start**, type **Remote Desktop Connection** (in Windows 7, click **Start**, click **All Programs**, click **Accessories**), and then click **Remote Desktop Connection**. The Remote Desktop Connection window opens.

5. Type **192.168.54.1** in the Computer text box. Click **Connect**. The Windows Security dialog box for the Windows Server computer opens.

6. Log on as an administrator. The Windows Server desktop appears. If necessary, click Yes in the Remote Desktop Connection dialog box.

7. Click the **Minimize** button on the horizontal bar at the top of the window to minimize the Remote Desktop session.

8. In the Command Prompt window, type **netstat** and press **Enter**. The computer displays information about the connection, indicating the protocol used, the state of the connection, the local address, the destination address, and the ports or service name used by each side of the connection. The state of the connection should be ESTABLISHED. What protocol is used by the Remote Desktop Connection? Figure 3-2 shows the output of the netstat command.

9. On *SERVER1*, press **CTRL+ALT+Del** if necessary and log on as an administrator. The Windows Server desktop appears and the Remote Desktop connection from *WORKSTATION1* is automatically ended.

10. Open the Command Prompt window.

11. In the Command Prompt window, type **netstat** and press **Enter**. How are the results of the netstat command different when run on the server?

12. Type **netstat -e** and press **Enter**. The computer displays information about the number of bytes sent and received, and about the number of packets sent and received. Table 3-2 shows options for the netstat command.

13. Type **ping 192.168.54.2** and press **Enter**. The computer indicates that it has received four replies from 192.168.54.2.

Figure 3-2   Typical output from the netstat command

Table 3-2   Options for the netstat command

Command	Action
netstat -a	Displays all connections and listening ports
netstat -e	Displays Ethernet statistics
netstat -s	Displays statistics per protocol
netstat -r	Displays the routing table
netstat -n	Displays numbers instead of names (usually used with the -a or -r options)

14. Type **netstat -e** again and press **Enter**. Has the number of packets sent and received increased?

15. Type **netstat -s** and press **Enter**. The computer displays information about individual protocols used.

16. Close the Remote Desktop Connection dialog box and log off both computers.

Certification Objectives

Objectives for the CompTIA Network+ Exam:

- 4.2 Given a scenario, analyze and interpret the output of troubleshooting tools
- 5.1 Analyze a scenario and determine the corresponding OSI layer

Review Questions

1. What protocol is used by Remote Desktop Connection?

    a. ICMP

    b. TCP

    c. UDP

    d. IP

2. About which protocols does the netstat -s command print information? (Choose all that apply.)

    a. ARP

    b. ICMP

    c. TCP

    d. UDP

3. At what layer of the OSI model does TCP work?

    a. Physical layer

    b. Data Link layer

    c. Network layer

    d. Transport layer

4. At what layer of the OSI model does IP work?

    a. Physical layer

    b. Data Link layer

    c. Network layer

    d. Transport layer

5. A user is having difficulty connecting to a remote Web site. After the user attempts to connect, the `netstat` command tells you that the connection state is established. Where in the OSI model is the problem probably located?

   a. At the Data Link layer

   b. At the Network layer

   c. At the Transport layer

   d. Somewhere above the Transport layer

6. Why doesn't the `netstat` command display any information about ICMP connections?

   a. ICMP does not function at the Transport layer.

   b. ICMP is not a true protocol.

   c. ICMP is a connectionless protocol.

   d. ICMP is considered unimportant.

Lab 3.3 Examining Ethernet Frames in Wireshark

Objectives

In this lab, you will capture and examine parts of an Ethernet frame using a software protocol analyzer called Wireshark. Every Ethernet frame contains a number of fields, including the 7-byte preamble (which tells the NIC that it is about to receive data), the 1-byte start-of-frame delimiter (which indicates that the frame is about to start), the 14-byte header (containing the destination MAC address, the source MAC address, and another field that depends on the frame type), 46 to 1500 bytes of data, and the 4-byte frame check sequence (FCS) field, which uses a cyclic redundancy check (CRC) to determine if the data in the frame has been corrupted. If the data field is not at least 46 bytes long, it will be padded by the sending host until it is 46 bytes long. Only the header, the data and any padding, and the FCS field are used to determine the size of the frame.

The dominant Ethernet frame type in modern networks is Ethernet II. The most important difference between the Ethernet II frame and other types of Ethernet frames is the type field in the header. This field contains a code for the protocol used, such as IP, IPX, or ARP, and makes it possible for Ethernet II frames to carry multiple types of protocols. (The Ethernet SNAP frame type also has a type field. However, it also uses additional fields, resulting in extra overhead.)

Note that neither Wireshark nor most other software protocol analyzers can capture the preamble and the FCS field. On most operating systems, these fields are discarded before they reach the operating system. To see these fields, you might need to use a dedicated hardware protocol analyzer such as RADCOM's PrismLite Integrated WAN/LAN/ATM Protocol Analyzer.

After completing this lab, you will be able to:

• Distinguish between the parts of an Ethernet frame

Materials Required

This lab will require the following:

- The network required in Lab 1.4, consisting of a computer named *SERVER1* running Windows Server 2012 R2 with an IP address of 192.168.54.1 and a computer named *WORKSTATION1* running Windows 8.1 or Windows 7 with an IP address of 192.168.54.2

- Administrative access to both computers

- The FTP service installed and configured from Lab 2.6

- The network protocol analyzer Wireshark (available from *wireshark.org*) installed on *SERVER1*

Most of the steps in this lab can also be completed using virtualization software such as VMware.

Estimated completion time: **45 minutes**

Activity

1. Log on to *SERVER1* as the administrator. The Windows Server desktop appears.

2. Click **Start**, type **Wireshark**, and then click **Wireshark**. The Wireshark Network Protocol Analyzer opens.

3. Click **Capture**, and then click **Start**.

4. The Wireshark window opens, displaying the number of frames of each type captured.

5. Open a Command Prompt window.

6. Type `ping -t 192.168.54.2` and press **Enter**. The computer begins pinging 192.168.54.2 and will continue to do so until you stop it.

7. Look at the Wireshark window. When the total number of frames captured is greater than 10, click **Stop**. A list of captured frames appears in the top pane, and details about the highlighted frame appear in the bottom two panes. Figure 3-3 shows an example of a captured frame.

8. Click a frame listed as ICMP in the Protocol column to highlight it. Detailed information about the frame appears in the bottom two panes.

9. In the middle pane, click the plus sign next to Ethernet II to expand the tree below it. Record the source and destination addresses.

10. Record the destination and source addresses in the Internet Protocol part of the frame. (This is part of the data field of the frame.) Was this frame sent from *SERVER1* or was it sent from *WORKSTATION1*?

11. In the Command Prompt window, press **CTRL+C** to stop the `ping` command, then type `ipconfig/all` and press **Enter**. What is the MAC address for this host? Does it match one of the addresses you recorded in Step 9?

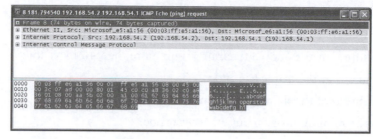

Figure 3-3 A captured frame
Source: The Wireshark Foundation

12. Type `arp -a` and press **Enter**. Look for the IP address of the other computer. Does its associated MAC address match one of the addresses you recorded in Step 9?

13. Look at the Type field below "Ethernet II." What is this frame's type? Does it match the protocol listed in Wireshark's protocol column? Why or why not?

14. Log off both computers.

Certification Objectives

Objectives for the CompTIA Network+ Exam:

- 2.1 Given a scenario, use appropriate monitoring tools

Review Questions

1. What is the purpose of the checksum?

   a. To ensure that data arrives in the proper sequence

   b. To ensure that data is properly encrypted and decrypted

   c. To ensure that data arrives at its intended destination

   d. To ensure that data arrives whole and intact

2. How many times is a checksum calculated when a frame of data is sent from a source computer to a destination computer that resides on the same segment?

   a. 1

   b. 2

   c. 3

   d. 4

3. What type of address identifies the source of data in a frame?

   a. MAC

   b. Logical

   c. Network

   d. Host

4. What is the purpose of padding in an Ethernet frame?

   a. To ensure that the data in the frame is exactly 1500 bytes long

   b. To ensure that the data in the frame is no more than 46 bytes long

   c. To signal that the frame has ended

   d. To ensure that the data in the frame is at least 46 bytes long

5. What is the minimum size of an Ethernet frame?

   a. 56 bytes

   b. 64 bytes

   c. 128 bytes

   d. 256 bytes

6. Which parts of an Ethernet frame are Wireshark and other protocol analyzers unlikely to capture? (Choose all that apply.)

   a. Header

   b. Frame check sequence

   c. Padding

   d. Preamble

Lab 3.4 Capturing Network Data in Wireshark

Objectives

Protocol analyzers such as Wireshark can also be used to look at the data contained in a frame. This data includes the Network layer packet, which itself contains data. If the data is not securely encrypted, sensitive information such as usernames and passwords can be captured. In this lab, you will use Wireshark to capture a frame from an FTP logon attempt. Because FTP does not encrypt this information, it will be readable.

After completing this lab, you will be able to:

- Read unsecured data from an Ethernet frame

Materials Required

This lab will require the following:

- The network required in Lab 1.4, consisting of a computer named *SERVER1* running Windows Server 2012 R2 with an IP address of 192.168.54.1 and a computer named *WORKSTATION1* running Windows 8.1 or Windows 7 with an IP address of 192.168.54.2

- Administrative access to both computers

- The FTP service installed and configured from Lab 2.6
- The network protocol analyzer Wireshark (available from *wireshark.org*) installed on *SERVER1*

Most of the steps in this lab can also be completed using virtualization software such as VMware.

Estimated completion time: **45 minutes**

Activity

1. Log on to *SERVER1* as the administrator. The Windows Server desktop appears.

2. Click **Start**, type **Wireshark**, and click **Wireshark**. The Wireshark Network Protocol Analyzer opens.

3. Click **Capture**, and then click **Start**.

4. The Wireshark window opens, displaying the number of frames of each type captured.

5. Log on to *WORKSTATION1* as the administrator. The Windows desktop appears.

6. Open the Command Prompt window.

7. In the Command Prompt window, type `ftp 192.168.54.1` and press **Enter**. The computer indicates that you have connected to 192.168.54.1 and that the remote computer is running the Microsoft FTP service.

8. Attempt to log on with your first name as the username and **happy** as the password. The attempt will fail.

9. Look at the Wireshark window on *SERVER1* and click **Stop**.

10. To find the log on information, click **Edit** and then click **Find Packet**.

11. Click **String** and, next to "Filter," enter your first name as you typed it when you attempted to log on.

12. Click **Find**. Note that the captured frame contains both the username and password that you used while attempting to log on to the FTP server.

13. Close Wireshark and log off both computers.

Certification Objectives

Objectives for the CompTIA Network+ Exam:

- 3.2 Compare and contrast common network vulnerabilities and threats
- 4.7 Given a scenario, troubleshoot and resolve common security issues

Review Questions

1. Which of the following is true about the major types of Ethernet frames?

   a. Each frame operates at the Network layer.

   b. Each frame contains the destination and source MAC addresses.

   c. Each frame has a different maximum size.

   d. Each frame uses a preamble at the end of the frame to signal the end of the frame.

2. The packet inside a frame contains which of the following?

   a. Source destination address

   b. Source MAC address

   c. FCS

   d. Source IP address

3. Which information is not included in an Ethernet frame's 14-byte header?

   a. Frame check sequence

   b. Source address

   c. Destination address

   d. Ethernet type

4. The largest possible data field in an Ethernet frame is:

   a. 500 bytes

   b. 1000 bytes

   c. 1500 bytes

   d. 2000 bytes

5. What is the most common Ethernet frame type used on modern networks?

   a. Ethernet II

   b. Ethernet 802.3

   c. Ethernet 802.2

   d. Ethernet SNAP

Lab 3.5 Using the Ping Utility to Troubleshoot a TCP/IP Network

Objectives

The ping utility (also known as the `ping` command) is one of the most basic tools used to check network connectivity in a TCP/IP network. Every operating system that supports the TCP/IP protocol suite also supports the ping utility, which works by sending a message using the ICMP protocol to the target asking for a reply. If the message reaches the target, it sends an ICMP reply. This indicates that you have network connectivity between the computer where you used the `ping` command and the computer you are trying to reach. Keep in mind, however, that ping does not tell you anything about network services running on the remote computer, nor does it tell you anything about the type or number of hops that the ICMP messages took to reach a host.

When you use ping to troubleshoot a connectivity problem, you should first verify that TCP/IP is working properly by pinging the loopback address (127.0.0.1) and the computer's own IP address. Then, you should ping each stop along the way to the remote host that you cannot reach to verify that you can reach each stop. For instance, if you cannot ping a router along the way to a remote host, this might indicate that the router is down and might explain why you cannot reach the remote host. (Note that some routers or firewalls might block ICMP packets and prevent ping from working properly.)

After completing this lab, you will be able to:

- Use ping to determine the source of problems in a TCP/IP network

- Isolate a problem by following a logical methodology

Materials Required

This lab will require the following:

- A computer running Windows Server 2012 R2, named *SERVER1* with two NICs

- One NIC configured with an IP address of 192.168.54.1 and a subnet mask of 255.255.255.0, and the other NIC configured with an IP address of 172.16.1.1 and a subnet mask of 255.255.255.0

- Routing and Remote Access configured on *SERVER1* so that it acts as a router

- A switch named *SWITCH1* connected (with a straight-through Cat 5 or better UTP cable) to the NIC on *SERVER1* that was configured with an IP address of 192.168.54.1

- A switch named *SWITCH2* connected (with a straight-through Cat 5 or better UTP cable) to the NIC on *SERVER1* that was configured with an IP address of 172.16.1.1

- A computer running Windows 8.1 or Windows 7 named *WORKSTATION1*, configured with an IP address of 192.168.54.2 and a subnet mask of 255.255.255.0, connected to *SWITCH1* with a straight-through Cat 5 (or better) UTP cable

- A second computer running Windows 8.1 or Windows 7 named *WORKSTATION2*, configured with an IP address of 172.16.1.2 and a subnet mask of 255.255.255.0, connected to *SWITCH2* with a straight-through Cat 5 (or better) UTP cable

- Administrative access to all three computers

Most of the steps in this lab can also be completed using virtualization software such as VMware.

Estimated completion time: **45 minutes**

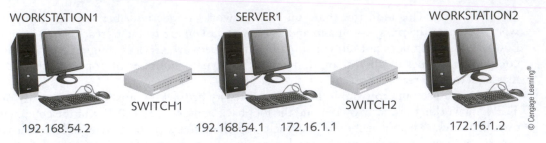

Figure 3-4   Network layout for Lab 3.5

Activity

1. Review the layout and IP addresses of the network in Figure 3-4.

2. Now you can determine if *WORKSTATION2* (which has an IP address of 172.16.1.2) is up and running. Review the following problem-isolation methodology. (Do not perform the steps yet; simply review them so that you have an overall view of how you will troubleshoot the network.)

   • Log on to the *WORKSTATION1* computer. Ping the local computer's loopback address, 127.0.0.1, to ensure that TCP/IP is installed.

   • Ping the local computer's IP address to ensure that the local computer's NIC is addressed and functioning properly.

   • Ping the near side of the router to ensure that the connection between 192.168.54.2 and 192.168.54.1 is operating properly. The term *near side* refers to the router's NIC with an IP address on the same network as the local computer.

   • Ping the far side of the router to ensure that the connection through the router is operating properly; specifically, this test ensures that the connection between 192.168.54.2 and 172.16.1.1 is functional. The term *far side* refers to the router's NIC that is on the path to a destination host with an IP address on a different network than the local computer.

   • Ping a computer on the network segment on the far side of the router; in this situation, the computer on the far side of the router is the *WORKSTATION2* computer. This ensures connectivity all the way from *WORKSTATION1* at 192.168.54.2 to *WORKSTATION2* at 172.16.1.2.

If you are working from home, you could modify the steps below to ping either side of your home Internet router.

   The following steps walk you through the procedure outlined in Step 2. For each ping test, ping issues a message indicating either success or failure. If ping returns an error at any step, you can assume that the problem lies with the connection at the particular step that produced the error.

3. Log on to *WORKSTATION1* as an administrator. The Windows desktop appears.

4. Open a Command Prompt window.

5. To determine if the local computer's NIC is operating correctly, type **ping 127.0.0.1** and then press **Enter**. Was the ping successful?

6. To determine if TCP/IP is operating properly, type **ping 192.168.54.2** and then press **Enter**. Was the ping successful?

7. To determine if the connection to the near side of the router is operating properly, type **ping 192.168.54.1** and then press **Enter**. Was the ping successful?

8. To determine if the router is operating properly, type **ping 172.16.1.1** and then press **Enter**. Was the ping successful?

9. To determine if a computer on the network segment on the far side of the router is operating properly, type **ping 172.16.1.2** and then press **Enter**. Was the ping successful?

10. Cover the link lights on each switch with a piece of paper or another obstruction. If the link lights on each computer's NICs are visible, place a box or another obstruction in front of each NIC.

11. Have your instructor or lab partner unplug one of the cables from one of the NICs in the back of the router. This should be done so that you cannot identify which cable has been removed.

12. Without looking at the link lights on the NICs or the switches, repeat Steps 7 through 9. Record the step that failed, and record the cable you think failed.

13. Remove the obstructions added in Step 10 and examine the link lights on the switches and on the NICs. Which cable was unplugged?

14. Plug in the cable that was unplugged in Step 11.

15. If you have a lab partner, repeat Steps 10 through 14 with your lab partner.

16. Log off *WORKSTATION1*.

Certification Objectives

Objectives for the CompTIA Network+ Exam:

- 4.1 Given a scenario, implement the following network troubleshooting methodology
- 4.2 Given a scenario, analyze and interpret the output of troubleshooting tools

Review Questions

1. What would you ping to determine whether TCP/IP was functioning properly on your computer?

   a. The gateway address

   b. The near side of the router

   c. The loopback address

   d. The far side of the router

2. Which of the following responses to a `ping` command issued on a Windows-based computer indicates that the ping test was successful?

    a. `Packets: Sent = 4, Received = 4, Lost = 0 (0% loss)`

    b. `Packets: Sent = 0, Received = 0, Lost = 0 (0% loss)`

    c. `Packets: Sent = 0, Received = 0, Lost = 4 (100% loss)`

    d. `Packets: Sent = 4, Received = 4, Lost = 4 (100% loss)`

3. When you issue a `ping` command, what Application layer protocol sends a message to the destination host?

    a. ARP

    b. RARP

    c. SNMP

    d. ICMP

4. Suppose you were troubleshooting a network connectivity problem between a workstation on a private LAN and a server on the Internet. As part of a logical troubleshooting methodology, what address would you ping after determining that the TCP/IP stack on the workstation was functioning properly?

    a. The workstation's loopback address

    b. The workstation's default gateway

    c. The private LAN's Internet name server

    d. The Internet server you're trying to reach

5. In the scenario described in Question 4, as part of a logical troubleshooting methodology, what address would you ping second?

    a. The workstation's loopback address

    b. The workstation's default gateway

    c. The private LAN's Internet name server

    d. The Internet server

6. Which of the following is the loopback address in IP version 4 addressing?

    a. 127.0.0.1

    b. 1.1.1.1

    c. 127.0.0.0

    d. 10.0.0.0

7. What type of message would you receive if you were trying to ping *www.comptia.org* from a Windows computer and misspelled the host's name as *wwv.comptia.org* in the `ping` command syntax?

    a. Host wwv.comptia.org not responding

    b. Ping request could not find host wwv.comptia.org. Please check the name and try again.

    c. Reply from www.comptia.org: bytes= 0

    d. Unknown host www.comptia.org

Lab 3.6 Using the Traceroute Utility to Troubleshoot a TCP/IP Network

Objectives

Another useful troubleshooting command in a TCP/IP network is the traceroute utility, which traces the path a packet travels as it goes over the network from a source to a destination node. This is particularly useful on large networks (including the Internet), as it can indicate at which hop along the route between two computers a problem exists. In smaller networks where you already know the network path, you can use the `ping` command instead. Note that on the Internet, firewalls and packet filtering can restrict the usefulness of the `traceroute` command (as well as the `ping` command).

On Windows machines, the `traceroute` command is known as `tracert`. Both the `tracert` command and the `traceroute` command begin by sending a packet to the destination host with a TTL (Time to Live) value of one. When the packet reaches the first router along the way, the TTL expires and the router sends an ICMP message back to the computer running the command. The command uses this ICMP message to identify the first router along the path. The computer increases the TTL value by one and sends another packet to the destination host. When the packet reaches the next router, the TTL expires and the next router sends an ICMP message. The command continues to increase the TTL value until it either reaches the destination or until a maximum number of routers have been tested (usually 30 by default). Although each variation of the command uses the same basic technique, the implementation varies slightly. The UNIX `traceroute` command sends UDP packets as test packets, whereas the Windows `tracert` command sends ICMP packets.

After completing this lab, you will be able to:

- Use the `traceroute` and `tracert` commands to trace the path to a destination
- Interpret both successful and unsuccessful `traceroute` responses

Materials Required

This lab will require the following:

- The lab setup built for Lab 3.5

Estimated completion time: **35 minutes**

Activity

1. Log on to *WORKSTATION1* as an administrator. The Windows desktop appears.

2. Open the Command Prompt window.

3. At the command prompt, type **tracert 172.16.1.2** and press **Enter**. The `tracert` command traces the path from *WORKSTATION1* to *WORKSTATION2*, showing the number of each hop, three round-trip response times, and the name or IP address for each hop. (Note that you can also use `tracert` with a domain name, such as *microsoft.com*.) Figure 3-5 shows an example of the output of the `tracert` command.

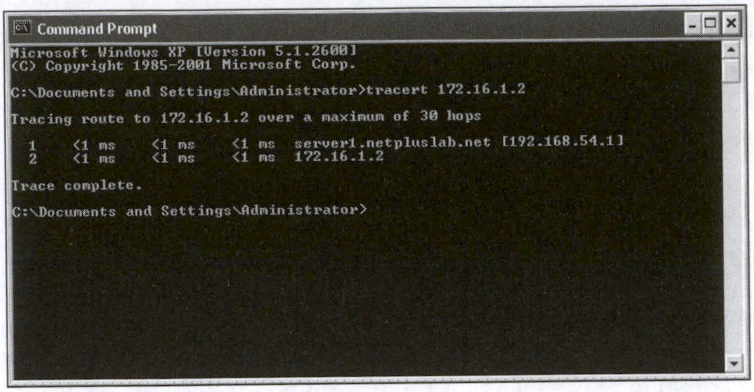

Figure 3-5   Typical output of the `tracert` command

4. Remove the cable from the NIC attached to *WORKSTATION2*.

5. Type **tracert 172.16.1.2** again and press **Enter**. Instead of recording two hops and stopping, the `tracert` command continues. However, after the first hop, the response times are replaced by asterisks and the IP address is replaced by "Request timed out." This indicates that the `tracert` command could not determine the path to the destination address after the first hop.

6. Replace the cable you removed from *WORKSTATION2* in Step 4.

7. Remove the cable from the NIC on *SERVER1* attached to *SWITCH1*.

8. Repeat Step 3. This time, the `tracert` command exits with the message "Destination host unreachable."

9. Replace the cable you removed in Step 7.

10. Enable the firewall on *WORKSTATION2* so that it blocks ICMP. Repeat Step 3. What message did the `tracert` command generate?

11. On a Windows computer connected to the Internet, repeat Steps 1 through 3. However, substitute the name of a Web site such as *www.cisco.com* or *www.google.com* for the IP address in Step 3. Note that firewalls and other security measures between this computer and the Web site, as well as the security configuration of the Web site itself, might prevent the `tracert` command from working as expected. Repeat with several different Web sites. Was every hop on a different network?

Certification Objectives

Objectives for the CompTIA Network+ Exam:

• 4.2 Given a scenario, analyze and interpret the output of troubleshooting tools

Review Questions

1. Which of the following commands can reveal the number of hops a packet takes between a source and target node?

   a. `ipconfig`

   b. `ping`

   c. `tracert`

   d. `ifconfig`

2. Which of the following commands can indicate whether a host is unreachable?

   a. `ping`

   b. `ipconfig`

   c. `ifconfig`

   d. `winipcfg`

3. Which of the following commands would you use to determine the relative location of network congestion between your Windows workstation and an Internet host?

   a. `netstat`

   b. `nbtstat`

   c. `tracert`

   d. `ipconfig`

4. If you attempted the `tracert` command on an Internet host and that host was not connected to the network, which of the following would the `tracert` command's response contain?

   a. Destination host unreachable

   b. Unknown host

   c. Host not responding

   d. Request timed out

5. What does a hop represent in the context of a `tracert` command?

   a. An Internet client

   b. A modem, hub, switch, or router

   c. A router

   d. A carrier's POP

Lab 3.7 Troubleshooting Web Client Problems

Objectives

In this lab, you will troubleshoot a problem with a Web client. Because the connection between a client and a host on the Internet usually relies on a great number and type of connections, problems might be difficult to identify and fix. Even if the nature of the problem is clear, you might not have any control over the network resources causing the problem. For this reason, coordination with other network administrators and other organizations is often essential to solving problems on the Internet.

In addition to verifying basic physical and logical network connectivity, you must also make sure that DNS is working properly. Issues involving DNS are a common source of problems with Web servers and Web browsers. If the Web server is operating correctly but the client is unable to use DNS to find its address, the client will be unable to reach the Web server. The effect is the same as if the Web server were not functioning properly. However, the Web server will typically be reachable through its IP address (if its IP address is known at all). DNS problems can occur for a variety of reasons, including incorrect DNS entries, misconfigured DNS servers, or even failure to pay domain name registration fees.

After completing this lab, you will be able to:

- Use a methodical troubleshooting approach to identify and solve a problem involving a Web client
- Investigate potential problems caused by DNS errors

Materials Required

This lab will require the following:

- A computer running Windows Server 2012 R2 named *SERVER1* with two NICs
- One NIC configured with an IP address of 192.168.54.1 and a subnet mask of 255.255.255.0, and the other NIC configured with an IP address of 172.16.1.1 and a subnet mask of 255.255.255.0
- Routing and Remote Access configured on *SERVER1* so that it acts as a router
- A switch named *SWITCH1* connected to the NIC on *SERVER1* that was configured with an IP address of 192.168.54.1 with a straight-through Cat 5 (or better) UTP cable
- A switch named *SWITCH2* connected to the NIC on *SERVER1* that was configured with an IP address of 172.16.1.1 with a straight-through Cat 5 (or better) UTP cable, as shown in Figure 3-6
- A computer running Windows 8.1 or Windows 7 named *WORKSTATION1*, configured with an IP address of 192.168.54.2 and a subnet mask of 255.255.255.0, connected to *SWITCH1* with a straight-through Cat 5 (or better) UTP cable

Figure 3-6   Network layout for Lab 3.6

- A computer running Windows Server 2012 R2 named *SERVER2*, configured with an IP address of 172.16.1.2 and a subnet mask of 255.255.255.0, connected to *SWITCH2* with a straight-through Cat 5 (or better) UTP cable

- IIS installed and running on *SERVER2*, with a file named default.htm containing the text "This is a test page" in C:\Inetpub\wwwroot

- The DNS server running on *SERVER1*, with an entry for *www.netpluslab.net* pointing to 172.16.1.2

- *WORKSTATION1* configured to use *SERVER1* as its DNS server

- Administrative access to all three computers

- A faulty network cable that is the same color as the network cables used in the other labs

- An instructor or classmate assigned to cause a problem in the network

Estimated completion time: **60–90 minutes**

Activity

1. Log on to *WORKSTATION1* as an administrator. The Windows desktop appears.

2. Open Internet Explorer.

3. In the address box, type **www.netpluslab.net** and then press **Enter**. A Web page opens with the text "This is a test page."

4. Close Internet Explorer.

5. Leave the room and ask your instructor or classmate to cause a network problem by performing one of the actions listed in Table 3-3.

6. After you return to the room, attempt to repeat Steps 1 through 3 on *WORKSTATION1*. You should be unable to open the Web page. Attempt to solve the problem using the following steps. If you solve the problem before completing all the steps, proceed to Step 17.

7. Attempt to determine the state of physical connectivity in the network. Check the status of the link lights on both switches and the NICs in *WORKSTATION1*, the router, and the Web server.

8. Attempt to determine the state of network connectivity. On *WORKSTATION1*, open the Command Prompt window and type **ping 127.0.0.1** and then press **Enter**. Success indicates that the TCP/IP stack on *WORKSTATION1* is working.

9. At the command prompt on *WORKSTATION1*, type **ping 192.168.54.1** and then press **Enter**. Success indicates that you can connect to the near NIC on the router.

10. Type **ping 172.16.1.1** and then press **Enter**. Success indicates that you can connect to the far NIC on the router.

11. Type **ping 172.16.1.2** and then press **Enter**. Success indicates that you can connect to the Web server.

Table 3-3 Possible actions to be performed by an instructor or classmate

Action	Instruction
Install faulty cable on server	Replace the network cable connecting the Web server to the switch with a faulty network cable.
Reconfigure the IP address on the Web server	a. Log on to *SERVER2* as the administrator. The Windows Server 2012 R2 desktop appears. b. Right-click **Start,** then click **Network Connections.** c. Right-click **Ethernet0** and click **Properties.** The Ethernet0 Properties window opens. d. Double-click **Internet Protocol Version 4 (TCP/IPv4).** The Internet Protocol Version 4 (TCP/IPv4) Properties window opens. e. Click the **Use the following IP address** option button. In the IP address text box, type **172.16.1.5.** In the Subnet mask text box, type **255.255.255.0.** f. Click **OK** twice, and then close any open dialog boxes or windows.
Change the DNS server on *WORKSTATION1*	a. On *WORKSTATION1*, right-click **Start,** then click **Network Connections.** The Network Connections dialog box opens. b. Right-click **Ethernet0** and click **Properties.** The Ethernet0 Properties window opens. c. Double-click **Internet Protocol Version 4 (TCP/IPv4).** The Internet Protocol Version 4 (TCP/IPv4) Properties window opens. d. Click the **Use the following DNS server addresses** option button. In the Preferred DNS server text box, type **192.168.154.1.** e. Click **OK** twice, and then close all open dialog boxes.
Change the DNS entry for *www.netpluslab.net*	a. Log on to *SERVER1* as the administrator. The Windows Server desktop appears and Server Manager opens. b. Click **Tools,** and then click **DNS.** The DNS Manager window opens. c. In the tree in the left pane of the window, click the arrow next to *SERVER1* to expand the tree underneath it. d. Click **Forward Lookup Zones** in the tree in the left pane. Icons for the forward lookup zones appear in the right pane.
	e. Right-click the **Netpluslab.net** icon and then click **Properties.** The netpluslab.net Properties window opens. f. Click the Name Servers tab. Click **Edit,** select the existing IP address and type **172.16.1.200** in the IP address text box to replace it, and then click **OK.** g. Close the DNS window.

12. If there is no network connectivity, at the command prompt on *WORKSTATION1*, type `ipconfig` and then press **Enter.** IP addressing information displays. Verify that the IP address is correct.

13. If you cannot find a problem with the IP addressing information on *WORKSTATION1*, repeat the previous step on *SERVER1* and *SERVER2*.

14. If you have verified network connectivity between *WORKSTATION1* and the Web server, on *WORKSTATION1* type **http://172.16.1.2** in the address box in Internet Explorer, and then press **Enter**. If you cannot open the Web page, this indicates a problem with DNS.

15. At the command prompt on *WORKSTATION1*, type **ipconfig /all** and then press **Enter**. Look through the IP addressing information to verify that *WORKSTATION1* is configured to use *SERVER1* (at 192.168.54.1) as its DNS server.

16. If *WORKSTATION1* is using the correct DNS server, type **nslookup www.netpluslab.net** and then press **Enter**. The IP address for *www.netpluslab.net* displays. Check to see if this matches the IP address of the Web server (172.16.1.2).

17. At this point, you should have been able to identify the problem. Fix it and repeat Steps 5 through 16, asking your instructor or classmate to perform a different action listed in Table 3-3.

Certification Objectives

Objectives for the CompTIA Network+ Exam:

- 4.1 Given a scenario, implement the following network troubleshooting methodology
- 4.2 Given a scenario, analyze and interpret the output of troubleshooting tools

Review Questions

1. What does the `nslookup` command reveal?

   a. A client's current connections

   b. A client's routing table entries

   c. The IP address of a given host name or vice versa

   d. The NetBIOS name based on a computer's IP address

2. If the link light on a switch port is not lit, what can you assume about the client connected to that switch's port?

   a. There are no connectivity problems with the client.

   b. The client cannot exchange data with the network.

   c. The client can exchange data only with other nodes on its segment.

   d. The client can exchange Network layer data, but not Transport layer data.

3. If a client does not have the correct DNS server address specified in its TCP/IP properties, which of the following will occur?

   a. The client cannot log on to or exchange data with the network.

   b. The client can exchange data with nodes on its local network, but not with nodes on other networks.

   c. The client can exchange data with nodes on local and external networks, but not by name.

   d. The client can exchange data with most, but not all, nodes on both its local and external networks by name.

4. What would happen if you assigned your Web server a new IP address that didn't match its DNS entry?

   a. It would be unavailable to clients.

   b. It would be available only to local clients, but not to clients accessing it over the Internet.

   c. It would be available to clients accessing it over the Internet, but not to local clients.

   d. It would still be available to all clients.

5. Which of the following tools will issue a simple pass/fail indication for a Cat 5 UTP cable?

   a. Cable checker

   b. Time domain reflectometer

   c. Multimeter

   d. Tone generator

6. True or False? Suppose you ping the IP address of a known Web server, and the response to your command indicates that the Web server is responding. It then follows that the Web server would successfully respond to HTTP requests from clients.

NETWORK DEVICES

Labs included in this chapter

- Lab 4.1 Viewing Ethernet Frames
- Lab 4.2 The Parallel Backbone
- Lab 4.3 Building a Daisy Chain
- Lab 4.4 Creating a Multi-Homed Computer by Installing Two NICs
- Lab 4.5 Activating Routing and Remote Access in Windows Server
- Lab 4.6 Activating a Routing Protocol in Windows Server
- Lab 4.7 Configuring a Bridging Firewall

CompTIA Network+ Exam Objectives

Objective	Lab
1.1 Explain the functions and applications of various network devices	4.2, 4.4, 4.5, 4.6, 4.7
1.5 Install and properly terminate various cable types and connectors using appropriate tools	4.2
1.6 Differentiate between common network topologies	4.3
1.9 Explain the basics of routing concepts and protocols	4.5, 4.6
1.12 Given a set of requirements, implement a basic network	4.2
2.1 Given a scenario, use appropriate monitoring tools	4.1
3.5 Given a scenario, install and configure a basic firewall	4.7
4.2 Given a scenario, analyze and interpret the output of troubleshooting tools	4.1, 4.6

All screenshots, unless otherwise noted, are used with permission from Microsoft Corporation.

Lab 4.1 Viewing Ethernet Frames

Objectives

A network protocol analyzer is software or a hardware device that reads packets or frames directly from a computer's NIC and allows you to view them or to save them for later viewing. This process is called capturing frames. A network protocol analyzer also decodes the frames captured so that you can look at the individual parts of the frame. Even though a network protocol analyzer captures frames, the packets are typically of the most interest to a network administrator.

Microsoft Network Monitor is a network protocol analyzer included with Windows Server, as well as with other versions of Windows. You can use a network protocol analyzer to examine the traffic on a network one frame at a time, or one part of a frame at a time. As you gain experience at looking at network traffic, you can also use Network Monitor to look for potential problems. For instance, you can look at Transport layer information in a series of packets to determine if the computer on the other end is sending data too quickly. After you gain a little experience with them, you'll find Network Monitor or other network protocol analyzers to be valuable troubleshooting tools.

It is important to keep in mind that a network protocol analyzer such as Network Monitor can be used to violate a user's privacy. As such, it should not be used carelessly or lightly.

After completing this lab, you will be able to:

- Use Network Monitor to look at captured frames

Materials Required

This lab will require the following:

- The network required in Lab 1.4, consisting of a computer named *SERVER1* running Windows Server 2012 R2 with an IP address of 192.168.54.1, and a computer named *WORKSTATION1* running Windows 8.1 or Windows 7 with an IP address of 192.168.54.2: This network can either be physical with two computers connected to a switch, or virtualized using software such as VMware

- The latest version of Network Monitor downloaded from the Microsoft download center and installed on *SERVER1*

- Administrative access to both *SERVER1* and *WORKSTATION1* as any ordinary user

 Most of the steps in this lab can also be completed using virtualization software such as VMware.

Estimated completion time: **60 minutes**

Activity

1. Log on to *WORKSTATION1* as an ordinary user. The Windows desktop appears.
2. Open a Command Prompt window.

Lab 4.1 Viewing Ethernet Frames   83

3. Type `ping -t 192.168.54.1` and press **Enter**. This sends ICMP packets continuously to *SERVER1*, and ensures that packets are available when you open Network Monitor.

> If the ping is unsuccessful, you may need to disable the firewall on either *SERVER1* or *WORKSTATION1*

4. Sign in to *SERVER1* as an administrator. Server Manager opens.

5. Click **Start**, type **Microsoft Network Monitor**, and then click the **Microsoft Network Monitor 3.4** icon. (Your version number might be different.) The Microsoft Network Monitor window opens, as shown in Figure 4-1.

6. In the Select Networks pane, ensure that Ethernet0 is checked.

7. Click **New Capture** on the toolbar, and then click **Start**. Network Monitor begins to capture packets, as shown in Figure 4-2. The Frame Summary pane shows information about the packets captured by Network Monitor.

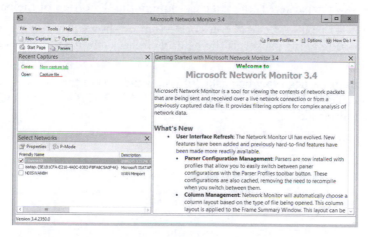

Figure 4-1   Microsoft Network Monitor

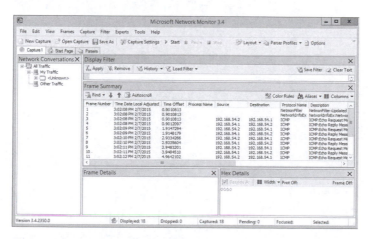

Figure 4-2   A network capture

8. When the number of frames captured is above 100, click **Stop** on the toolbar.

9. Locate a frame with "ICMP" in the Protocol Name field and click that row. The list of frames remains in the Frame Summary pane, a detailed description of each part of the selected frame appears in the Frame Details pane, and a representation of the frame in hexadecimal appears in the Hex Details pane. See Figure 4-3 for an example of a captured frame.

   By clicking the plus signs (+) in the Frame Details pane, you can display detailed information about each part of the packet. In the Frame section, Network Monitor shows detailed information about the frame itself. What is the total frame length for the frame you've chosen?

10. Click the plus sign (+) next to "Ethernet." Network Monitor shows detailed information about the Ethernet portion of the frame. What is the source address of the packet? What is the destination address of the packet? What is the Ethernet type?

11. Click the plus sign (+) next to "Ipv4." Network Monitor shows detailed information about the IP portion of the packet. What is the source address of the packet? What is the destination address of the packet? Is there a checksum in the IP portion of the packet?

12. Click the plus sign (+) next to "Icmp." Network Monitor shows detailed information about the ICMP portion of the packet. Is there another checksum for this portion of the packet?

13. Close Network Monitor. Click **No** when asked if you want to save the capture. Click **No** if asked to save unsaved entries in the database. On *WORKSTATION1*, press **CTRL+C** to stop the `ping` command.

14. Log off both computers.

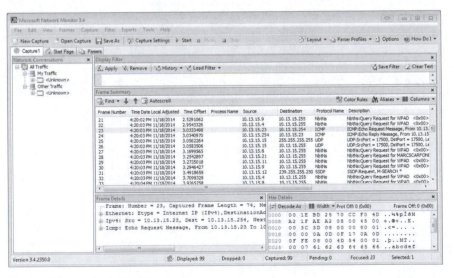

Figure 4-3   An individual frame

Certification Objectives

Objectives for the CompTIA Network+ Exam:

- 2.1 Given a scenario, use appropriate monitoring tools
- 4.2 Given a scenario, analyze and interpret the output of troubleshooting tools

Review Questions

1. At what layer in the OSI model were the source and destination addresses for the packet in Step 11 located?

2. In the frame you examined in Steps 9 through 13, which portions of the packet calculated a CRC checksum? What layers of the OSI model do they correspond to?

3. A user is unable to reach your company's Web site. From the user's workstation, you can ping the remote Web server. How might you use Network Monitor or another network protocol analyzer to troubleshoot the problem? (Choose all that apply.)

   a. By checking to see if the workstation is sending packets to the Web server

   b. By checking to see if the server is sending packets to the workstation

   c. By checking the workstation's IP configuration

   d. By checking the workstation's ARP configuration

4. Which protocols can be seen using Network Monitor? (Choose all that apply.)

   a. ICMP

   b. ARP

   c. TCP

   d. UDP

5. About which OSI layer does Network Monitor *not* provide information?

   a. Physical layer

   b. Data Link layer

   c. Network layer

   d. Transport layer

Lab 4.2 The Parallel Backbone

Objectives

In this lab, you will build a network that includes a variation of a parallel backbone. In a parallel backbone, each network segment has two or more connections to the central router or switch. If one connection fails, each segment can still connect to the rest of the network through the other connection.

The disadvantage to using a parallel backbone is cost. Depending on the type of devices used in the network and the logical topology, a parallel backbone might entail additional cabling, additional network devices, or additional configuration of network devices. As a network administrator, you must often choose between price and reliability. In most networks, only the most important devices have redundant network connections. For instance, a failure of the server that handles a company's billing might cost the company a substantial amount of money. The cost of a parallel backbone can be offset by the money that could be lost during such an outage. For a workstation, however, a parallel backbone might not be cost effective.

After completing this lab, you will be able to:

- Create a parallel backbone network

Materials Required

This lab will require the following:

- Two computers running Windows Server 2012 R2, one named *SERVER1* and the other named *SERVER2*, each with two NICs with RJ-45 connectors but without IP addresses configured

- Routing and Remote Access Service (RRAS) installed but not enabled on both computers

- Access as the administrator to both computers

- Two Ethernet switches

- Four straight-through Cat 5 (or better) UTP cables

 To complete this lab virtually, you will have to configure both server images to have separate network adapters.

Estimated completion time: **60 minutes**

Activity

1. Power on the two computers and the two switches.

2. Plug one of the cables into a NIC in *SERVER1*. Plug the other end of the cable into one of the switches. The link lights on the switches and on the NIC illuminate.

3. Plug another cable into the second NIC in *SERVER1*. Plug the other end of this cable into the other switch (that is, the switch you did not use in Step 2). Both NICs on *SERVER1* are now connected to different switches. The link lights on the switch and on the NIC illuminate.

4. Plug a third cable into a NIC on *SERVER2*. Plug the other end of this cable into one of the switches.

5. Plug the fourth cable into the second NIC on *SERVER2*. Plug the other end of this cable into the other switch. Both NICs on *SERVER2* are now plugged into different switches, and each server is now connected to each switch. Figure 4-4 shows the network cabling for this lab.

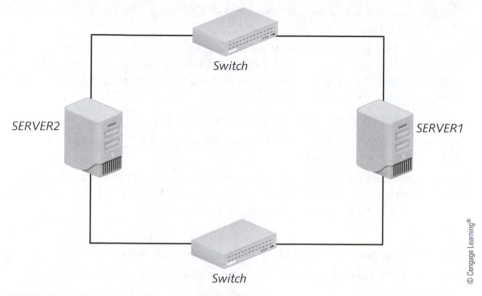

Figure 4-4   Parallel backbone network cabling

6. Sign in to *SERVER1* as the administrator. Server Manager opens.

7. In Server Manager, click the IP address next to the first Ethernet connection.

8. Right-click Ethernet0 and click **Properties**. The Ethernet0 Properties window opens.

9. Double-click **Internet Protocol Version 4 (TCP/IPv4)**. The Internet Protocol Version 4 (TCP/IPv4) Properties window opens.

10. Select the **Use the following IP address** option button. Enter **192.168.54.1** in the IP address text box and **255.255.255.0** in the Subnet mask text box. Select the **Use the following DNS Server addresses** option button, and enter **192.168.54.1** in the Preferred DNS server text box.

11. Click the **Advanced** button. The Advanced TCP/IP Settings dialog box opens.

12. Click **Add** beneath the IP addresses list box. The TCP/IP Address dialog box opens.

13. Now you will configure a secondary IP address. Enter **10.1.1.1** in the IP address text box and **255.255.255.0** in the Subnet mask text box.

14. Click **Add**. The dialog box closes, and the new IP address appears below "IP addresses" in the Advanced TCP/IP Settings dialog box.

15. Click **OK** three times to close the Ethernet0 Properties window. Click **Close** to close the Ethernet0 Status window.

16. Double-click **Ethernet1**. The Ethernet1 Status window opens.

17. Click **Properties**. The Ethernet1 Properties window opens.

18. Double-click **Internet Protocol Version 4 (TCP/IPv4)**. The Internet Protocol Version 4 (TCP/IPv4) Properties window opens.

19. Select the **Use the following IP address** option button. Enter **192.168.56.1** in the IP address text box and **255.255.255.0** in the Subnet mask text box. Select the **Use the following DNS Server addresses** option button, and enter **192.168.54.1** in the Preferred DNS server text box.

20. Click **OK** twice to close the Ethernet1 Properties window.

21. In Server Manager, click **Tools**, then click **Routing and Remote Access**. The Routing and Remote Access window opens.

22. Right-click **SERVER1 (local)** in the left pane of the Routing and Remote Access window. Select **Configure and Enable Routing and Remote Access** from the shortcut menu. The Routing and Remote Access Server Setup Wizard opens.

23. Click **Next**.

24. Select the **Custom configuration** option and then click **Next**.

25. Click the **LAN routing** check box to select it and then click **Next**.

26. Click **Finish**. A dialog box opens, indicating that the service has been installed and asking if you would like to start the service.

27. Click **Start service**. The service starts.

28. If necessary, click the **right-pointing arrow** next to *SERVER1 (local)* to expand the tree. In the left pane of the Routing and Remote Access window, click the **right-pointing arrow** to expand the tree below IPv4 if the tree is not already expanded. Right-click **General**, then select **New Routing Protocol** from the shortcut menu. The New Routing Protocol dialog box opens.

29. Double-click **RIP Version 2 for Internet Protocol**. The dialog box closes, and RIP appears below IPv4 in the tree in the left pane of the Routing and Remote Access window.

30. Right-click **RIP** in the tree in the left pane, and then click **New Interface** from the short-cut menu. The New Interface for RIP Version 2 for Internet Protocol dialog box opens.

31. Double-click **Ethernet0**. The RIP Properties – Ethernet0 Properties window opens.

32. Click **OK**.

33. Repeat Steps 29 through 32 for Ethernet1.

34. Right-click **SERVER1 (local)** in the left pane, point to **All Tasks** in the shortcut menu, and then click **Restart**. The Routing and Remote Access Service restarts.

35. On *SERVER2*, repeat Steps 6 through 10 entering **192.168.54.2** in the IP address text box and Preferred DNS server text box in Step 10.

36. On *SERVER2*, repeat Step 15. Note that it is only necessary to click OK twice in this case.

37. On *SERVER2*, repeat Steps 16 through 32, entering **192.168.56.2** in the IP address text box and **192.168.54.2** in the Preferred DNS server text box in Step 19.

38. On *SERVER2*, open a Command Prompt window.

39. Type `ping 10.1.1.1` and press **Enter**. You see a message indicating that the computer has received four replies from the remote computer. (If the `ping` command is unsuccessful, switch the cables attached to *SERVER2's* NICs, and verify that the link light on each NIC and hub is illuminated as expected.)

40. Remove one of the cables attached to *SERVER2*. (However, leave all of the cables attached to *SERVER1*.)

41. Type `ping 10.1.1.1` and press **Enter**. You see a message indicating that the computer has received four replies from the remote computer despite the removal of the cable.

42. Log off both computers.

Certification Objectives

Objectives for the CompTIA Network+ Exam:

- 1.1 Explain the functions and applications of various network devices
- 1.5 Install and properly terminate various cable types and connectors using appropriate tools
- 1.12 Given a set of requirements, implement a basic network

Review Questions

1. What is an advantage of using a parallel backbone over a collapsed backbone?
   a. A collapsed backbone requires too many connecting devices.
   b. A parallel backbone uses redundant connections and is more reliable.
   c. A collapsed backbone uses redundant connections, which costs more money.
   d. A parallel backbone uses fewer redundant connections, which costs less money.

2. What is the purpose of using the routing protocol in this lab?
   a. Each server can choose a different path when the current path fails.
   b. The network administrator does not have to configure static routes.
   c. It has no purpose.
   d. Each server saves the appropriate IP addresses in its ARP cache.

3. Which of the following is true about the use of parallel backbones in real-life networks?
   a. Parallel backbones are used when redundant connections are not possible.
   b. Parallel backbones are used whenever possible because they are so inexpensive.
   c. Parallel backbones only work in Ethernet networks.
   d. Parallel backbones are used for important servers and networks because they are more expensive to build.

4. In this lab, you configured the hubs and the two servers in a ring. How does the topology in this lab differ from a ring topology such as Token Ring? (Choose all that apply.)

   a. Each host transmits when necessary.

   b. A single workstation or server in a simple ring topology could take down the entire ring.

   c. Each host passes a token to the next host.

   d. The topology in this lab is an example of an active topology.

5. For which of the following network devices is redundancy least important?

   a. The network backbone cabling

   b. Server

   c. User workstations

   d. A central switch

Lab 4.3 Building a Daisy Chain

Objectives

In this lab, you will create a daisy chain, which is simply a linked series of devices, one after another. Ideally, daisy chains are something to avoid. But in reality, they're often found in small networks despite their limitations. Rather than running multiple lines from a central switch, some network administrators will cut costs and only run a single cable to connect several devices by adding a second switch.

In any daisy chain, you run the risk of expanding the network beyond its physical limitations. Adding unnecessary intermediary devices increases the network latency and can result in high error rates, data transmission problems, or reduced throughput. These problems might also be intermittent and, hence, more difficult to identify and troubleshoot.

Ordinarily, you must use a crossover cable to connect two switches. However, many switches have an uplink port. An uplink port allows you to use a straight-through cable instead. One end of the straight-through cable is attached to the uplink port, and the other end is attached to an ordinary switch. In other cases, the switch might autodetect whether the uplink port functions as an uplink port or as an ordinary port.

After completing this lab, you will be able to:

- Identify common enterprise backbone topologies
- Build a simple version of a common enterprise backbone

Materials Required

This lab will require the following:

- Four Ethernet switches set at a common speed
- Five straight-through Cat 5 (or better) UTP cables

- Three crossover Cat 5 (or better) UTP cables, if required, to connect the switches

- A computer running Microsoft Windows 8.1 or Windows 7 named *WORKSTATION1*, with an RJ-45 NIC running at the same speed as the switches and with an IP address of 192.168.54.2 and a subnet mask of 255.255.255.0

- A computer running Microsoft Windows 8.1 or Windows 7 named *WORKSTATION2*, with an RJ-45 NIC running at the same speed as the switches and with an IP address of 192.168.54.3 and a subnet mask of 255.255.255.0

- Access as an administrator to both computers

VIRTUAL LAB

This lab could also be adapted to a virtual environment using network virtualization software, such as GNS3 or Cisco's Packet Tracer.

Estimated completion time: **45 minutes**

Activity

1. Power on each switch and computer.

2. Plug one of the Cat 5 cables into a port in one of the switches. Plug the other end of this cable into the uplink port of one of the other switches. On both switches, a link light illuminates. If the switches do not have uplink ports or if the lights do not illuminate, use a crossover cable to connect the switches instead. The uplink port is designed to allow two switches to be connected with a straight-through cable, but not all switches have uplink ports.

3. Connect one of the remaining two switches to one of the two switches you connected in Step 2. Connect the remaining switch to the switch you just connected. Now you have a chain of four switches. Each connection on each switch should have an illuminated link light.

4. Plug one end of one of the Cat 5 cables into a data port on one of the switches. Plug the other end into the NIC in the back of one of the computers. A link light illuminates on both the switch and the NIC.

5. Repeat Step 4 by connecting the other computer into the switch at the other end of the chain. Figure 4-5 shows the network cabling for this lab.

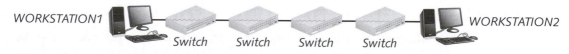

WORKSTATION1   Switch   Switch   Switch   Switch   WORKSTATION2

Figure 4-5   Daisy-chain network cabling

© 2016 Cengage Learning®

6. Log on to *WORKSTATION1* as an administrator. The Windows desktop appears.

7. Open a Command Prompt window.

8. Type `ping 192.168.54.3` and press **Enter**. You see a message indicating that the computer has received four replies. (If you see an error message instead, go to the next step.)

9. Repeat the previous step, examining the lights on each switch for errors. (Typically, a light on a switch will blink red or will not blink at all if the switch is experiencing errors.) Do you see any error lights on any of the switches?

10. Log off the computer.

Certification Objectives

Objectives for the CompTIA Network+ Exam:

- 1.6 Differentiate between common network topologies

Review Questions

1. What type of port connects one switch to another in a daisy-chain fashion?

   a. Output port

   b. Patch panel port

   c. Uplink port

   d. External port

2. When connectivity devices are connected in a daisy-chain fashion, what type of backbone do they create?

   a. Parallel

   b. Serial

   c. Collapsed

   d. Distributed

3. What type of network access method is used on an Ethernet switch?

   a. CSMA/CA

   b. CSMA/CD

   c. Demand priority

   d. Token passing

4. Which of the following is the most common frame type on modern Ethernet networks?

   a. Ethernet II (DIX)

   b. Ethernet 802.2 (Raw)

   c. Ethernet SNAP

   d. Ethernet 902.3 (Novell proprietary)

5. What is risky about daisy-chaining switches on a network? (Choose all that apply.)

    a. Too many switches will cause errors in addressing data for its proper destination.

    b. Too many switches can cause increased network latency.

    c. Too many switches can result in reduced throughput.

    d. Too many switches will increase the possibility for errors in data encryption and decryption.

Lab 4.4 Creating a Multi-Homed Computer by Installing Two NICs

Objectives

Network adapters are connectivity devices that enable a workstation, server, printer, or other node to receive and transmit data over the network media. In most modern network devices, NICs contain the data transceiver, which is the device that transmits and receives data signals.

NICs operate at both the Physical layer and the Data Link layer of the OSI model because they apply data signals to the wire and assemble or disassemble data frames. They do not, however, analyze the data from higher layers. A router, on the other hand, operates at the Network layer of the OSI model and can interpret higher-layer logical addressing information.

In this lab, you will perform the first step in creating a multi-homed computer consisting of a single computer with two NICs. A multi-homed computer has more than one NIC. Multi-homed computers function as a router and are used to interconnect dissimilar networks; the presence of two NICs in a computer allows it to connect to two different networks. Other types of networks may be connected by using different types of interfaces.

After completing this lab, you will be able to:

- Physically install NICs
- Make a multi-homed computer using two NICs
- Configure TCP/IP properties on NICs

Materials Required

This lab will require the following:

- A computer named *SERVER1* running Windows Server 2012 R2 without any NICs installed
- At least two PCI bus slots available on *SERVER1*
- Administrative access to *SERVER1*
- Two Ethernet PCI NICs with RJ-45 connectors listed on the Windows Server Catalog Hardware Compatibility List (HCL); at the time of this writing, you can find the Windows Server Catalog at *windowsservercatalog.com*
- Two Ethernet switches compatible with the NICs

- Two straight-through Cat 5 (or better) UTP cables
- A toolkit with a Phillips-head screwdriver, a ground mat, and a ground strap

To complete this lab virtually, you will have to configure the virtual image of *SERVER1* to have two network adapters.

Estimated completion time: **60 minutes**

Activity

1. Power off the computer.

2. Unplug the power cord from the computer, and then place the computer on the ground mat.

3. Place the ground strap on your wrist and attach it to the ground mat underneath the computer.

4. Remove any screws from the computer's case.

5. Remove the computer case.

6. Choose a vacant PCI slot on the system board where you will insert the NIC. Remove the metal slot cover from the slot you will use.

7. Place the NIC in the slot, pushing it firmly and straight down into place.

8. Attach the NIC to the system unit with the Phillips-head screwdriver. This secures the NIC in place.

9. Replace the cover.

10. Reinsert the screws on the cover.

11. Connect one end of one cable to the NIC. Connect the other end of the same cable to one of the switches (hubs).

12. Plug in the computer and turn it on. Plug in the switch. Link lights on both the switch and the back of the NIC turn green. On some NICs, there might also be a yellow light or a flashing yellow light. If the link lights do not illuminate, verify that the cables are connected properly.

13. After *SERVER1* is running, look at the lights on the NIC and at the port lights on the switch. They should be on. If they are not on, check the cabling. You might also need to turn off the computer, unplug it, and verify that the NIC is firmly seated inside the computer.

14. Log on to the server as the administrator. A dialog box might open indicating that the server has discovered new hardware. Also, a wizard might open and attempt to install new hardware. If so, click **Cancel** to close the wizard.

15. In Server Manager, open Network Connections by clicking the IP address next to the Ethernet connection.

16. Right-click the name of your Ethernet connection and click the **Properties** button. The Ethernet0 Properties dialog box opens.

If you're using Windows 7, the Ethernet adapter might be called Local Area Connection.

17. Double-click **Internet Protocol Version 4 (TCP/IPv4)**. The Internet Protocol Version 4 (TCP/IPv4) Properties dialog box opens.

18. Select the **Use the following IP address** option button. The IP address, Subnet mask, and Default gateway text boxes are enabled.

19. In the IP address text box, type **172.16.1.1**.

20. In the Subnet mask text box, type **255.255.255.0**.

21. Leave the Default gateway text box blank.

22. Click **OK**. A dialog box might open, indicating that the DNS server list is empty and that the computer will configure itself as the DNS server. If so, click OK again. You return to the Ethernet Properties dialog box.

23. Click **OK** again to close the Ethernet Properties dialog box.

24. Repeat Steps 15 through 23 with the second NIC. The second NIC should appear as Ethernet1 or equivalent. When repeating Step 19, use an IP address of 192.168.54.1. You have now built a multi-homed computer. You will finish making this computer a router in Lab 4.5.

25. Log off the computer.

Certification Objectives

Objectives for the CompTIA Network+ Exam:

- 1.1 Explain the functions and applications of various network devices

Review Questions

1. Which of the following devices only operates at the Physical layer of the OSI model?

    a. NIC

    b. Hub or repeater

    c. Bridge

    d. Router

2. What type of address does a router interpret?

    a. Physical address

    b. MAC address

    c. Block ID

    d. Network address

3. What is the minimum total size of an Ethernet frame?

   a. 6 bytes

   b. 12 bytes

   c. 46 bytes

   d. 64 bytes

4. On a typical 100Base-T network, where would you find transceivers?

   a. In the NICs

   b. In the operating systems

   c. In the UPSs

   d. In the cabling

5. Which of the following is a difference between a router and a hub?

   a. A router is less sophisticated than a hub.

   b. A router operates at the Transport layer of the OSI model, whereas a hub operates at the Data Link layer of the OSI model.

   c. A router operates at the Network layer of the OSI model, whereas a hub operates at the Physical layer of the OSI model.

   d. A router regenerates signals, whereas a hub interprets addressing information to ensure that data is directed to the proper destination.

6. In which of the following networking scenarios would a router be the optimal connectivity device?

   a. A home network with five users who want to share documents that are stored on one of the five workstations

   b. A WAN that connects a college physics department with a classroom in a high school on the other side of town

   c. A LAN that connects 10 users, a server, and a printer at a small business

   d. A peer-to-peer LAN that connects eight users to provide a shared database

7. What is the most likely purpose of the hubs in this lab?

   a. To connect the computer to different networks

   b. To determine, by checking the link lights, whether the NIC has been installed correctly

   c. To determine, by checking the link lights, whether you have configured the IP addresses on the NICs correctly

   d. To allow the NICs to operate at the Network layer

Lab 4.5 Activating Routing and Remote Access in Windows Server

Objectives

In this lab, you will configure the multi-homed computer you created in Lab 4.4 to be a simple router and add a static route to its routing table. When a router receives a packet from a computer or another router, it looks in its routing table to see where it should send the packet. A routing table consists of a list of all the networks the router knows about and the next hop for each of these networks. Each route consists of a destination network and the next hop where the router should send packets to reach the destination. The next hop might be the IP address of the next router on the path to the destination or the network interface card closest to it. A router has separate routing tables for each routable protocol (such as TCP/IP or IPX/SPX) it runs.

For instance, suppose a router receives a packet with a destination address of 10.100.17.29. It looks in its routing table for a route that matches this address. It finds the route and sees that packets for 10.100.17.29 should be sent out to the router at 10.100.17.1. Then it sends the packet to 10.100.17.1.

When the router at 10.100.17.1 receives the packet, it looks at its routing table for a matching route. The matching route tells the router to send the packet out its Ethernet NIC. It sends the packet out its Ethernet NIC, to the destination computer. In this manner, routers can send packets over long paths consisting of many hops.

To fill its routing table, a router must learn the routes it needs to use. One way in which routers learn routes is by looking at the addresses on their own interfaces. Network administrators can also add routes directly into a routing table. Routes configured by a network administrator are known as static routes.

Note that most network administrators will use dedicated routing hardware whenever possible, rather than a software router such as the one you will configure in this lab. Dedicated routing hardware will typically be faster, more stable, and have more features than a software router.

After completing this lab, you will be able to:

- Activate and configure Routing and Remote Access Service on a Windows Server server
- Show the routing table of a Windows Server server configured as a network router
- Add a static route to a Windows Server server configured as a network router

Materials Required

This lab will require the following:

- The network built at the end of the Lab 4.4
- A computer named *SERVER1* running Windows Server 2012 R2 with two NICs with Routing and Remote Access Service installed

- One NIC on *SERVER1* configured with an IP address of 192.168.54.1 and a subnet mask of 255.255.255.0

- The other NIC on *SERVER1* configured with an IP address of 172.16.1.1 and a subnet mask of 255.255.255.0

- Two computers running Windows 8.1 or Windows 7 with NICs compatible with the switches or hubs

- One of the Windows 8.1 or Windows 7 computers named *WORKSTATION1* and configured with an IP address of 192.168.54.2 and a default gateway of 192.168.54.1

- The other Windows 8.1 or Windows 7 computers named *WORKSTATION2* and configured with an IP address of 172.16.1.2 and a default gateway of 172.16.1.1

- Access to both Windows 8.1 or Windows 7 computers as the local administrator

- Two straight-through Cat 5 (or better) UTP cables

This lab can be completed virtually using virtualization software such as VMware.

VIRTUAL LAB

Estimated completion time: **75 minutes**

Activity

1. Plug in each NIC in *SERVER1* to one of the hubs. Log on to *SERVER1* as the administrator.

2. On *SERVER1*, select **Tools**, and then click **Routing and Remote Access**.

3. In the left pane of the dialog box, click the name of the server to select it. Click **Action**, and, if necessary, click **Configure and Enable Routing and Remote Access**. The Routing and Remote Access Server Setup Wizard opens.

4. Click **Next**. The Configuration dialog box opens, listing several options for configuring this computer as a router.

5. Select the **Custom configuration** option, and then click **Next**. The Custom Configuration dialog box opens.

6. Click the **LAN routing** check box to place a checkmark in it. Click **Next**.

7. Click **Finish**. The Routing and Remote Access Server Setup Wizard saves your settings and starts the Routing and Remote Access Service.

8. A dialog box opens, indicating that the Routing and Remote Access Service is ready to use. Click **Start service** to start the service. A dialog box indicating that the service is initializing opens briefly. Close the Routing and Remote Access dialog box.

9. Plug the RJ-45 connector of one of the Cat 5 cables into one of the switches. Plug the other end of the cable into the NIC in the back of one of the workstation computers.

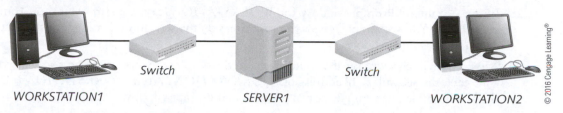

Figure 4-6   Network layout for Lab 4.5

10. Repeat the previous step, connecting the other computer to the other switch. The workstation computers should each be plugged into different switches, while *SERVER1* should be plugged into both switches. This allows traffic from *WORKSTATION1* to travel through *SERVER1* to *WORKSTATION2*. Figure 4-6 shows the network cabling.

11. Log on to *WORKSTATION1* as an administrator. The Windows desktop appears.

12. Open a Command Prompt window.

13. Type **ping 172.16.1.2** and press **Enter**. If the output does not indicate that the computer has received four replies from 172.16.1.2, repeat Steps 9 and 10 before continuing, switching the switches to which each computer is attached.

14. Repeat Steps 11 and 12 with *WORKSTATION2*. The Windows server is now acting as a router. This means that it accepts packets from *WORKSTATION1* and uses its routing table to determine where to send the packets so that they reach their destination, *WORKSTATION2*.

15. At the command prompt, type **ping 192.168.54.2** and press **Enter**. The output indicates that this computer has received four replies from the other computer. You have successfully used the Windows server as a router.

16. Next, you will configure a secondary IP address on *WORKSTATION2*. Right-click **Start**, and select **Network Connections**. The Network Connections dialog box opens.

17. Right-click the **Ethernet0** icon and then click **Properties** from the shortcut menu.

18. Double-click **Internet Protocol Version 4 (TCP/IPv4)**. The Internet Protocol Version 4 (TCP/IPv4) Properties dialog box opens. Click **Advanced**. The Advanced TCP/IP Settings dialog box opens.

19. Click **Add** beneath the IP addresses heading at the top of the dialog box. The TCP/IP Address dialog box opens.

20. Type **10.1.1.1** in the IP address text box. Type **255.0.0.0** in the Subnet mask text box.

21. Click **Add**. You have just configured this computer with a second IP address, which it can also use to communicate with other computers. You return to the Advanced TCP/IP Settings dialog box.

22. Click **OK** to close the Advanced TCP/IP Settings dialog box, click **OK** to close the Internet Protocol Version 4 (TCP/IPv4) Properties dialog box, and then click **OK** to close the Ethernet0 Properties dialog box.

23. In the Command Prompt window for *WORKSTATION1*, type **ping 10.1.1.1** and press **Enter**. You see a reply (displayed four times on the screen) indicating that the destination host is unreachable.

24. Next, you will check to see if a route exists on the Windows Server computer so that you can reach the secondary IP address on *WORKSTATION2* from *WORKSTATION1*. On the Windows Server computer, open a Command Prompt window.

25. Type **route print** and press **Enter**. The computer displays a list of its interfaces and its routing table. Notice that there is no route to any IP address or network beginning with 10. See Figure 4-7 for an example of a routing table on a Windows Server like *SERVER1* in this lab.

26. Recall that when you typed ping 10.1.1.1 in Step 23, the computer responded with "Destination host unreachable" four times. Now you will configure a static route on *SERVER1* so that *WORKSTATION1* can reach 10.1.1.1. Type **route add 10.0.0.0 mask 255.0.0.0 172.16.1.2** and press **Enter**. This tells the router to add a route to any machine with a network number of 10.0.0.0 and a subnet mask of 255.0.0.0 through the computer with the IP address of 172.16.1.2.

27. Type **ping 10.1.1.1** and press **Enter**. The computer responds with "Reply from 10.1.1.1" four times.

28. Type **route print** and press **Enter**. The computer displays its routing table. In the Network Destination column, you should see the route you added in Step 26, 10.0.0.0.

29. Return to the Command Prompt window you opened earlier on *WORKSTATION1*. Type **ping 10.1.1.1** and press **Enter**. The computer responds with "Reply from 10.1.1.1" four times. You have now successfully used the static route you configured on the Windows server.

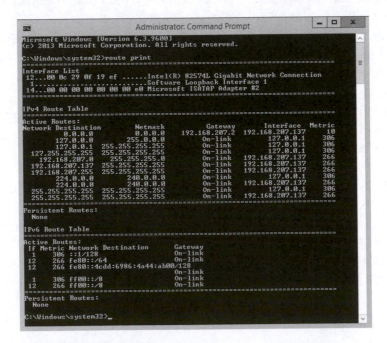

Figure 4-7 Routing table

30. Finally, you will look at the route used by packets to reach 10.1.1.1. Type `tracert` `10.1.1.1` and press **Enter**. The computer displays the route that packets take to reach the address 10.1.1.1.

31. Log off all three computers.

Certification Objectives

Objectives for the CompTIA Network+ Exam:

- 1.1 Explain the functions and applications of various network devices
- 1.9 Explain the basics of routing concepts and protocols

Review Questions

1. What is the purpose of a routing table on a TCP/IP-based network?

    a. To associate the NetBIOS names of nodes with their IP addresses

    b. To associate the IP addresses of nodes with their host names

    c. To associate the IP addresses of nodes with their locations on the network

    d. To associate the host names of nodes with their MAC addresses

2. Which of the following most fully describes what a successful response from the `ping` command indicates?

    a. A node is powered on.

    b. A node is physically connected to the network.

    c. A node is running the Windows Server operating system.

    d. A node is connected to the network and is running TCP/IP successfully.

3. What does the `tracert` command show?

    a. The path taken by packets to the destination address

    b. The MAC address of the destination address

    c. Whether the remote host supports TCP/IP

    d. The operating system run by the host at the destination address

4. What command would you use to add a node's IP address, subnet mask, and network location interface to a routing table?

    a. `route add`

    b. `add host`

    c. `add node`

    d. `route open`

5. In the default `ping` command on a computer running Windows, how many replies will you receive if the test is successful?

   a. 1

   b. 2

   c. 3

   d. 4

6. What menu option sequence would you choose to set up Routing and Remote Access Service on a Windows Server 2012 computer?

   a. Start, Control Panel, Network Connections, Routing and Remote Access

   b. Start, Administrative Tools, Routing and Remote Access

   c. Start, All Programs, Accessories, Routing and Remote Access

   d. Start, Control Panel, Routing and Remote Access

Lab 4.6 Activating a Routing Protocol in Windows Server

Objectives

Configuring more than a handful of static routes on a network is time consuming and error-prone. Many networks consist of hundreds or even thousands of routes. For instance, at the time of this writing, the Internet routing table consists of around 500,000 static routes. If you used static routes to maintain the routing tables on your routers, you would need to configure each static route on each router. Imagine configuring 500 or more routes on 50 routers! Additionally, each time you added a new network, you would need to configure a new route on each router.

To simplify network administration, most networks of any size use a routing protocol to help routers learn routes. A router running a routing protocol tells connected routers, or neighbors, about the networks it knows about. In turn, it learns all the routes its neighbors know about. In this way, it can discover all the routes in the network. Routing protocols also allow routers to find the best routes to a destination. Finally, routing protocols allow routers to recover from outages. If a router fails, other routers will learn this from information sent by the routing protocol. If another route to the destination is available, they will use it.

In this lab, you will configure Routing Information Protocol (RIP) version 2 on a computer running Windows Server. RIP is a relatively simple routing protocol, which is supported on many network devices and servers. However, keep in mind that routing protocols can be quite complex and that mistakes with routing protocols can cause large outages. The BGP protocol, for example, is commonly used for large Internet backbones.

After completing this lab, you will be able to:

- Explain the function of various routing protocols
- Install a routing protocol on a Windows server

Materials Required

This lab will require the following:

- A computer named *SERVER1* running Windows Server 2012 R2, with two NICs
- One NIC on the *SERVER1* computer configured with an IP address of 192.168.54.1 and a subnet mask of 255.255.255.0
- The other NIC on the *SERVER1* computer configured with an IP address of 172.16.1.1 and a subnet mask of 255.255.255.0
- A computer named *SERVER2* running Windows Server 2012 R2, with a NIC, an IP address of 192.168.54.2, a subnet mask of 255.255.255.0, and no default gateway
- Routing and Remote Access disabled on both computers
- Two Ethernet switches
- Three straight-through Cat 5 (or better) UTP cables
- Access as the administrator to both computers

This lab can be completed virtually using virtualization software such as VMware.

Estimated completion time: **45 minutes**

Activity

1. Connect each of the NICs in *SERVER1* to a separate switch with Cat 5 cables.
2. Connect the NIC in *SERVER2* to one of the switches with the remaining Cat 5 cable.
3. Log on to *SERVER2* as the administrator.
4. Open a Command Prompt window.
5. Now you will verify that you have network connectivity with *SERVER1*. Type **ping 192.168.54.1** and press **Enter**. The computer indicates that it has received four replies. If instead you see a timeout error (or other error), *SERVER2* is plugged into the wrong switch. Take the cable plugged into *SERVER2*'s NIC, remove the end attached to the switch, and plug it into the other switch. Repeat this step.
6. Now you will attempt to reach the IP address of *SERVER1*'s other NIC. Type **ping 172.16.1.1** and press **Enter**. You see four messages indicating that the destination host is unreachable.
7. Type **route print** and press **Enter** to show the computer's routing table. Record the networks listed in the Network Destination column and the corresponding subnet masks in the Netmask column.
8. Log on to *SERVER1* as the administrator.
9. Open a Command Prompt window.

10. Type **route print** and press **Enter**. The computer displays its routing table. Record the routes you see as you did in Step 7.

11. On *SERVER1*, select **Tools**, and then click **Routing and Remote Access**. The Routing and Remote Access dialog box opens.

12. In the left pane, select **SERVER1**, click **Action** on the menu bar, and then click **Configure and Enable Routing and Remote Access**. The Routing and Remote Access Server Setup Wizard appears.

13. Click **Next**. The Configuration dialog box opens, listing several options for configuring this computer as a router.

14. Select the **Custom configuration** option, and then click **Next**. The Custom Configuration dialog box opens.

15. Click the **LAN routing** check box to place a check in it and then click **Next**.

16. Click **Finish**. The Routing and Remote Access Server Setup Wizard saves your settings and starts the Routing and Remote Access Service.

17. A dialog box opens, indicating that the Routing and Remote Access Service is ready to use. Click **Start service** to start the service. A dialog box indicating that the service is initializing opens briefly.

18. In the left pane of the Routing and Remote Access dialog box, click the right-pointing arrow next to the *SERVER1* (local) icon, if necessary. A tree containing several nodes appears below the *SERVER1* icon. Click the right-pointing arrow next to the IPv4 node. More options appear underneath the IPv4 node, including an icon named "General."

19. Right-click the **General** icon and then click **New Routing Protocol** from the shortcut menu. The New Routing Protocol dialog box opens, as shown in Figure 4-8.

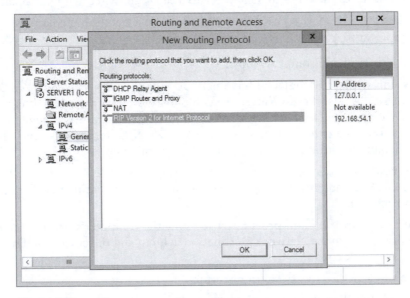

Figure 4-8 Adding a new routing protocol

20. Click **RIP Version 2 for Internet Protocol**, and then click **OK**. An RIP icon appears in the left pane on the same tree as the General icon while the Windows server installs the Routing Information Protocol.

21. Right-click the new **RIP** icon in the tree in the left pane, and then click **New Interface**. The New Interface for RIP Version 2 for Internet Protocol dialog box opens.

22. Click **Ethernet0**, if necessary, and then click **OK** to add the interface. The RIP Properties – Ethernet0 Properties dialog box opens.

23. Click **OK** to close the dialog box and finish adding the interface. If necessary, select RIP in the left pane. An icon for Ethernet0 appears in the right pane of the Routing and Remote Access dialog box.

24. Repeat Steps 21 through 23 for Ethernet1.

25. Right-click the **SERVER1 (local)** icon. On the shortcut menu, point to **All Tasks**, then click **Restart**. A dialog box opens briefly indicating that the Routing and Remote Access Service is restarting.

26. Enable Routing and Remote Access on *SERVER2* by repeating Steps 11 through 23 and Step 25. After RIP for IP is installed on both computers, they will dynamically share their routing tables within a minute.

27. Wait one minute. In the left pane of the Routing and Remote Access dialog box on *SERVER2*, right-click the **RIP** icon, and then click **Show Neighbors**. The SERVER2 – RIP Neighbors dialog box opens, showing the IP address of *SERVER1*. If you do not see the IP address of *SERVER1* in this dialog box, wait another minute and repeat this step.

28. In the Command Prompt window on *SERVER2*, type **ping 172.16.1.1** and press **Enter**.

29. Type **route print** and press **Enter**. What additional routes do you see now that you didn't see in Step 10?

30. Repeat Step 29 on *SERVER1*.

Certification Objectives

Objectives for the CompTIA Network+ Exam:

- 1.1 Explain the functions and applications of various network devices
- 1.9 Explain the basics of routing concepts and protocols
- 4.2 Given a scenario, analyze and interpret the output of troubleshooting tools

Review Questions

1. What does RIP stand for?

   a. Regulated Interaction Protocol

   b. Routing Information Protocol

   c. Response Interpretation Protocol

   d. Registered Installation Protocol

2. True or False? To determine the best path to transfer data, routers communicate using routing protocols such as TCP/IP.

3. What additional routes did you find in Step 29?

4. Which routing protocol is commonly used for Internet backbones?

   a. OSPF

   b. RIP for IP

   c. EIGRP

   d. BGP

5. When might the best path *not* equal the shortest distance between two nodes? (Choose all that apply.)

   a. When a communications link has been recently added to the network

   b. When a communications link is suffering congestion

   c. When a router experiences routing protocol errors

   d. When the media on the shortest path is slower than the media on the best path

Lab 4.7 Configuring a Bridging Firewall

Objectives

A firewall is a gateway used to connect two or more networks and to control the traffic allowed to cross a network. A firewall is often used to protect a network from potentially malicious traffic on the Internet. For example, the firewall is typically configured to allow users on the protected network, or inside the firewall, to use network resources on the Internet. Many firewalls can control traffic with varying degrees of ease anywhere from the Data Link layer up to the Application layer.

In many ways, the distinction between a firewall and a router is fuzzy. Many routers can also filter traffic. Like a router, a firewall can be a dedicated piece of hardware or software configured on a server. The function of a firewall also overlaps somewhat with that of a router. A firewall can use a handful of static routes, or it can run a routing protocol like a router.

However, a firewall does not need to be a router at all. In this lab, you will configure a computer running Windows Server 2012 R2 as both a bridge and a firewall. A bridge is a gateway device that operates at Layer 2 of the OSI model, and does not require Layer 3 configuration. However, a bridging firewall can use information at Layer 3 and higher in the packets it receives to decide whether to forward them.

In this lab, you will configure the firewall to selectively prevent one computer from being able to ping the other. When one computer pings a second computer, it sends an ICMP echo request packet. The second computer sends an ICMP echo reply packet to acknowledge the ping. When the first computer receives the ICMP echo reply packet from the second computer, it knows that the ping has been successful. A firewall can prevent computers outside the firewall from pinging computers inside the firewall by filtering ICMP echo request packets. If the computers inside the firewall do not receive the ICMP echo request packets, they will never send ICMP echo reply packets. Thus, computers outside the firewall will not be able to successfully ping computers inside the firewall. At the same time, the firewall will not prevent computers inside it from pinging computers outside the firewall.

After completing this lab, you will be able to:

- Configure a computer running Windows Server as a simple firewall
- Configure the Windows Server 2012 R2 firewall to filter ICMP echo request packets

Materials Required

This lab will require the following:

- The network built at the end of Lab 4.4
- A computer named *SERVER1* running Windows Server 2012 R2 with two NICs with Routing and Remote Access Service installed
- One NIC on the *SERVER1* computer configured with an IP address of 192.168.54.1 and a subnet mask of 255.255.255.0
- Another NIC on the *SERVER1* computer configured with an IP address of 172.16.1.1 and a subnet mask of 255.255.255.0
- Two computers running Windows 8.1 or Windows 7 with NICs compatible with the switches
- One of the Windows 8.1 or Windows 7 computers named *WORKSTATION1* and configured with an IP address of 192.168.54.2 and a default gateway of 192.168.54.1
- The other Windows 8.1 or Windows 7 computer named *WORKSTATION2* and configured with an IP address of 172.16.1.2 and a default gateway of 172.16.1.1
- Access to both Windows 8.1 or Windows 7 computers as the local administrator
- Two straight-through Cat 5 (or better) UTP cables

Estimated completion time: **30 minutes**

Activity

1. Connect one end of a cable to one of the switches. Connect the other end of the cable to *WORKSTATION1*.
2. Repeat the previous step, connecting the other switch to *WORKSTATION2*.
3. Connect one end of a cable to one of the switches. Connect the other end of the cable to one of the NICs in *SERVER1*.
4. Repeat the previous step, connecting the other switch to *SERVER1*. Now both *WORKSTATION1* and *WORKSTATION2* are connected to different switches, and each switch is connected to one of the NICs on *SERVER1*.
5. Log on to *WORKSTATION1* as an administrator. The Windows desktop appears.
6. Open a Command Prompt window.

7. Type `ping 172.16.1.2` and press **Enter** to confirm that *WORKSTATION1* can successfully ping *WORKSTATION2*. Now you will configure *SERVER1* as a firewall.

8. Log on to *SERVER1* as the administrator.

9. On *SERVER1*, click **Tools**, and then click **Windows Firewall with Advanced Security**.

10. Click **Inbound Rules**, then right-click **Inbound Rules** and click **New Rule**.

11. Select **Custom** and then click **Next**.

12. If necessary, select **All programs** and then click **Next**.

13. Next to Protocol type, select **ICMPv4** and click **Next**.

14. Confirm that this rule applies to any local and remote IP addresses and click **Next**.

15. Select **Block the connection**, click **Next**, and click **Next** again.

16. Name the rule **Ping Block** and click **Finish**.

17. The computer will now drop ICMP echo request packets sent to *WORKSTATION2*.

18. In the Command Prompt window on *WORKSTATION1*, type `ping 172.16.1.2` and press **Enter**. The computer indicates four times that it is unable to reach the destination host.

19. Delete Ping Block rule and log off each computer.

Certification Objectives

Objectives for the CompTIA Network+ Exam:

- 1.1 Explain the functions and applications of various network devices
- 3.5 Given a scenario, install and configure a basic firewall

Review Questions

1. Which of the following could serve as firewalls? (Choose all that apply.)

   a. A modem

   b. A Windows server

   c. A repeater

   d. A Linux server

2. True or False? A firewall can run a routing protocol like a router.

3. What is the highest level of the OSI model in which a firewall can operate?

   a. Data Link

   b. Network

   c. Transport

   d. Application

4. A gateway connects two different types of networks, two different types of communications protocols, or two different computer architectures. Which of the following is *not* considered a gateway?

   a. A router connecting a Token Ring

   b. A computer translating application data from TCP/IP to IPX/SPX

   c. A computer translating voice signals into data and transmitting it over a TCP/IP network

   d. A file and print server communicating with clients using both TCP/IP and IPX/SPX

5. You have configured a device that runs the OSPF routing protocol, but whose primary purpose is to prevent unwanted Internet traffic from reaching your company's LAN. Which of the following is true about this device?

   a. It is a router because it runs a routing protocol.

   b. It is a router because its primary purpose is to control traffic.

   c. It is a firewall because it runs a routing protocol.

   d. It is a firewall because its primary purpose is to control traffic.

6. Which of the following statements about a bridge is false?

   a. Without IP addressing information, a bridge will not be seen with the `tracert` command.

   b. Bridges require no Layer 3 addressing.

   c. Bridges decide which packets to forward based on their Layer 3 headers.

   d. Bridges operate at the Data Link layer.

Lab 5.1 Learning Media Characteristics

Objectives

In this lab, you will learn about the costs and characteristics of network media and networking and computer equipment. This will give you experience in comparing costs of network components and network media. It will also give you an idea of the equipment needed to set up a network and of the total costs involved in doing so.

Bear in mind that the cost of a particular medium includes not only the cost of the cable, but also the installation cost, the maintenance costs, and the cost of replacing the medium if it becomes obsolete in the future. Additionally, the cost of networking and computer equipment and software will vary widely, depending on the vendor, the equipment chosen, and the licensing terms.

After completing this lab, you will be able to:

- Identify the costs and characteristics of Category 5 UTP cable

Materials Required

This lab will require the following:

- Access to a retail or online store that sells computer networking equipment
- Pencil and paper

Estimated completion time: **30–90 minutes**

Activity

1. Visit a retail computer store (such as Best Buy or Radio Shack) that sells Ethernet Category 5 cable, computers, software, and networking supplies. Alternately, visit a Web site (such as *cdw.com*) that specializes in computers, software, and networking supplies. In Table 5-1, record the Web address or the name of the store.

2. In Table 5-1, record the cost of Category 5 cable sold by the foot. If the store does not sell cable by the foot, divide the price of the longest Category 5 cable you can find by its length in feet.

3. In Table 5-1, record the cost of Category 5e, Category 6, Category 6a, or Category 7 cable as you did in the previous step.

4. In Table 5-1, record the cost and model information for a low-end, four-port Ethernet switch with RJ-45 connections.

5. In Table 5-1, record the cost and model information for a 16-port switch with RJ-45 connections.

6. In Table 5-1, record the cost and model information for an 802.11n wireless access point or a home router that includes a wireless access point.

NETWORK CABLING

Labs included in this chapter

- Lab 5.1 Learning Media Characteristics
- Lab 5.2 Creating a UTP Crossover Cable to Connect Two Computers
- Lab 5.3 Comparing Throughput
- Lab 5.4 Understanding How a Category 5 Cable Fails
- Lab 5.5 Connecting Two Switches with Fiber-Optic Cable
- Lab 5.6 Using a Network Cable Tester

CompTIA Network+ Exam Objectives

Objective	Lab
1.5 Install and properly terminate various cable types and connectors using appropriate tools	5.2, 5.5
2.1 Given a scenario, use appropriate monitoring tools	5.3
2.2 Given a scenario, analyze metrics and reports from monitoring and tracking performance tools	5.3
4.2 Given a scenario, analyze and interpret the output of troubleshooting tools	5.4, 5.6
4.4 Given a scenario, troubleshoot and resolve common copper cable issues	5.4, 5.6
5.4 Given a scenario, deploy the appropriate wired connectivity standard	5.1

7. In Table 5-1, record the cost and model information for a typical desktop computer. If you have difficulty deciding on a model, choose one that is intermediate in price.

8. In Table 5-1, record the cost and model information for a typical laptop computer. If you have difficulty deciding on a model, choose one that is intermediate in price.

9. In Table 5-1, record the cost of an Ethernet NIC with an RJ-45 connection for a desktop. If your desktop computer already has an onboard NIC, record the cost as "Included."

10. In Table 5-1, record the cost and model information for a PCMCIA or USB NIC with an RJ-45 connection for a laptop. If your laptop computer already has an onboard NIC, record the cost as "Included."

11. In Table 5-1, record the cost and model information for a wireless network card that is compatible with the desktop computer you listed in Step 7. If your desktop already has an integrated wireless card, record the cost as "Included."

12. In Table 5-1, record the cost and model information for a wireless network card that is compatible with the laptop you listed in Step 8. If your laptop already has an integrated wireless card, record the cost as "Included."

13. In Table 5-1, record the cost of the full version of Windows 8.1 or Windows 7. If your computers come already bundled with Windows, record the cost as "Included."

14. Assume that you need to connect 50 workstations and 20 laptops to a network and that all of them must run Windows 8.1 or Windows 7. Calculate the cost of these computers and their operating systems, assuming you use the computers you identified in Steps 7 and 8. Record this information in Table 5-1.

15. Assume that each workstation and each laptop requires 50 feet of cable. Calculate the cost of the total amount of Category 5 cable needed. For comparison, also calculate the cost of the total amount of the Category 5e, Category 6, Category 6a, or Category 7 cable you found in Step 3. Record this information in Table 5-1.

16. Assume that each workstation will use a wired connection and that each laptop will use both a wired and a wireless connection. Calculate the total cost of all of the wired and wireless NICs. Record this information in Table 5-1.

17. Assume that one wireless access point will be required. (Additional wireless access points might be required depending on the physical layout of the building and other factors.) How many hubs or switches are required to connect all the workstations and all the laptops to the network at the same time? Calculate the total cost for switches and the wireless access point. Record this information in Table 5-1.

18. Calculate the total cost of the network using Category 5 cable by adding up the totals you calculated in Steps 14 through 17. Record this information in Table 5-1. Do not include in the total the cost of the other cabling you calculated in Step 15.

19. For comparison, calculate the total cost of the network using the highest-quality cable you could find (Category 6 or 7). Record this information in Table 5-1. Do this by summing the totals you calculated in Steps 14 through 17. Do not include in the total the cost of the Category 5 cabling.

Table 5-1 Cost information for Lab 5.1

Store or Web site name:		
Item	**Cost**	**Notes**
Category 5 cable, per foot		
Highest-quality cable available, per foot		
Low-end, four-port Ethernet switch		Model:
16-port switch		Model:
802.11n wireless access point or home router		Model:
Desktop computer		Model:
Laptop computer		Model:
Ethernet NIC for a desktop		Model:
PCMCIA or USB NIC for a laptop		Model:
Wireless network card for a desktop		Model:
Wireless network card for a laptop		Model:
Windows 8.1 or Windows 7		
50 workstations and 20 laptops with operating systems		
Category 5 cable to connect all 50 workstations and 20 laptops		
Category 5e, 6, 6a, or 7 cable to connect all 50 workstations and 20 laptops		
Wired and wireless NICs for desktops and laptops		
One wireless access point and a sufficient number of hubs or switches to connect all the workstations and laptops to the network		
Total cost of the network with Category 5 cable		
Cost of the network with highest-quality cable available		Type of cable:

Certification Objectives

Objectives for the CompTIA Network+ Exam:

- 5.4 Given a scenario, deploy the appropriate wired connectivity standard

Review Questions

1. What type of connector does a 100Base-T network require?

   a. RJ-11

   b. BNC

   c. AUI

   d. RJ-45

2. What is the signal rate for Cat 5e cable?

   a. 16 MHz

   b. 100 MHz

   c. 350 MHz

   d. 500 MHz

3. Which of the following is commonly used to protect UTP cable from EMI?

   a. Conduit

   b. STP

   c. Crossover cable

   d. Lead shielding

4. What is the maximum throughput of a 100Base-TX network?

   a. 5 Mbps

   b. 10 Mbps

   c. 50 Mbps

   d. 100 Mbps

5. The 1000Base-TX standard requires _____ cabling or better.

   a. Cat 3

   b. Cat 5

   c. Cat 5e

   d. Cat 6

Lab 5.2 Creating a UTP Crossover Cable to Connect Two Computers

Objectives

You might find it necessary to make cables from time to time. The phrase "making cables" actually refers to the process of properly attaching connectors to the ends of a length of cable. Many companies make their own cables to save money. Additionally, knowing how to make cables makes it easier to troubleshoot cabling problems.

Normal patch cables, also known as straight-through cables, have wire terminations on either end that are identical. Another kind of cable is a crossover cable. In this type of cable, the transmit and receive pins in one of the cable's plugs must be reversed. A crossover cable allows two workstations to connect directly to each other (without a connectivity device between them).

This lab walks you through the steps of attaching the ends to a Category 5 cable. For a visual demonstration of various techniques, try searching YouTube for "making a crossover cable."

After completing this lab, you will be able to:

- Make a crossover Category 5 cable
- Directly connect two computers with an RJ-45 crossover cable by plugging one end of the cable into the NIC of one computer and the other end of the cable into the NIC of the second computer
- Use a cable tester to ensure cable integrity

Materials Required

This lab will require the following:

- At least 10 feet of Category 5 (or better) UTP cable without connectors
- Two RJ-45 connectors (or more if necessary)
- Two computers named *WORKSTATION1* and *WORKSTATION2* running Windows 8.1 or Windows 7, configured to be in a workgroup named NETPLUS, with an Ethernet NIC
- Administrative access to both computers
- A network crimper
- A wire stripper
- A cable tester
- A wire cutting tool

Estimated completion time: **60 minutes**

Activity

1. Use the wire cutter to make a clean cut at both ends of the UTP cable.

2. Use the wire stripper to remove one inch (or less) of the sheath from one end of the UTP cable. Do not strip the insulation from the individual wires inside the UTP cable, and take care not to damage the insulation on the twisted pairs inside.

3. Slightly separate the four wire pairs, but keep the pairs twisted around each other.

4. Hold the RJ-45 connector so that the opening faces you and the plastic flap is on the bottom. Push the wires into the RJ-45 connector so that each wire is in its own slot in the connector, in the order shown in Table 5-2. Use a crimping tool to punch down the cable. You have now completed one end of the cable.

5. Repeat Steps 2 and 3 for the other end of the twisted-pair cable.

6. Hold the RJ-45 connector so that the opening faces you and the plastic flap is on the bottom, just as you did in Step 4. If you flip the RJ-45 connector over, the cable will not work. Push the wires into the RJ-45 connector so that each wire is in its own slot in the order shown in Table 5-3. Use a crimping tool to punch down the cable. This crosses the transmit and receive wires (both positive and negative), which allows the computers to communicate when connected. After completing this step, your crossover cable will be ready to use. Figure 5-1 shows an example of a crossover cable attached to a cable tester.

Table 5-2   Pin numbers and color codes for creating a TIA/EIA 568A straight-through cable end

Pin number	Pair number	Use	Color
1	2	Transmit	White with green stripe
2	2	Receive	Green
3	3	Transmit	White with orange stripe
4	1	Receive	Blue
5	1	Transmit	White with blue stripe
6	3	Receive	Orange
7	4	Transmit	White with brown stripe
8	4	Receive	Brown

Table 5-3   Pin numbers and color codes for creating a TIA/EIA 568B crossover cable end

Pin number	Pair number	Use	Color
1	3	Transmit	White with orange stripe
2	3	Receive	Orange
3	2	Transmit	White with green stripe
4	1	Receive	Blue
5	1	Transmit	White with blue stripe
6	2	Receive	Green
7	4	Transmit	White with brown stripe
8	4	Receive	Brown

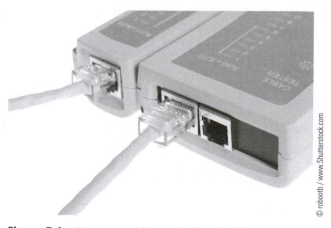

Figure 5-1   Crossover cable attached to a cable tester

7. Plug each end of the cable into the cable tester. If the cable tester determines there are any problems with your cable, remove the ends of the cable with a wire cutter and repeat the first six steps of this lab. Otherwise, skip to the next step. Making a cable properly on the first try is difficult.

8. Remove the cable ends from the cable tester.

9. Connect one end of the cable to the NIC of *WORKSTATION1*.

10. Connect the other end of the same cable to the NIC of *WORKSTATION2*. The lights on each NIC turn on.

11. Log on to *WORKSTATION1* using an administrative account. The Windows desktop appears.

12. Right-click **Start**, and then click **Network Connections**. Or if you're using Windows 7, open the Control Panel, click **Network and Internet**, click **Network and Sharing Center**, and then click **Change adapter settings**. The Network Connections dialog box opens.

13. Right-click the **Ethernet0** icon or, in Windows 7, Local Area Connection. Select **Properties** from the shortcut menu that appears. The Ethernet0 or, in Windows 7, Local Area Connection Properties window opens.

14. Double-click **Internet Protocol Version 4 (TCP/IPv4)**. The Internet Protocol Version 4 (TCP/IPv4) Properties dialog box opens.

15. Click the **Use the following IP address** option button. In the IP address text box, enter **192.168.54.2**. In the Subnet mask text box, enter **255.255.255.0**. Click **OK** and then click **OK** again.

16. Repeat Steps 11 through 15 on *WORKSTATION2*, using an IP address of 192.168.54.3.

17. On *WORKSTATION2*, open the Command Prompt window.

18. Type `ping 192.168.54.2` and press **Enter**. The computer indicates that it has received four replies, demonstrating that the two computers can communicate with each other over the new cable.

19. On *WORKSTATION1*, open a Command Prompt window.

20. Type `ping 192.168.54.3` and press **Enter**. The computer indicates that it has received four replies from the remote computer.

21. Log off both computers.

Certification Objectives

Objectives for the CompTIA Network+ Exam:

- 1.5 Install and properly terminate various cable types and connectors using appropriate tools

Review Questions

1. How much power does standard PoE provide?

   a. 15.4 watts

   b. 25.5 watts

   c. 45 watts

   d. Unlimited

2. What is one use for a crossover cable?

   a. To connect a hub and a workstation

   b. To connect a workstation to a wall jack

   c. To connect two workstations directly

   d. To connect a workstation to a modem

3. Which of the following tools would be useful in creating a patch cable for a 100Base-T network?

   a. Screwdriver

   b. Crimper

   c. Soldering iron

   d. Pliers

4. What type of cable would connect a workstation to the wall jack in the work area of a 100Base-T network?

   a. Straight-through cable

   b. Crossover cable

   c. Coaxial cable

   d. Punch-down cable

5. In twisted-pair wire, how does the twist ratio affect transmission? (Choose all that apply.)

   a. The more twists per inch, the less cross-talk transmission will suffer.

   b. The more twists per inch, the slower the transmission.

   c. The more twists per inch, the more attenuation transmission will suffer.

   d. The more twists per inch, the faster the transmission.

6. What is the maximum speed at which Category 3 UTP can transmit data?

   a. 1 Mbps

   b. 10 Mbps

   c. 100 Mbps

   d. 1 Gbps

7. What type of cable is required for 100Base-FX?

   a. Coaxial cable

   b. UTP

   c. STP

   d. Fiber-optic cable

Lab 5.3 Comparing Throughput

Objectives

As a network administrator, you will often have to choose between different types of media, even within the same network. Throughput is often an important consideration in choosing between different network media. For instance, servers typically require faster media than most workstations, and some workstations will require faster media than others. Additionally, the types of applications in use on the network will also play a role in the types of media used. Some applications, such as streaming video, require more bandwidth than others.

When comparing media types, it is often helpful to look at the actual transmission rates under realistic conditions. The *actual* transmission rates will often differ from the theoretical transmission rates. Many factors will prevent a computer from transmitting or receiving data at the theoretical rate. These include the quality of the cabling, noise, and the ability of the computer on either end to send or receive data. Additionally, the bandwidth used by other computers on the network can limit the available bandwidth. Also, you will often need to verify that many applications work as expected with the intended media. With applications such as streaming video or IP telephony (VoIP), factors such as latency and transmission rate make a big difference in whether users can successfully use the application. Testing new applications under realistic conditions can help you make the best decision possible about the type of network media you will use in your network.

After completing this lab, you will be able to:

- Measure the throughput on an Ethernet network
- Compare throughput on networks using different media
- Recognize that actual throughput might not reach the maximum throughput specified for a network

Materials Required

This lab will require the following:

- A computer named *SERVER1* running Windows Server 2012 R2 and configured as a domain controller for the netpluslab.net domain with an IP address of 192.168.54.1 and a subnet mask of 255.255.255.0
- A computer named *WORKSTATION1* running Windows 8.1 or Windows 7 in the netpluslab.net domain and configured with an IP address of 192.168.54.2 and a subnet mask of 255.255.255.0
- Access as the administrator to *SERVER1*
- Two switches with RJ-45 ports configured so that each port is in the same VLAN
- Ethernet NICs with RJ-45 connectors in each computer, so that each computer can transmit data at the rate of the hubs or switches
- Two straight-through Category 5 (or better) UTP cables that can be used to connect the computers to a hub

- One crossover Category 5 (or better) UTP cable that can be used to connect the two hubs directly
- On *SERVER1*, a shared folder named NETPLUS that can be accessed by the netplus user in the netpluslab.net domain; this folder should contain a large file (>50 MB), such as a video file or a compressed folder

Estimated completion time: **25–30 minutes**

Activity

1. Connect the computers to the first hub or switch.
2. On *SERVER1*, log on as the administrator. Windows Server Manager opens.
3. Select **Tools**, and then click **Performance Monitor**. The Performance Monitor window opens.
4. Select **Performance Monitor** in the Monitoring Tools folder.
5. Right-click the graph in the right pane. Select **Add Counters** from the shortcut menu. The Add Counters dialog box opens, as shown in Figure 5-2.
6. Click **Network Interface** in the list of available counters and then click the computer's NIC in the Instances of selected object list box.
7. Expand the **Network Interface** category and click **Bytes Total/sec** in the list below Network Interface. Click **Add**. The Bytes Total/sec counter is added to the list of counters that will be monitored.

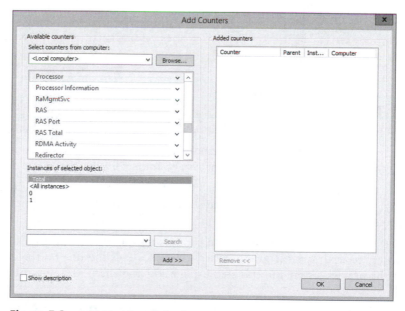

Figure 5-2   Add Counters dialog box

8. Click **OK**. The Add Counters dialog box closes.

9. If the Performance window shows any counters besides Bytes Total/sec at the bottom of the right pane of the Performance window, click these counters to highlight them. Press the **Delete** key to delete them. You now see the NIC's current bandwidth.

10. Log on to *WORKSTATION1* with an administrative account. The Windows desktop appears.

11. Open **File Explorer**. The This PC window opens. (In Windows 7, click the **Start** button, and then click **Computer**. The Computer window opens.)

12. Click the Computer tab, and then click **Map network drive**. The Map Network Drive window opens.

13. If necessary, choose drive letter **Z:** from the drop-down menu next to the Drive list box. Type `\\192.168.54.1\netplus` in the Folder text box and then click **Finish**.

14. A message box opens, indicating that you are attempting to connect to \\192.168.54.1\netplus. The Connect to 192.168.54.1 window opens. (The window might not appear if the password is the same on both computers. If so, go to Step 16.)

15. In the User name text box, enter **netplus@netpluslab.net**. In the Password text box, enter the password for the netplus account. Click **OK**. A window showing the contents of the shared netplus folder on the server is displayed.

16. Open the Command Prompt window.

17. Type `mkdir C:\temp` and press **Enter**. The computer creates a new directory.

18. Type `notepad test.bat` and press **Enter**. A dialog box opens asking if you want to create the file.

19. Click **Yes**. The Notepad window opens.

20. In Notepad, enter the following three lines, substituting the correct filename for *filename*:

```
:Copy
copy Z:\filename C:\temp
goto COPY
```

21. Exit Notepad. A dialog box opens, asking if you want to save your changes. Click **Save**.

22. At the command prompt, type `test` and press **Enter**. The batch file continuously copies the file to *WORKSTATION1* from the shared folder on *SERVER1*.

23. Look at the graph on *SERVER1*. If the line is flat and at the very bottom or the very top of the graph, right-click the graph and select **Properties** from the shortcut menu. Otherwise, go to Step 26.

24. On *SERVER1*, click the **Graph** tab. In the Maximum text box, enter **500** and click **OK**. The computer redraws the graph with the new scale. If the line on the graph is still flat, repeat the previous step and this step using 5000 and then 50,000 until the line is in the middle of the graph.

25. After a minute, look at the Average box at the bottom of the graph and record the number of bytes received per second. Multiply this number by 8 to find the number of bits received per second. Record the number of bits received per second and compare it with the bandwidth of the hub.

26. At the command prompt on *WORKSTATION1*, press **CTRL+C** to stop the batch file. Type **Y** and press **Enter** when asked to terminate the batch job.

27. Leave *WORKSTATION1* connected to the first hub but connect *SERVER1* to the second hub. Connect the two hubs directly with a crossover cable. The lights on each NIC turn on.

28. At the command prompt on *WORKSTATION1*, type **test** and press **Enter**.

29. Watch the graph on *SERVER1*. After a minute, record the number of bytes received per second. Multiply this number by 8 to find the number of bits received per second and compare it with the bandwidth of the hubs.

30. At the command prompt on *WORKSTATION1*, press **CTRL+C** to stop the batch file. Type **Y** and press **Enter** when asked to terminate the batch job. On *SERVER1*, close the Performance Monitor window.

31. Compare the number of bits received per second through the single hub you recorded in Step 25 with the number of bits received per second through two hubs you recorded in Step 29.

32. Log off both computers.

Certification Objectives

Objectives for the CompTIA Network+ Exam:

- 2.1 Given a scenario, use appropriate monitoring tools
- 2.2 Given a scenario, analyze metrics and reports from monitoring and tracking performance tools

Review Questions

1. Increasing the twist ratio makes twisted-pair cabling more resistant to _____.
   a. Stretching
   b. Fire
   c. Cross-talk
   d. Attenuation

2. What might cause a 100Base-TX network to experience an average throughput of less than 100 Mbps? (Choose all that apply.)
   a. Heavy traffic on the network
   b. Excessive noise
   c. Too many protocols bound on the server
   d. A mix of different network operating systems on the servers

3. What does the "T" in 10Base-T and 100Base-T stand for?

   a. Transmission

   b. Transport layer

   c. Twisted-pair

   d. Transparent

4. What type of cable is required for a 100Base-T network?

   a. Cat 3 or higher

   b. Cat 5 or higher

   c. Cat 6 or higher

   d. Cat 7 or higher

5. Where would you find a plenum cable?

   a. Above the ceiling tiles in an office

   b. In an outdoor cable trench that leads to a building

   c. Between a hub and a punch-down panel

   d. Between a workstation and a wall jack

Lab 5.4 Understanding How a Category 5 Cable Fails

Objectives

Verifying the integrity of network cabling is often an important first step in solving network problems. In the OSI model, the network media is at the Physical layer. If the network media is not functioning properly, the layers above the Physical layer will not function properly either. It is important to keep in mind that damage to cabling might not be immediately obvious, and might result in odd or intermittent problems. For instance, a damaged or miswired cable might cause excess noise. Although data might be transmitted through the cable, protocols at higher levels of the OSI model will need to retransmit data. The problem might also become worse over time, eventually preventing data from being transmitted through the cable at all.

Network cabling should be protected as much as possible. It can be damaged slowly over time by factors such as excessive heat or pressure, or it can be damaged quickly by a user's foot or a backhoe outside. The better protected network cabling is, the longer it will last.

In this lab, you will use an incorrectly made cable to simulate a network problem. Although cables can be damaged in many different ways, it is also important to verify that network cabling is properly installed in the first place. If you do not verify proper installation of network cabling, you might find it difficult to distinguish between a problem with the original installation and cabling damaged after the installation. This can prevent you from finding the ultimate source of the problem and fixing it properly.

After completing this lab, you will be able to:

- Identify the problem associated with an incorrectly wired Category 5 (or better) UTP cable

- Use a basic RJ-45 network cable tester (optional)

Materials Required

This lab will require the following:

- At least 10 feet of Category 5 (or better) UTP cable
- Four RJ-45 connectors
- A computer named *WORKSTATION1* running Windows 8.1 or Windows 7 in the NETPLUS workgroup with an Ethernet NIC with RJ-45 connectors, configured with an IP address of 192.168.54.2 and a subnet mask of 255.255.255.0
- A computer named *WORKSTATION2* running Windows 8.1 or Windows 7 in the NETPLUS workgroup with an Ethernet NIC with RJ-45 connectors, configured with an IP address of 192.168.54.3 and a subnet mask of 255.255.255.0
- File and Printer Sharing for Microsoft Networks installed on both computers
- Administrative access to both computers
- A network crimper
- A wire stripper
- A wire cutting tool
- A network cable tester
- A miswired Category 5 UTP cable created by your instructor (optional)
- Completion of Lab 5.2

Estimated completion time: **60 minutes**

Activity

1. If you already have a miswired cable, skip to Step 5. Otherwise, you can create one with the following steps.

2. Perform Steps 1 through 4 of Lab 5.2 for one end of the twisted-pair cable.

3. Repeat Steps 1 through 3 of Lab 5.2 for the other end of the twisted-pair cable.

4. On the second end of the twisted-pair cable, push the wires into the RJ-45 connector so that each wire is in its own slot and so that the colors match the pin numbers listed in Table 5-4. Using a crimping tool, punch down the end of the cable. This results in an incorrectly made cable.

5. Connect one end of the cable to each computer. If the network adapter lights on each computer do not illuminate, proceed with the next step. If they do, you accidentally made a correctly wired cable, and you need to begin this lab again.

6. Log on to *WORKSTATION1* with an administrative account. The Windows desktop appears.

7. Open a Command Prompt window.

8. Type **ping 192.168.54.3** and press **Enter**. The computer indicates that the request timed out four times.

Table 5-4   Pin numbers and color codes for creating an incorrect cable end

Pin number	Pair number	Color
1	4	Brown
2	4	White with brown stripes
3	1	White with blue stripes
4	3	White with orange stripes
5	3	Orange
6	1	Blue
7	2	White with green stripes
8	2	Green

© 2016 Cengage Learning®

9. Repeat Steps 6 through 8 on *WORKSTATION2*, attempting to ping the IP address 192.168.54.2 instead.

10. If you have a basic cable tester, use it to test the cable for problems. What information does the cable tester give you?

11. Using the wire cutting tool, cut the incorrectly wired end of the cable about one inch from the RJ-45 connector. The RJ-45 connector should drop off.

12. Rewire and recrimp the connector to make a crossover cable as described in Lab 5.2; this connector should be wired according to the specifications in Table 5-3. Test the cable again if you have a cable tester and then connect one end of the cable to the NIC in each of the computers.

13. In the Command Prompt window on *WORKSTATION1*, type **ping 192.168.54.3** and press **Enter**. The computer indicates that it has received four replies from *WORKSTATION2*.

14. In the Command Prompt window on *WORKSTATION2*, type **ping 192.168.54.2** and press **Enter**. The computer indicates that it has received four replies from *WORKSTATION1*.

15. Log off both computers.

Certification Objectives

Objectives for the CompTIA Network+ Exam:

- 4.2 Given a scenario, analyze and interpret the output of troubleshooting tools
- 4.4 Given a scenario, troubleshoot and resolve common copper cable issues

Review Questions

1. What organization is responsible for establishing structured wiring standards?

   a. TIA/EIA

   b. ANSI

   c. ITU

   d. FCC

2. What pin number is used for transmitting a positive signal on an RJ-45 straight-through patch cable?

   a. 1

   b. 2

   c. 5

   d. 6

3. Which of the following could be a symptom of a damaged patch cable between a workstation and the wall jack on a UTP network? (Choose all that apply.)

   a. The workstation cannot send or receive data to or from the network.

   b. The workstation and other workstations in the same office cannot send or receive data to or from the network.

   c. The workstation can send data to the network, but cannot receive data from the network.

   d. All workstations on the same segment can send data to the network, but cannot receive data from the network.

4. How many wire pairs are in a typical Category 5 cable?

   a. 2

   b. 3

   c. 4

   d. 6

5. How does bend radius affect transmission?

   a. Transmission will not be successful until the bend radius has been reached.

   b. Transmission cannot occur at the bend radius.

   c. Transmission will be unreliable after the bend radius is exceeded.

   d. Transmission will be less secure after the bend radius is exceeded.

6. What problem could be caused by laying cable in the ceiling tiles six inches above a bank of fluorescent lights?

   a. Increased latency

   b. EMI

   c. Fire hazard

   d. Decreased bend radius

Lab 5.5 Connecting Two Switches with Fiber-Optic Cable

Objectives

In this lab, you will connect two switches with fiber-optic cable. Although UTP cable is less fragile, less expensive, and easier to handle than fiber, fiber can allow the transfer of more information over greater distances than UTP cable. Additionally, electrical interference does not affect fiber.

A port used to connect two switches is often called an uplink port. An uplink port often uses faster media than the other ports on the switch, but not always. Traffic between the two switches will be transmitted through the uplink ports. If the other ports on the switch transmit a lot of traffic between the two switches, the uplink port might become saturated. This will reduce throughput for any traffic that must go through the two switches. If the uplink ports use a faster media than the other ports on the switch, it becomes more difficult (or impossible) to saturate the link between the two ports.

After completing this lab, you will be able to:

- Connect two switches using multimode fiber

Materials Required

This lab will require the following:

- A computer named *WORKSTATION1* running Windows 8.1 or Windows 7 with a NIC and with an IP address of 192.168.54.2 and a subnet mask of 255.255.255.0

- A computer named *WORKSTATION2* running Windows 8.1 or Windows 7 with a NIC and with an IP address of 192.168.54.3 and a subnet mask of 255.255.255.0

- Administrative access to both computers

- A shared folder on *WORKSTATION2* named NETPLUS

- Two switches, named *SWITCH1* and *SWITCH2*, with fiber uplink ports (with any necessary configuration to act as uplink ports), the appropriate connectors, and all ports configured in the same VLAN

- Installation of any adapters, such as Gigabit Interface Converters (GBICs), necessary for operation of the uplink ports

- A length of fiber-optic cable with the appropriate connectors to attach to the two switches

- Two Category 5 (or better) UTP cables with RJ-45 connectors

Other fiber connectors may be used as appropriate.

Estimated completion time: **20 minutes**

Activity

1. Plug the RJ-45 connector at one end of a UTP cable into the NIC of *WORKSTATION1*. Plug the RJ-45 connector at the other end of the cable into one of the RJ-45 ports on *SWITCH1*. Link lights on the switch and on the NIC light up.

2. Repeat the previous step, connecting *WORKSTATION2* to *SWITCH2*.

3. If necessary, remove the plugs from one of the fiber uplink ports on *SWITCH1*. Fiber ports often come with a plug to protect the port from dust and other damage.

   As fiber ports may emit invisible laser radiation when they do not contain a cable, do not stare into an open port. Avoid looking into one while the switch is powered on.

4. Grasp the connector at one end of the fiber-optic cable. Making sure that the SC connector is properly oriented, push it into the uplink port on *SWITCH1* until the connector snaps into place. Link lights on both switches light up.

5. Log on to *WORKSTATION1* using an administrative account. The Windows desktop appears.

6. Open a Command Prompt window.

7. Type `ping 192.168.54.3` and press **Enter**. The computer indicates that it has received four replies.

8. Repeat Steps 5 through 7 on *WORKSTATION2*, and then ping the IP address 192.168.54.2.

9. Log off both computers.

Certification Objectives

Objectives for the CompTIA Network+ Exam:

- 1.5 Install and properly terminate various cable types and connectors using appropriate tools

Review Questions

1. Which of the following is *not* an advantage of fiber cables over UTP cables?

   a. Fiber is not susceptible to electric interference, whereas UTP cable is.

   b. Fiber is less fragile than UTP cable.

   c. Fiber is more expensive than UTP cable.

   d. Fiber can transmit data over longer distances than UTP cable.

2. You work for a small ISP. Which fiber technology would be best for connecting to your telecommunications carrier over a distance of 2.8 miles?

   a. 1000Base-LX

   b. 1000Base-SX

   c. 10 GBase-SR

   d. 1000Base-T

3. In which of the following situations would it be possible to use a UTP cable standard such as 1000Base-CX over a fiber-optic cable standard such as 1000Base-LX or 1000Base-T?

   a. When connecting two data centers over distances of 2 km or less

   b. When connecting short distances of 25 meters or less between network devices and servers inside a single data center

   c. When connecting short distances of 200 meters or less between network devices and workstations inside a building

   d. When connecting buildings inside a campus over distances of 500 meters or less

4. Which of the following problems could cause signal loss in fiber-optic cable?

   a. Cross-talk between strands of fiber in multimode fiber cables

   b. Cross-talk between cables in single mode fiber cables

   c. Electromagnetic interference caused by power lines near the cables

   d. Dirty connectors

5. 100Base-FX requires multimode fiber cable with two or more strands. How are these strands used to transmit and receive data? (Choose all that apply.)

   a. One strand is used for both transmission and reception in both full- and half-duplex.

   b. Both strands are used for transmission and reception in full-duplex.

   c. One strand is used for transmission and the other is used for reception in half-duplex.

   d. Both strands are used for transmission and reception in full-duplex, whereas there is no half-duplex for 100Base-FX.

Lab 5.6 Using a Network Cable Tester

Objectives

Network cable testers are useful tools when troubleshooting network cabling. A basic cable tester may only check a single kind of cable for common problems such as an open or short circuit. More sophisticated testers can perform a variety of tests and will not only tell you if a cable is working, but will also determine the nature and location of the problem.

In this lab, you will become familiar with the basic functions of a network cable tester and, if possible, use one to check a variety of cables for problems.

After completing this lab, you will be able to:

- Perform basic tests with a network cable tester

Materials Required

This lab will require the following:

- A network cable tester capable of testing UTP cable
- Access to a retail or online store that sells computer networking equipment
- Pencil and paper

Estimated completion time: **40 minutes**

Activity

1. Determine the manufacturer, make, and model number for your cable tester.
2. If you don't have the product manual, see if additional information is available either on the manufacturer's Web site or as a downloadable PDF.
3. Use the manual, Web site, and the Internet to answer the following questions. Record the answers on a separate piece of paper. If your network tester does not have a particular test, record N/A for not available.

    a. What kinds of media can it test? Be sure to record specific categories such as Cat 5 and Cat 6 as well as general categories like UTP and COAX.

    b. Does the tester come with a detachable or separate remote terminator that attaches to the other side of the UTP cable being tested? What is the function of the remote terminator?

    c. Does the tester determine the length of the cable? How is this determined?

4. Does the cable tester detect a short in the UTP cable? Does it determine where in the cable the short is located?
5. Can it detect both near end and far end open wires?
6. Does the cable tester test for a miswire?
7. Does it test for split pairs? Why are split pairs a problem?
8. Does your cable tester perform any other notable tests on UTP cable?
9. Using the skills you developed in Lab 5.2, create a wire with a split pair. Use Table 5-2 to determine the wiring of both ends except switch the wires for pins 1 and 3 on both ends.
10. Did the cable tester find this problem?

Certification Objectives

Objectives for the CompTIA Network+ Exam:

- 4.2 Given a scenario, analyze and interpret the output of troubleshooting tools
- 4.4 Given a scenario, troubleshoot and resolve common copper cable issues

Review Questions

1. A higher twist ratio causes less _____ but more attenuation.

   a. Shielding

   b. Cost

   c. Noise

   d. Cross-talk

2. How many pairs of wires are used for transmission in Gigabit Ethernet?

   a. 4

   b. 3

   c. 2

   d. 1

3. What is the maximum throughput of a 100Base-TX network?

   a. 5 Mbps

   b. 10 Mbps

   c. 50 Mbps

   d. 100 Mbps

4. A TIA/EIA 568A pinout on one side and a 568B pinout on the other will make a _____ cable.

   a. Straight-through

   b. Patch

   c. Crossover

   d. Rollover

5. This kind of cable can be used to connect a computer to the console port of a router.

   a. Straight-through

   b. Patch

   c. Crossover

   d. Rollover

WIRELESS NETWORKING

Labs included in this chapter

- Lab 6.1 Adding a Windows Client to a Hidden Wireless Network
- Lab 6.2 Adding a Linux Client to a Wireless Network
- Lab 6.3 Installing a Wireless Router
- Lab 6.4 Securing a Wireless Network
- Lab 6.5 Investigating Wireless Access Points
- Lab 6.6 Using Wireless Network Monitoring Software

CompTIA Network+ Exam Objectives

Objective	Lab
2.7 Install and configure wireless LAN infrastructure and implement the appropriate technologies in support of wireless capable devices	6.1, 6.2, 6.3, 6.4, 6.5, 6.6
3.3 Given a scenario, implement network hardening techniques	6.4, 6.6
4.3 Given a scenario, troubleshoot and resolve common wireless issues	6.1, 6.6

Lab 6.1 Adding a Windows Client to a Hidden Wireless Network

Objectives

In this lab, you will add a host to a wireless network. Wireless networks allow a user to connect to the network without cabling. This makes it possible to use a networked computer in a cafeteria, outdoors, in a coffee shop, and in many other places.

However, wireless networks come with a number of disadvantages. They do not have the throughput that some wired networks provide. Throughput also varies depending on reception, and good reception might not be possible from all locations. Wireless signals are affected by sources of electronic noise, including natural sources like the weather and solar activity, and artificial sources, such as fluorescent lights and microwave ovens. Finally, wireless networks might not be as secure as cabled networks. An unsecured wireless access point might mean that anyone with a wireless card in the next building or in the parking lot could gain access to your network resources.

After completing this lab, you will be able to:

- Add a Windows client to a wireless network

Materials Required

This lab will require the following:

- A computer (ideally a laptop) named *WORKSTATION1* running Windows 8.1 or Windows 7 with a wireless network card configured so that Windows manages wireless settings (instead of using the network card's client software to manage wireless settings)

- A wireless access point named *netplus* (or another name supplied by your instructor) configured with an IP address of 192.168.1.1 and a subnet mask of 255.255.255.0 that does not broadcast its SSID

- The wireless access point configured to give out DHCP addresses between 192.168.1.2 and 192.168.1.254 (or some portion of that range) and a subnet mask of 255.255.255.0

- Any additional settings needed to connect the Windows 8.1 or Windows 7 computer to this wireless access point

> Estimated completion time: **30 minutes**

Activity

1. Log on to *WORKSTATION1* as an administrator. The Windows desktop appears.

2. Click **Start**, type **Network and Sharing Center**, and press **Enter**. The Network and Sharing Center window opens.

3. Click **Set up a new connection or network**, click **Manually connect to a wireless network**, and then click **Next**. This displays the dialog box shown in Figure 6-1.

4. Enter **netplus** (or the name of the wireless access point) in the Network name text box. Configure any additional settings as indicated by your instructor and then click **Next**.

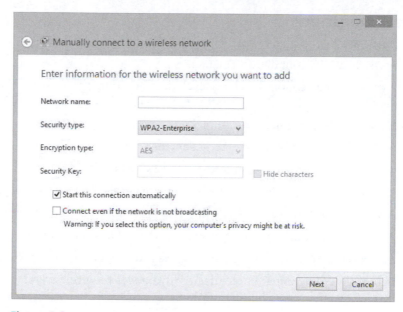

Figure 6-1   Manually connecting to a wireless network

5. After you've connected to the network, close any open windows.

6. Now you can test your connectivity to the wireless network. Open a Command Prompt window.

7. Type `ping 192.168.1.1` and press **Enter**. The computer indicates that it has received four replies.

8. If the Windows computer is a laptop, type `ping -t 192.168.1.1` and press **Enter**. The `ping` command begins running continuously, and will not stop until you end it. Pick up the laptop and walk away from the wireless access point. How far can you walk away from the wireless access point before the computer indicates that it is unable to reach 192.168.1.1?

9. Press **CTRL+C** to stop the `ping` command.

10. Use the technique from Steps 8 and 9 to walk in different directions and, on a separate piece of paper, draw a rough map of the range of your wireless network.

11. Note if the range is identical in all directions. If not, what do you think caused the differences?

12. When you're finished, log off the computer.

Certification Objectives

Objectives for the CompTIA Network+ Exam:

- 2.7 Install and configure wireless LAN infrastructure and implement the appropriate technologies in support of wireless capable devices

- 4.3 Given a scenario, troubleshoot and resolve common wireless issues

Review Questions

1. How is a wireless NIC different from a NIC that requires a cable?

   a. A wireless NIC contains an antenna.

   b. A wireless NIC contains a chip, which does additional processing at higher levels of the OSI model.

   c. A wireless NIC requires an external power source.

   d. A wireless NIC requires an external antenna.

2. In which of the following ways does a wireless LAN differ from an Ethernet LAN?

   a. A wireless LAN requires additional protocols in the TCP/IP suite.

   b. A wireless LAN uses completely different protocols than an Ethernet LAN.

   c. A wireless LAN uses different techniques at the Physical layer to transmit data.

   d. A wireless LAN uses different techniques at the Data Link layer to transmit frames.

3. Which of the following are potential disadvantages of wireless LANs as compared with cabled LANs? (Choose all that apply.)

   a. Controlling access to a wireless LAN is more difficult.

   b. Issues such as the location of buildings and the weather can affect connectivity to a wireless LAN.

   c. The additional protocols required by wireless LANs create additional overhead.

   d. Signal strength can be affected by many sources of electronic noise.

4. Why is a wireless signal susceptible to noise?

   a. Wireless NICs are usually poorly made.

   b. Wireless transmissions cannot be shielded like transmissions along an Ethernet cable.

   c. Wireless NICs do not support the network protocols necessary for error correction.

   d. Wireless NICs rely on the upper levels of the OSI model for error correction.

5. You have been hired as a network consultant by the East Coast Savings bank. East Coast Savings would like to implement a wireless LAN, but with high standards of security. What sort of restrictions would you recommend placing on the wireless LAN?

   a. Wireless LAN users have the same access as users attached to the Ethernet network.

   b. Wireless LAN users may surf the Web, but may not access the rest of the bank's network.

   c. Wireless LAN users may surf the Web, but may not access the rest of the bank's network without special security software.

   d. Wireless LAN users must use their own wireless ISP.

Lab 6.2 Adding a Linux Client to a Wireless Network

Objectives

In this lab, you will add a Linux host to a wireless network using the Network Manager service, which can be accessed and configured through an applet in the GNOME environment. This makes connecting to a wireless network relatively easy, like in Windows, and only involves a small number of steps. Without the graphical network manager, the connection would have to be manually configured at the command line.

After completing this lab, you will be able to:

- Add a Linux client to a wireless network

Materials Required

This lab will require the following:

- A computer (ideally a laptop) running a current version of Linux such as Ubuntu or Fedora named *LINUX1*, with a wireless network card, and Network Manager installed
- A wireless access point named *netplus* (or another name supplied by your instructor) configured with an IP address of 192.168.1.1 and a subnet mask of 255.255.255.0
- The wireless access point configured to give out DHCP addresses between 192.168.1.2 and 192.168.1.254 (or some portion of that range) and a subnet mask of 255.255.255.0
- Any additional settings needed to connect the Linux computer to this wireless access point

> Estimated completion time: **30 minutes**

Activity

1. Power on the *LINUX1* and log on as root. The desktop appears.
2. If Network Manager is not already active, start it by opening a terminal and typing **sudo /sbin/service NetworkManager start**.
3. Once the system has had a few minutes to discover any available wireless networks, click the network icon in the notification area at the top to view them.
4. Select the wireless network named *netplus* by clicking it. If netplus has been set up with a password, enter it now to connect.
5. Test your wireless connection by moving back to the terminal and typing **ping 192.168.1.1** and pressing **Enter**. The computer indicates that it has received four replies.
6. Close any open applications and log off the computer.

Certification Objectives

Objectives for the CompTIA Network+ Exam:

- 2.7 Install and configure wireless LAN infrastructure and implement the appropriate technologies in support of wireless capable devices

Review Questions

1. What term is used to describe when a mobile user moves out of one access point's range and into the range of another?

   a. Reassociation

   b. Deassociation

   c. Reallocation

   d. Extending the service set

2. What is the administrator's default account called in Linux?

   a. Admin

   b. Administrator

   c. default

   d. root

3. Where is the Network Manager service located?

   a. /user

   b. /sbin/service

   c. /etc/NetworkManager

   d. /Network/Manager

4. Describe how you could use Network Manager to switch between networks.

5. What Linux command is used to test network connections?

   a. `root`

   b. `sudo`

   c. `ping`

   d. `start`

Lab 6.3 Installing a Wireless Router

Objectives

In this lab, you will set up a basic unsecured wireless router. Then, in Lab 6.4, you will also implement some essential security features on the router. A wireless router is often used at home or with small peer-to-peer networks to allow several computers to wirelessly connect to an ISP and share an Internet connection. The router can also provide additional features such as functioning as a firewall or a DHCP server.

After completing this lab, you will be able to:

- Set up a basic wireless router

Materials Required

This lab will require the following:

- A computer (ideally a laptop) running Windows 8.1 or Windows 7 with a wireless network card
- An unconfigured wireless router with setup CD or user's manual
- A Cat 5 (or better) network cable

> Estimated completion time: **30 minutes**

Activity

1. If your router comes with a setup CD/DVD, run the setup program on your Windows computer. Follow the instructions in the manual on how to disconnect the Internet connection from your Windows computer and connect it to the router.

2. Physically connect your computer to a network port on the router using a Cat 5 (or better) straight-through cable. (Be sure to connect to one of the LAN ports on the router, not the Internet port.)

3. Plug in the router and turn it on.

4. Firmware on the router contains a configuration program that can usually be accessed using a Web browser. Determine the IP address of the router either by consulting the manual or by asking your instructor.

5. In your browser's address box, enter the IP address of the router (e.g., 192.168.1.1) and press **Enter**.

6. If necessary, sign in to the utility using a default password.

7. Verify that the main router configuration page is visible. The page will most likely have a drop-down menu with categories such as Setup, Wireless, and Security. Figure 6-2 shows the basic settings page for a NETGEAR wireless router.

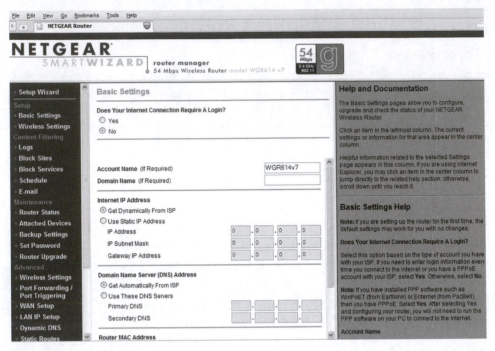

Figure 6-2 The NETGEAR router Basic Settings page

8. For most situations, the default settings should work without any changes. However, the router should be secured by changing the default password, enabling wireless encryption (preferably WPA2), and so on. Securing a router is covered in Lab 6.4. The setup program should take you through the process of configuring your router.

9. Even if you're choosing not to secure your router, it's always a good idea to change your router's default password so other people cannot change the settings.

10. Spend some time examining the basic features of your router and then make the following changes:

    • Enable DHCP.

    • Set the range of assigned addresses to begin at 192.168.1.100.

    • Change the Network Name (SSID) to *NETLAB*.

    • Set the Wireless Channel to *Auto*.

11. If necessary, reconnect your Internet connection so it correctly syncs up with the router.

12. Shut down the Windows computer and disconnect the patch cable from the router.

13. Boot the Windows computer and use the steps in Lab 6.1 to wirelessly connect to the Internet.

14. Close any open programs and log off the computer.

Certification Objectives

Objectives for the CompTIA Network+ Exam:

- 2.7 Install and configure wireless LAN infrastructure and implement the appropriate technologies in support of wireless capable devices

Review Questions

1. How is a wireless router's configuration utility usually accessed?

    a. By flashing the RAM BIOS

    b. Through a Web browser

    c. With the Windows Cfgrtr utility

    d. From the command line

2. Why is it a good idea to change your wireless router's password?

    a. So other people cannot change the router's settings

    b. So you won't forget it

    c. To make it the same as your logon password

    d. The default password is most likely too complex

3. What type of connection is used to attach to the network port on a wireless router?

    a. None, it is wireless

    b. USB

    c. Serial

    d. Straight-through patch cable

4. Which of the following Wi-Fi standards has the highest effective throughput?

    a. 802.11g

    b. 802.11a

    c. 802.11b

    d. 802.11n

5. Wireless access points are assigned a unique name or _____.

    a. FHSS

    b. DSSS

    c. CSMA

    d. SSID

Lab 6.4 Securing a Wireless Network

Objectives

Wireless routers are often used to connect a laptop to a small peer-to-peer or home network. Without adequate security, a wireless router can leave your network open to a wide range of threats. In this lab, you will learn how to implement some of the more common security features often found on wireless routers.

After completing this lab, you will be able to:

- Secure a wireless router

Materials Required

This lab will require the following:

- A computer (ideally a laptop) running Windows 8.1 or Windows 7 with a wireless network card
- An unconfigured wireless router with the included setup CD or user's manual

Estimated completion time: **30 minutes**

Activity

1. Install an unsecured wireless router as described in Lab 6.3.

2. Most wireless routers can be configured through a Web browser. Use a browser to open your router's configuration program; typically, this is done by accessing the router's configuration page at, for example, *http://192.168.1.1*.

3. Although configuration programs can vary from router to router, they are usually menu-driven and fairly easy to navigate. Use the router's configuration pages to implement the following changes. When in doubt, consult the documentation included with the router.

4. Begin by updating the router's firmware either through the configuration program or from the manufacturer's Web site. This will help address any known security flaws with the router.

5. Set a strong password for the router itself. The default passwords for all common router models are available on the Internet; for example, the default password of many Linksys routers is *admin*. With this information, an attacker can easily access the router's configuration program and disable any security features.

6. Change the name of the wireless network, or SSID (service set identifier), from the default name. The default SSID on most Linksys routers is *linksys*.

7. Turn off SSID broadcasting so your network does not show up in a list of available networks. This will not stop determined attackers, but it will prevent the network from appearing as available to casual wireless users in your area.

8. Disable remote administration so your router can only be configured by a computer that is physically attached.

9. Enable some form of encryption such as WEP, WPA, or WPA2. WPA and especially WPA2 are strongly preferred because WEP encryption can be easily broken by knowledgeable attackers. However, using WEP encryption is preferable to using no encryption at all.

10. Use MAC filtering to create a list of computers that are allowed access to the network. This too will prevent casual users from accessing your network, but can be overcome by an advanced user employing a wireless sniffer.

11. Connect to the router with your wireless computer and test your wireless connection by opening your browser and navigating to a site on the Internet.

12. When you're finished, reset the router to its factory defaults and log off your computer.

Certification Objectives

Objectives for the CompTIA Network+ Exam:

- 2.7 Install and configure wireless LAN infrastructure and implement the appropriate technologies in support of wireless capable devices

- 3.3 Given a scenario, implement network hardening techniques

Review Questions

1. What does *SSID* stand for?

   a. Service set identifier

   b. Security service Internet domain

   c. Security station identification

   d. Simple security Internet device

2. WEP, WPA, and WPA2 are all forms of wireless _____.

   a. access

   b. routers

   c. services

   d. encryption

3. You can limit access to certain computers with _____.

   a. encryption

   b. MAC filtering

   c. remote administration

   d. a strong password

4. A rogue access point set up to look like a legitimate access point is called a(n) _____.

   a. guest network

   b. evil twin

   c. remote bridge

   d. password sniffer

5. A major security weakness of WEP is the fact that it uses a _____ network key.

   a. 48-bit

   b. shared

   c. dynamic

   d. single-use

Lab 6.5 Investigating Wireless Access Points

Objectives

In this lab, you will compare several wireless access points and choose the solution that best meets your needs. A wireless local area network (WLAN) connects computers through a wireless NIC to a device called a wireless access point (WAP or AP). WLANs use a variety of standards that offer different features such as range and throughput.

After completing this lab, you will be able to:

- Compare wireless access points in terms of price and features
- Identify wireless access point hardware

Materials Required

This lab will require the following:

- Pencil and paper
- A computer with Internet access
- An ordinary user account on the computer

Estimated completion time: **30 minutes**

Activity

1. Log on to the computer as an ordinary user. The Windows desktop appears.

2. Open a Web browser such as Internet Explorer and browse the Web sites of several distributors that sell networking equipment, including wireless access points. Common manufacturers of wireless access points include Cisco/Linksys, D-Link, and 3Com.

3. Use these sites to find access points from at least two different manufacturers that meet the following criteria:

   - 802.11g and 802.11n support
   - Power over Ethernet (PoE)
   - Ceiling mounted
   - Plenum rated
   - IPv6 support
   - WPA2 encryption

4. On a separate piece of paper, record the make, model number, price, and a brief list of distinguishing features for each of the access points that you found.

5. Which access point is the best value?

6. Did you have any trouble finding information on the equipment?

7. When you're finished, log off the computer.

Certification Objectives

Objectives for the CompTIA Network+ Exam:

- 2.7 Install and configure wireless LAN infrastructure and implement the appropriate technologies in support of wireless capable devices

Review Questions

1. Which wireless networking standard operates in both the 2.4-GHz and 5-GHz bands?

   a. 802.11a

   b. 802.11b

   c. 802.11g

   d. 802.11n

2. What feature will eliminate the need for a separate electrical outlet for your WAP?

   a. PoE

   b. WPA

   c. WPA2

   d. 802.11n

3. Why is plenum-rated cable often a requirement for ceiling-mounted access points?

   a. Ceiling-mounted APs are more than seven feet off the ground.

   b. They work at higher speeds.

   c. They need to operate at higher temperatures.

   d. In the case of a fire, they do not give off toxic fumes.

4. In an enterprise-wide WLAN, coverage can be extended across multiple access points by joining them to the same _____.

   a. ESS

   b. WPA

   c. MAC

   d. MIMO

5. Some wireless access points can associate a client's MAC address with a port on a switch allowing a client to stay connected to a _____ as it moves throughout an area.

   a. DSSS

   b. FHSS

   c. RTS/CTS

   d. VLAN

Lab 6.6 Using Wireless Network Monitoring Software

Objectives

Wireless network monitoring software can be used to examine your own wireless network and look for other nearby networks that may cause interference. This kind of software can usually capture details about networks, such as their network name or SSID, whether they use encryption, and their broadcasting frequency. Some programs will also capture and analyze packets transmitted on the WLAN. In this lab, you will use a common wireless network detector from Nirsoft called WirelessNetView.

After completing this lab, you will be able to:

- Monitor your wireless network for performance and security issues

Materials Required

This lab will require the following:

- A computer (ideally a laptop) running Windows 8.1 or Windows 7 with a wireless network card and Internet access

- The wireless router setup in Lab 6.3

- An administrative account on the computer

Estimated completion time: **20 minutes**

Activity

1. Log on to the computer as an administrator. The Windows desktop appears.

2. Download and install **WirelessNetView** from *nirsoft.net* under the Network Monitoring Tools section.

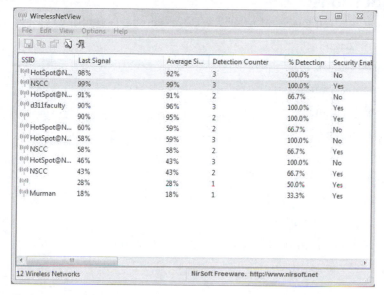

Figure 6-3   WirelessNetView showing available networks

3. Run **WirelessNetView**.

4. Click **File**, and then **Clear Networks List**.

5. After a few minutes, the WirelessNetView window should fill with all of the available networks, as shown in Figure 6-3.

6. Use WirelessNetView to determine if your wireless network is set up as you expected.

7. Double-click on your own network and record your network's SSID, authentication type, channel number, and maximum speed.

8. If other networks are also visible, answer the following questions:
   a. Are any unsecured networks visible?
   b. Do any other networks use the same channel number as your network?

9. If possible, walk with your laptop while monitoring the signal strength. How far from the wireless router could you get before the signal strength dropped by 10 percent.

10. Create a more detailed map of wireless signal strength like the one you created in Lab 6.1.

11. When you're finished, exit WirelessNetView and log off the computer.

Certification Objectives

Objectives for the CompTIA Network+ Exam:

- 2.7 Install and configure wireless LAN infrastructure and implement the appropriate technologies in support of wireless capable devices

- 3.3 Given a scenario, implement network hardening techniques

- 4.3 Given a scenario, troubleshoot and resolve common wireless issues

Review Questions

1. Determining the frequencies of nearby WLANs can be useful for avoiding _____.

    a. client saturation

    b. the near-far effect

    c. simultaneous connections

    d. overlapping channels

2. Other WLANs can be a source of _____.

    a. interference

    b. attenuation

    c. reflection

    d. diffraction

3. How many channels are available on the 2.4-GHz band?

    a. 6

    b. 11

    c. 12

    d. 24

4. A map of the Wi-Fi coverage and interference in an area is called a(n) _____ map.

    a. signal

    b. heat

    c. zone

    d. address

CHAPTER SEVEN

CLOUD COMPUTING AND REMOTE ACCESS

Labs included in this chapter

- Lab 7.1 Configuring a Dial-Up Remote Access Server
- Lab 7.2 Creating a VPN with the Point-to-Point Tunneling Protocol
- Lab 7.3 Remotely Connecting to a Windows Server
- Lab 7.4 Remotely Managing a Computer
- Lab 7.5 Remotely Managing a Linux Server
- Lab 7.6 Plaintext Versus Encrypted Protocols

CompTIA Network+ Exam Objectives

Objective	Lab
1.2 Compare and contrast the use of networking services and applications	7.1, 7.2, 7.3, 7.5
1.4 Explain the characteristics and benefits of various WAN technologies	7.1
3.2 Compare and contrast common network vulnerabilities and threats	7.5, 7.6
3.3 Given a scenario, implement network hardening techniques	7.4
4.2 Given a scenario, analyze and interpret the output of troubleshooting tools	7.6

All screenshots, unless otherwise noted, are used with permission from Microsoft Corporation.

149

Lab 7.1 Configuring a Dial-Up Remote Access Server

Objectives

In this lab, you will create a remote access server (RAS) and connect to it from a client. With a remote access server, users may access network resources from home or on the road, even if they don't have access to an Internet connection. A salesperson, for example, might be on the road a large percentage of the time and have no network access besides her dial-up connection. By dialing into a dial-up server with Routing and Remote Access Service (RRAS), she can check email, share files, and use the network just as if she were locally connected to the network.

In Windows Server 2012 R2, keep in mind that you need to specifically enable a user to dial in remotely to the Windows server. Even if the server has a modem and is configured to accept incoming calls, it may still reject a call if a user does not have dial-in permission for security reasons.

After completing this lab, you will be able to:

- Configure RRAS to allow a Windows Server 2012 R2 computer to accept dial-up connections

Materials Required

This lab will require the following:

- A computer running Windows Server 2012 R2 named *SERVER1* in the NETPLUS workgroup, with ICS disabled and Routing and Remote Access installed but not activated
- Two NICs on *SERVER1,* one configured with an IP address of 192.168.54.1 and a subnet mask of 255.255.255.0 and the other configured with an IP address of 172.16.1.1 and a subnet mask of 255.255.255.0
- A shared folder on *SERVER1* named *NETPLUS* containing at least one text file
- A computer running Windows 8.1 or Windows 7 named *WORKSTATION1*
- Administrative access to both computers
- A user account named *netplus* configured on *SERVER1* with the rights needed to dial in to the server
- Modems installed and configured on both machines
- Access to two outside analog phone lines in the same or different locations or to two digital-to-analog converters (to prevent digital phone lines from ruining the modems)
- The telephone number of the phone line to which *SERVER1* is attached
- Two phone cords with RJ-11 connectors on both ends that are long enough to reach the wall outlet

Estimated completion time: **60 minutes**

Activity

1. Connect one end of a phone cord to the back of the modem installed on *SERVER1,* and connect the other end to the wall outlet.

2. Repeat the previous step with the Windows 8.1 or Windows 7 computer.

3. Log on to *SERVER1* as the administrator. The Windows Server Manager appears.

4. Click **Tools,** and then click **Routing and Remote Access.** The Routing and Remote Access dialog box opens.

5. Right-click the **SERVER1 (local)** icon in the left pane of the dialog box. In the shortcut menu, click **Configure and Enable Routing and Remote Access.** The Routing and Remote Access Server Setup Wizard opens.

6. Click **Next.** The wizard asks you for information on how to configure the Routing and Remote Access Service.

7. If necessary, select the **Remote access (dial-up or VPN)** option. Click **Next.**

8. Click the **Dial-up** check box to select it. Click **Next.** The wizard shows you information about the interfaces to which dial-up users will connect. Select your interface, then click **Next.**

9. The wizard asks you to choose how IP addresses will be assigned to remote clients. Figure 7-1 shows an example of this dialog box in the Routing and Remote Access Server Setup Wizard.

10. Make sure that the **Automatically** button is selected, and click **Next.** The wizard asks how you would like to configure authentication.

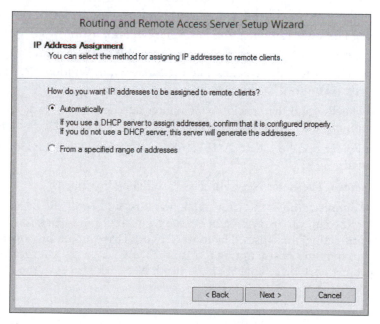

Figure 7-1   Assigning IP addresses to remote clients

11. Make sure that the **No, use Routing and Remote Access to authenticate connection requests** option is selected, and click **Next**. The computer indicates that you have completed the wizard.

12. Click **Finish**. A dialog box opens indicating that to support the relaying of DHCP messages from remote access clients, you must configure the DHCP Relay Agent.

13. Click **OK**. Message boxes appear indicating that the service is initializing. The Routing and Remote Access Server Setup Wizard closes. Log on to *WORKSTATION1* as an administrator. The Windows desktop appears.

14. On *WORKSTATION1*, right-click the network icon in the taskbar, click **Open Network and Sharing Center**, and click **Set up a new connection or network**. Select **Connect to the Internet** and click **Next**. In the "How do you want to connect?" Window, click **Dial-up**.

15. Enter the phone number of *SERVER1* in the Dial-up phone number text box.

16. Enter the appropriate username and password to connect to *SERVER1*.

17. Enter **Netplus Lab** in the Connection name text box.

18. Make sure that **Allow other people to use this connection** is selected and click **Create**. Click **Close** in the "The connection to the Internet is ready to use" window.

19. Right-click **Start** and click **Network Connections**. Or, in Windows 7, right-click the network icon, click **Open Network and Sharing Center**, then click **Change adapter settings.** The Network Connections dialog box opens.

20. Right-click the **Netplus Lab** icon and select **Connect** in the shortcut menu.

21. In the User name text box, enter **netplus**. In the Password text box, enter the password you used in Step 16. Click **Connect**. The modem connects to the remote access server.

22. A dialog box indicating that you have connected successfully opens. Click **OK**. You have successfully logged on to the remote access server.

23. Right-click **Start**, and then click **File Explorer**. Or, in Windows 7, right-click **Start**, then click **Open Windows Explorer.**

24. Click **This PC**, and then click the **Computer** tab. Or, in Windows 7, click **Computer**. On the menu bar, click **Map network drive**. The Map Network Drive dialog box opens.

25. In the Folder text box, enter **\\192.168.54.1\NETPLUS**. Click **Connect using different credentials**.

26. Click **Finish**. The Enter Network Password dialog box opens.

27. Type **Administrator** in the User name text box, and enter the password for the Administrator account on *SERVER1* in the Password text box. Click **OK**. The Enter Network Password dialog box closes. The Map Network Drive dialog box opens briefly, indicating that the computer is attempting to map the network drive. After it closes, an icon for the mapped network drive appears underneath Network Drives in the This PC or Computer window.

28. Double-click the icon for the mapped network drive. A folder containing the name of at least one text file appears.

29. Double-click the text file. The text file opens.

30. Close the text file and log off both computers.

Certification Objectives

Objectives for the CompTIA Network+ Exam:

- 1.2 Compare and contrast the use of networking services and applications
- 1.4 Explain the characteristics and benefits of various WAN technologies

Review Questions

1. What does RAS stand for?

   a. Remote authentication service

   b. Remote access server

   c. Remote accounting service

   d. Remote addressing server

2. Which of the following best describes a modem's function?

   a. To encapsulate Data Link layer protocols as Network layer protocols before transmitting data over the PSTN

   b. To separate data into frames as it is transmitted from the computer to the PSTN, and then strip data from frames as it is received from the PSTN

   c. To encrypt data as it is transmitted from the computer to the PSTN, and then decrypt data as it is received from the PSTN

   d. To convert a source computer's digital pulses into analog signals for the PSTN, and then convert analog signals back into digital pulses for the destination computer

3. What is another common term for *Public Switched Telephone Network*?

   a. Plain old telephone service

   b. Basic rate telephone service

   c. Limited access telephone service

   d. Transcontinental public telephone service

4. Which of the following types of dial-up connections would result in the best performance from the client's perspective?

   a. A PPP dial-up connection to an RRAS server that allowed the client to launch an application from the RRAS server

   b. A PPTP dial-up connection to an RRAS server that allowed the client to launch an application from another server on the LAN

   c. A SLIP dial-up connection to an RRAS server that allowed the client to log on to an application server on the LAN and run an application from that application server

   d. A PPTP dial-up connection to an RRAS server that allowed the client to log on to a Citrix terminal server and use ICA to run an application

5. Why do most remote clients (for example, those that dial in to an RRAS server) use DHCP and not static IP addressing?

   a. DHCP allows more efficient use of a limited number of IP addresses

   b. DHCP ensures that the client is authorized to access the network

   c. DHCP ensures that the client is assigned a valid IP address

   d. DHCP allows the client to use the same IP address each time he or she dials in to the LAN

Lab 7.2 Creating a VPN with the Point-to-Point Tunneling Protocol

Objectives

Dialing in to a remote access server can be quite slow and expensive if many users have to dial long distance. One way to reduce the time and cost of using a remote access server is to create a virtual private network (VPN) through the Internet. In a VPN, users connect to the remote access server over an encrypted channel through a public network. A VPN provides remote users the same access as they would get from a remote access server. As long as they have a connection to the Internet, users can have a fast and secure connection to their network.

Through a VPN, remote devices act as if they are directly connected to a remote switch. In many types of VPNs, a virtual network interface is created on both ends, just as if the two endpoints were directly linked by a single cable. Each virtual network interface has an IP address, just as a normal interface does. However, this IP address is associated with a logical NIC rather than a physical one, and is therefore often called a *virtual IP address*.

In this lab, you will create a VPN using the Point-to-Point Tunneling Protocol (PPTP). PPTP creates virtual NICs on the server and client. Traffic between each virtual NIC is encrypted so that a malicious user with a protocol analyzer cannot view the contents. Although there may be many network devices between the client and the server, the PPTP tunnel makes the client and server seem to be attached to the same hub.

Other protocols, including IPsec, can also be used to carry VPN traffic. VPNs run on a wide variety of hardware, including servers with several different operating systems, routers, firewalls, and dedicated VPN hardware such as Cisco's ASA 5500 Series devices. As VPN traffic requires additional processing and can use a lot of CPU time, many devices will off-load processing of VPN traffic onto a special chip or module.

After completing this lab, you will be able to:

- Configure a VPN with PPTP between a client computer and a Windows Server 2012 R2 computer

Materials Required

This lab will require the following:

- A computer running Windows Server 2012 R2 named *SERVER1* with two NICs, one configured with an IP address of 192.168.54.1 and a subnet mask of 255.255.255.0 and the other configured with an IP address of 172.16.1.1 and a subnet mask of 255.255.255.0

- Routing and Remote Access disabled on *SERVER1*

- A shared folder on *SERVER1* containing at least one text file

- A computer running Windows 8.1 or Windows 7 named *WORKSTATION1* with a NIC configured with an IP address of 192.168.54.2 and a subnet mask of 255.255.255.0

- Each NIC on both computers connected with straight-through Cat 5 (or better) UTP cables to a single switch

- Administrative access to both computers

- An account on *SERVER1* with a known password and sufficient rights to connect to *SERVER1*

Most of the steps in this lab can also be completed in a virtual environment using virtualization software such as VMware.

Estimated completion time: 30 minutes

Activity

1. Log on to *SERVER1* as the administrator. The Windows Server Manager appears.

2. Click **Tools**, and then click **Routing and Remote Access**. The Routing and Remote Access dialog box opens.

3. In the left pane of the dialog box, right-click **SERVER1 (local)**. In the shortcut menu, select **Configure and Enable Routing and Remote Access**. The Routing and Remote Access Server Setup Wizard opens.

4. Click **Next**. The wizard displays configuration options for the Routing and Remote Access Service.

5. Select the **Virtual private network (VPN) access and NAT** option and click **Next**. The wizard asks you to select at least one interface that connects this server to the Internet.

6. Select the name of your network interface such as **Ethernet0** and click **Next**. The wizard asks you to select options for IP address assignment.

7. If necessary, select **Automatically** and click **Next**. The wizard asks you to select options for managing multiple remote access servers.

8. If necessary, select **No, use Routing and Remote Access to authenticate connection requests** and click **Next**. The wizard indicates that you have finished.

9. Click **Finish**. A Routing and Remote Access dialog box might open, indicating that you must make further configuration changes to support the relay of DHCP messages. If not, go to Step 11.

10. Click **OK**. A dialog box opens, indicating that the Routing and Remote Access Service is starting. The dialog box closes, and the tree underneath *SERVER1* (local) has expanded.

11. Click Ports, then right-click **Ports** on the tree underneath *SERVER1* (local), and select **Properties** in the shortcut menu. The Ports Properties dialog box opens. See Figure 7-2.

12. Click **WAN Miniport (PPTP)** to select it and then click **Configure**. The Configure Device – WAN Miniport (PPTP) dialog box opens.

13. Click the **Demand-dial routing connections (inbound and outbound)** check box to remove the check. Click **OK** twice.

14. Right-click **SERVER1 (local)**. In the shortcut menu, point to **All Tasks**, and then click **Restart**. The Routing and Remote Access Service restarts.

15. Log on to *WORKSTATION1* as an administrator. The Windows desktop appears.

16. Right-click the Network icon on the taskbar.

17. Click **Open Network and Sharing Center**. The Network and Sharing Center window opens.

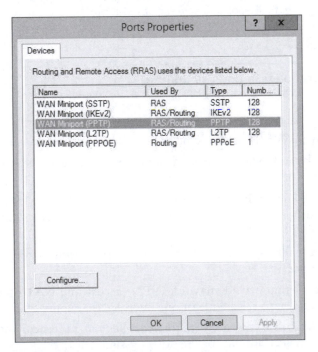

Figure 7-2 The Ports Properties dialog box

18. Click **Set up a new connection or network**. The Set Up a Connection or Network window opens.

19. Scroll down and select **Connect to a workplace** and click **Next**.

20. If necessary, select the **No, create a new connection option**, and then click **Next**.

21. Click **Use my Internet connection (VPN)**.

22. In the Before you connect... dialog box, click **Let me decide later** radio button and click **Next**. Enter **192.168.54.1** as the Internet address and **NetPlus** as the Destination name and click **Create**. Click **NetPlus** under Networks in the right pane and click **Connect**.

23. Enter the username and password for the account that can connect to *SERVER1* in the User name and Password text boxes. Click **OK**. The Connecting NetPlus dialog box opens, indicating that the computer is being registered on the network.

24. Open a Command Prompt window.

25. Type **ipconfig** and press **Enter**. The computer displays the IP address for each NIC on the computer, including the virtual NIC. (Note that the virtual NIC is named PPP adapter NetPlus.) What is the IP address of the virtual interface?

26. On *SERVER1*, open a Command Prompt window.

27. Type **ipconfig** and press **Enter**. The computer displays the IP address for each NIC on the computer, including the virtual NIC for the VPN. Note that the name of the virtual NIC is PPP Adapter RAS Server (Dial In) Interface. What is the IP address of the virtual interface on *SERVER1*?

28. On WORKSTATION1, open File Explorer and, if necessary, click the Computer tab.

29. On the menu bar, click **Map network drive**. The Map Network Drive dialog box opens.

30. In the Folder text box, enter **\\192.168.54.1\NETPLUS**. Click **Connect using different credentials**.

31. Click **Finish**. The Windows Security dialog box opens.

32. Type **Administrator** in the User name text box, and enter the password for the Administrator account on *SERVER1* in the Password text box. Click **OK**. The Windows Security dialog box closes. The Map Network Drive dialog box opens briefly, indicating that the computer is attempting to map the network drive. After it closes, an icon for the mapped network drive appears underneath Network Drives in the This PC (Computer) window.

33. Double-click the icon for the mapped network drive. A folder containing the name of at least one text file appears.

34. Double-click the text file. The text file opens.

35. Close the text file and log off both computers.

Certification Objectives

Objectives for the CompTIA Network+ Exam:

- 1.2 Compare the function and application of various network devices

Review Questions

1. What does the *T* in PPTP stand for?

   a. Tunneling

   b. Transmission

   c. Transport

   d. Telecommunications

2. What is one reason an organization might employ a VPN rather than simply allow users to dial directly in to their remote access server?

   a. VPNs always provide better performance than direct-dial connections.

   b. VPNs allow more users to connect to the LAN simultaneously.

   c. VPNs are less expensive for connecting a large number of remote users.

   d. VPNs prevent the need for firewalls between access servers and the Internet.

3. In this lab, you connected a workstation to a server using a VPN. Which of the following is true about the VPN connection you created in this lab?

   a. It uses physical IP addresses.

   b. It uses virtual IP addresses on the workstation end.

   c. It uses virtual IP addresses on both ends.

   d. It requires a modem for connection.

4. Which of the following transmission methods is most apt to be used by VPN clients?

   a. PSTN

   b. T-1

   c. Frame Relay

   d. SONET

5. What is the most common public network used with VPNs?

   a. ARPANET

   b. The Internet

   c. NetBEUI

   d. AppleTalk

Lab 7.3 Remotely Connecting to a Windows Server

Objectives

It is often necessary to connect to a Windows Server from a remote location. This can be invaluable for administration or troubleshooting. For instance, suppose that a problem with a particular server occurs while you are at home. Without some means of accessing the computer remotely, you must go to the computer to fix the problem.

By connecting remotely, you can often fix the problem without ever leaving home. Remote Desktop Services (called Terminal Services in Server 2008) allows a network administrator or support personnel to log on to a remote Windows server almost as if the network administrator were at the console.

By default, Terminal Services on Windows Server (called Terminal Services in Server 2008) is configured in Remote Administration mode. You can also configure it in Application Server mode. Application Server mode allows users to log on to the server and run applications. This has several advantages. First, network administrators can manage applications from one location. Otherwise, each application must be managed for each user's computer. Second, Terminal Services allows a network administrator to take over a particular user's session. This allows you to see exactly what the user sees. Finally, computers connecting to a computer running Terminal Services in Application Server mode, or a terminal server, may use a wide variety of hardware and operating systems. The terminal server does the bulk of the processing for applications run in Terminal Services. This leaves users free to access the terminal server from older computers, or from less powerful computers, called thin clients.

One disadvantage of allowing users to connect to a terminal server is cost. Using Terminal Services in Application Server mode requires additional licensing, whereas running Terminal Services in Remote Administration mode does not. In this lab, you will enable remote desktop on Windows Server 2012 R2 and connect to it from a Windows client.

After completing this lab, you will be able to:

- Configure remote desktop connection on Windows Server 2012 R2

Materials Required

This lab will require the following:

- A computer running Windows Server 2012 R2 named *SERVER1*, with a NIC configured with an IP address of 192.168.54.1 and a subnet mask of 255.255.255.0

- The server can be a member of a domain or a workgroup, although the steps will vary depending on your configuration

- A computer named *WORKSTATION1* running Windows 8.1 or Windows 7, with a NIC configured with an IP address of 192.168.54.2 and a subnet mask of 255.255.255.0

- Administrative access to each computer

- Each computer connected to a switch with straight-through Cat 5 or better UTP cables

Most of the steps in this lab can also be completed in a virtual environment using virtualization software such as VMware.

Estimated completion time: **45 minutes**

Activity

1. Log on to *SERVER1* as the administrator. The Windows Server Manager appears.

2. Right-click **Start**, click **Control Panel**, click **System and Security**, and click **System**.

3. Click **Remote settings**, if necessary, select **Allow remote connections to this computer**, click **OK**, and close the System window.

4. In Server Manager, click **Tools,** and then click **Active Directory Users and Computers.** The Active Directory Users and Computers window opens.

5. Click the **Builtin** folder under *netpluslab.net*.

6. In the right pane, double-click **Remote Desktop Users,** click the **Members tab,** and click **Add.** The Select Users, Contacts, Computers, Service Accounts, or Groups window opens.

7. Click **Advanced** and click **Find Now.**

8. Select **Administrator** and click **OK.**

9. Click **OK** twice more to close the Remote Desktop Users Properties Box.

10. Now you will log on to *SERVER1* (from *WORKSTATION1*) while it is still configured in Remote Administration mode. Log on to *WORKSTATION1* as an administrator. The Windows desktop appears.

11. Click **Start,** type **remote desktop connection,** and then click **Remote Desktop Connection.** The Remote Desktop Connection dialog box opens, as shown in Figure 7-3.

12. Enter **192.168.54.1** in the Computer text box. Click **Connect.** The Windows Security dialog box opens for *SERVER1*. Log on to the remote computer as the administrator. The Windows Server desktop appears.

13. Minimize the Remote Desktop Connection dialog box by clicking the horizontal line on the bar at the top of the screen.

14. Repeat Steps 11 through 12. Did Remote Desktop Connection allow you to open two sessions at the same time? If not, how was it prevented?

15. Log off both computers.

Certification Objectives

Objectives for the CompTIA Network+ Exam:

- 1.2 Compare and contrast the use of networking services and applications

Figure 7-3   Remote Desktop Connection dialog box

Review Questions

1. Which of the following are reasons you might implement Terminal Services instead of a remote access server? (Choose all that apply.)

   a. No modems required with Terminal Services

   b. Central configuration and control of applications on the terminal server

   c. No modems required on clients

   d. No need to configure security on the terminal server

2. What is the difference between configuring a Windows Server 2012 R2 computer to accept Remote Desktop Connection and configuring it to run Terminal Services?

   a. Remote Desktop Connection requires additional licensing.

   b. Terminal Services requires each client to have a modem.

   c. Terminal Services allows no more than two simultaneous connections.

   d. Terminal Services allows more than two simultaneous connections.

3. What is one way a network administrator can effectively troubleshoot a user's problem in a Terminal Services session that can't be done with a remote access server?

   a. Speaking with the user over the phone

   b. Examining the terminal server's error logs

   c. Taking over the user's session temporarily

   d. Rebooting the server

4. Which of the following is a potential disadvantage of Terminal Services?

   a. It requires additional licensing.

   b. It requires the client to be running Windows 8.1.

   c. It requires the client to have a high-speed connection such as a T-1.

   d. It requires the server to have a minimum of 1 GB of RAM.

Lab 7.4 Remotely Managing a Computer

Objectives

Common management tasks, such as installing updates, do not have to be performed while directly logged on to a local computer. Through Computer Management, you can perform many of these functions remotely. You can start and stop services on the remote computer, look at system information, and browse the Event Viewer. The Event Viewer is where you can view information about error messages and other events that have occurred on the computer. If you need to administer a network with many users and many computers, this can save you significant time.

After completing this lab, you will be able to:

- Remotely manage Windows computers

Materials Required

This lab will require the following:

- The network on the NETPLUSLAB.NET domain such as the one built at the end of Lab 1.4

 Most of the steps in this lab can also be completed in a virtual environment using virtualization software such as VMware.

Estimated completion time: **40 minutes**

Activity

1. Log on to *SERVER1* as the administrator for the netpluslab.net domain. The Windows Server Manager appears.

2. Click **Tools**, and click **Computer Management**. The Computer Management window opens.

3. Click the **Disk Management** icon below "Storage." How many hard disks are on the server, how large are they, and with what file system have they been configured?

4. Click the **Event Viewer** icon in the tree in the left pane of the window. A list of the event logs available appears in the right pane of the window.

5. In the left pane, expand **Event Viewer** and **Windows Logs**, and then click the **System** node. A list of events in the System event log appears in the center pane. Double-click the top event. The Event Properties window opens, showing detailed information about the event.

6. Click the down arrow on the right side of the window. The Event Viewer moves to the next event. Repeat a few times to see more events.

7. Close the Event Properties window by clicking **Close**.

8. Right-click **Computer Management (Local)** at the top of the tree in the left pane of the window. Select **Connect to another computer** in the shortcut menu. The Select Computer dialog box opens.

9. In the Another computer text box, type **WORKSTATION1** and click **OK**. The icon at the top of the left pane of the window changes to Computer Management (WORKSTATION1).

10. Click the right arrow next to "System Tools" to expand the tree underneath it. Repeat this step with the Services and Applications icon. Figure 7-4 shows the Computer Management dialog box for *WORKSTATION1* as you manage the computer remotely.

11. Repeat Steps 4 through 7 to look at events on *WORKSTATION1*. Does *WORKSTATION1* have as many types of event logs as *SERVER1*?

12. Log on to *WORKSTATION1* as the administrator of the NETPLUSLAB domain. The Windows desktop appears.

13. Open the Control Panel.

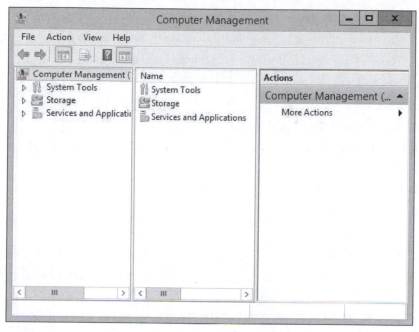

Figure 7-4   Managing *WORKSTATION1* remotely

14. Click the **System and Security** category.

15. Click the **Administrative Tools**.

16. Double-click the **Services** icon. The Services window opens.

17. Look for Windows Update. Its status should be "Running."

18. On *SERVER1*, click the **Services** icon in the left pane of the Computer Management window. A list of the services running on *WORKSTATION1* appears in the right pane of the window.

19. Right-click the **Windows Update** icon. In the shortcut menu, select **Stop**. A dialog box opens briefly, indicating that Windows is attempting to stop the service. The status disappears.

20. On *WORKSTATION1*, press **F5** to refresh the Services window. Look at the status of Windows Update in the Services window. It is now blank, indicating that the service is not running.

21. Right-click **Windows Update** in the Services window. In the shortcut menu, select **Start**. A dialog box opens briefly, indicating that Windows is attempting to start the service. The status changes to "Started."

22. Log off both computers.

Certification Objectives

Objectives for the CompTIA Network+ Exam:

- 3.3 Given a scenario, implement network hardening techniques

Review Questions

1. Which of the following is a potential advantage of being able to manage computers remotely?

   a. You will not need to log on to each individual computer.

   b. It eliminates the need for authentications.

   c. It uses less CPU time.

   d. It prevents security problems.

2. Which Windows Server utility would you use to find events that have happened on a particular server?

   a. Device Manager

   b. Disk Defragmenter

   c. Command Prompt

   d. Event Viewer

3. Why are you able to log on to the remote computer without supplying a username and password?

   a. No username or password is necessary.

   b. Active Directory handles authentication on the remote computer for you.

   c. Active Directory does not require authentication for remote computers.

   d. Your computer automatically supplies the username and password without the help of Active Directory.

4. True or False? Only the domain administrator can manage remote computers.

5. When you select Services from the Administrative Tools menu on a Windows Server 2012 R2 computer, what will you see?

   a. All services currently available on the Windows Server

   b. All services currently running on the Windows Server

   c. All services currently running on the Windows Server and its clients

   d. All services currently running on the Windows Server and other servers in the same domain

Lab 7.5 Remotely Managing a Linux Server

Objectives

Linux servers can be managed remotely much as they can be managed at the console, through a variety of tools. Almost all versions of Linux support Telnet servers. A Telnet server is a daemon that allows you to open a remote terminal session over a network. The Telnet client, usually just called Telnet, is available on most modern operating systems. However, the Telnet protocol does not use any encryption. As a result, Telnet is rapidly being replaced by the Secure Shell (SSH) protocol. The sshd daemon runs an SSH server, and the SSH program allows you to log on to an SSH server.

From a remote terminal window opened with the SSH program, you can do nearly anything that you can do on the system console. On a computer running the X Window software, you can also run any GUI program on the remote computer. X Window software is installed by default on most Linux computers, and can be installed on Windows computers as well. Remote terminal sessions run through either the SSH program or the Telnet program have only a few minor differences.

In this lab, you will remotely connect to a Linux computer using a common SSH client called PuTTY.

After completing this lab, you will be able to:

- Log on to a Linux computer remotely using SSH

Materials Required

This lab will require the following:

- A computer running a current version of Linux such as Ubuntu or Fedora named *LINUX1*, configured with no firewall

- *LINUX1* configured with an IP address of 192.168.54.5 and a subnet mask of 255.255.255.0

- A user named *netplus* and knowledge of the root password

- A computer running Windows 8.1 or Windows 7 named *WORKSTATION1* and configured with an IP address of 192.168.54.3

- Access to PuTTY, an SSH and Telnet client (available at putty.org)

- Both computers connected to a switch or hub with straight-through Cat 5 (or better) UTP cables

Most of the steps in this lab can also be completed in a virtual environment using virtualization software such as VMware.

Estimated completion time: **40 minutes**

Activity

1. Log on to *WORKSTATION1* as an administrator.

2. Open Internet Explorer.

3. In the address box, type **www.putty.org** and press **Enter**. The main PuTTY Web page opens.

4. Click **here** to download PuTTY.

5. Click **putty.exe** to download the latest release version of PuTTY.

6. Click **Run**. The PuTTY Configuration window opens, as shown in Figure 7-5.

7. Specify the destination you want to connect to as **192.168.54.5** and click **Open**.

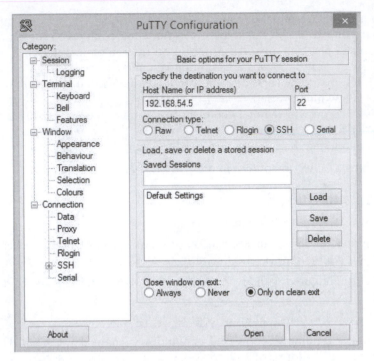

Figure 7-5   The PuTTY Configuration window

8. Log on to *LINUX1* as the netplus user. The desktop appears.

9. Open a terminal window.

10. Type the password and press **Enter**. The prompt changes to `[linux1@192.168.54.5]$`, indicating that you are now logged on to *LINUX1*.

11. Type **su -** and press **Enter**. The Password prompt appears. Type root's password and press **Enter**. The prompt now ends in a pound sign (#), indicating that you are logged on as the root user.

12. Type **ifconfig** and press **Enter**. The computer displays information about the network card installed in it. In addition to the NIC in the computer (most likely named eth0 or eth1), the computer displays information about the lo NIC, or the loopback. This is a virtual (or software-only) NIC, primarily used for testing. A loopback NIC is configured by default on most devices that use TCP/IP. What are the names and IP addresses of the NICs on the computer?

13. Type **exit** and press **Enter**. Type **exit** and press **Enter** again to exit from *LINUX1*. The prompt in the terminal window changes back to indicate that you are no longer the root user.

14. Type **ifconfig** and press **Enter**. The computer indicates that the command cannot be found.

15. Now you will attempt to run the `ifconfig` command by typing the full path of the command. Type **/sbin/ifconfig** and press **Enter**. The computer displays information

about the network cards on the computer. (The netplus user cannot find the `ifconfig` command without supplying the full pathname because the environment for the netplus user is different from that of the root user.)

16. Type **exit** and press **Enter**. Type **exit** and press **Enter** again to exit the SSH session on *LINUX1*.

17. Log off both computers.

Certification Objectives

Objectives for the CompTIA Network+ Exam:

- 1.2 Compare and contrast the use of networking services and applications
- 3.2 Compare and contrast common network vulnerabilities and threats

Review Questions

1. What is the difference between the SSH protocol and the Telnet protocol?

    a. The Telnet protocol is encrypted.

    b. The Telnet protocol is faster than the SSH protocol.

    c. SSH is encrypted.

    d. SSH can only be used between Linux or UNIX servers.

2. Which of the following commands could you use to display a Linux computer's IP address?

    a. `ipconfig`

    b. `ssh`

    c. `ipdisplay`

    d. `ifconfig`

3. Why might a virtual NIC be configured on a Linux computer?

    a. Because an additional IP address is needed for a Web server

    b. For the computer to act as a router between two networks

    c. For redundancy

    d. For load balancing

4. The `ssh` command allows you to open a remote terminal window on another computer. What is the major difference between working in an SSH session on a remote computer in another city, and working directly at the console of the remote computer?

    a. You cannot power cycle the remote computer.

    b. You cannot run GUI programs in the SSH session.

    c. You cannot run terminal programs such as top or ps while working in an SSH session.

    d. You cannot log on to other remote computers while working in an SSH session.

5. In this lab, how could you tell whether a terminal window was for the local computer or for an SSH session on a remote computer?

   a. The prompt indicated the name of the remote computer.

   b. There was no way to tell.

   c. The prompt indicated the name of the program being run.

   d. The computer beeped when you logged on to a remote computer.

Lab 7.6 Plaintext Versus Encrypted Protocols

Objectives

Most of the older communications programs still in use, such as FTP or Telnet, use plaintext. Using such a program to administer a server or a network device can make it easy for an intruder to steal account information using a protocol analyzer.

In this lab, you will use a protocol analyzer to examine the dangers of using plaintext protocols. An administrator who carelessly uses a plaintext protocol such as FTP or Telnet to manage a server might compromise its security. An intruder with a protocol analyzer can easily find the password and use it to log on to the server. Once intruders have compromised a server, they often install a protocol analyzer to find account names and passwords, which they can use to compromise other servers. Use of encrypted protocols such as SSH instead of FTP or Telnet makes compromise of account information more difficult.

It is important to keep in mind that, although a protocol analyzer is an important and valuable tool for network administrators, using a protocol analyzer to obtain the passwords of users or to eavesdrop on their communications without their consent is unethical and illegal. In addition, you should always have clear and specific consent before using a protocol analyzer. This is especially true on a network that is not yours, such as a customer network. On networks that you manage, you should determine whether use of a protocol analyzer is permissible before using one. In some high-security environments, such as a financial or military institution, you might be prohibited from using a protocol analyzer at all. In other environments, you should make sure that you have explicit permission to use a protocol analyzer when necessary.

After completing this lab, you will be able to:

- Describe the difference between encrypted and unencrypted network protocols

Materials Required

This lab will require the following:

- A computer running Windows Server 2012 R2 named *SERVER1*, configured with an IP address of 192.168.54.1 and a subnet mask of 255.255.255.0

- IIS and the File Transfer Protocol (FTP) Publishing Service installed and running on *SERVER1*

- A user named *netplus* on *SERVER1* with a known password

- A computer running Windows Server 2012 R2 named *SERVER2*, configured with an IP address of 192.168.54.2 and a subnet mask of 255.255.255.0

- The Wireshark protocol analyzer (available from *wireshark.org*) and, if necessary, the WinPcap packet capture library (available from *winpcap.org/*) installed on *SERVER2*

- Access to *SERVER1* and *SERVER2* as the administrator

- A computer running a current version of Linux such as Ubuntu or Fedora named *LINUX1*, configured with the firewall disabled, with SELinux disabled, and with the GNOME Desktop Environment

- *LINUX1* configured with an IP address of 192.168.54.5 and a subnet mask of 255.255.255.0

- A computer running Windows 8.1 or Windows 7 named *WORKSTATION1*, configured with an IP address of 192.168.54.3 and a subnet mask of 255.255.255.0

- A user named *netplus* on *LINUX1* with a known password and a known password for the root account

- Cygwin 1.7.x (available at cygwin.com) installed on *WORKSTATION1*, with the openssh and openssl packages in the Net category installed in addition to the default packages

- Access to the Windows 8.1 or Windows 7 computer as the netplus user

- All four computers connected to a switch with straight-through Cat 5 (or better) UTP cables

Most of the steps in this lab can also be completed in a virtual environment using virtualization software such as VMware.

Estimated completion time: **30 minutes**

Activity

1. Log on to *SERVER1* as the administrator. The Windows Server Manager appears.

2. Click **Tools**, and then click **Internet Information Services (IIS) Manager.** The Internet Information Services (IIS) Manager window opens.

3. If necessary, click the right arrow next to *SERVER1* to expand the tree in the left pane. If a window pops up and asks if you want to get started with Microsoft Web Platform, click **No**. In the left pane, right-click **Sites** and click on **Add FTP Site**. Name your site **FTP** and select the physical path (most likely C:\inetpub\ftproot). Click **Next**.

4. Select an IP address of 192.168.54.1 (from the drop down menu) and select **No SSL**. Click **Next**.

5. Select **Basic** as the Authentication type, allow access for **All users**, and give users **Read** and **Write** permissions. Click **Finish**.

6. Log on to *SERVER2* as the administrator. The Windows Server Manager appears.

7. Click **Start**, type **wireshark**, and click **Wireshark** when it appears. The Wireshark Network Analyzer window opens.

8. On the menu bar, click **Capture**, click **Interfaces**, and then click the **Options** button that corresponds to your network adapter. The Wireshark: Capture Options window opens.

9. In the Capture Filter text box, enter **192.168.54.3**. This configures Wireshark to capture only packets being sent from or to IP address 192.168.54.3.

10. Click **Start**. Wireshark begins to capture any packets sent to or from 192.168.54.3.

11. Log on to *WORKSTATION1* as an administrator. The Windows desktop appears.

12. Open a Command Prompt window.

13. Type `ftp 192.168.54.1` and press **Enter**. The FTP program prompts for the username.

14. Type `netplus` and press **Enter**. The FTP program displays the Password prompt.

15. Type the password for the netplus account. The FTP program indicates that the netplus user has logged on.

16. Type `dir`. The computer displays any files that might be present in the root directory of the FTP server.

17. Type `quit` to exit the FTP program.

18. On *SERVER2*, click **Stop** in the Wireshark dialog box. Wireshark displays the captured packets, as shown in Figure 7-6.

19. In the Filter text box, type **ftp** and press **Enter**. The computer displays only those packets that have FTP in the Protocol field.

20. In the top pane, click the first packet. In the middle pane, click the plus next to File Transfer Protocol (FTP). Detailed information about the FTP portion of the packet appears. (You might need to scroll down to see it all.) Click any plus signs you see beneath File Transfer Protocol (FTP) so that more information appears beneath them.

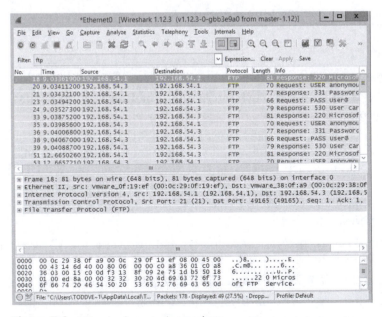

Figure 7-6 Wireshark capturing packets

Source: The Wireshark Foundation

21. In the top frame, click the first packet again. Using the ↓ key, scroll down through the list of packets. Look for a packet containing the text *Request: PASS* and a password. Does this password match the password you typed in Step 15?

22. Scroll through the remaining packets. Do you see everything that you typed when you were logged on to the FTP server?

23. Now you will use a protocol analyzer to view an encrypted SFTP session. In the Wireshark window on *SERVER2*, click **Capture** and then click **Start**. The Wireshark dialog box opens, asking if you would like to save the capture file.

24. Click **Continue without Saving**.

25. Wireshark begins capturing packets again.

26. On *WORKSTATION1*, run **Cygwin Terminal**. A terminal window named ~ opens.

27. Type **sftp netplus@192.168.54.5** and press **Enter**. The computer might indicate that the authenticity of the host cannot be established and ask if you would like to continue connecting. If so, type **yes**. The computer prompts for the netplus user's password.

28. Type the password for the netplus user account on *LINUX1* and press **Enter**. The computer displays the sftp> prompt.

29. Type **dir**. The computer displays the names of any files in the home directory of the netplus user on *LINUX1*.

30. Type **quit**. The computer closes the SFTP connection.

31. On *SERVER2*, click **Stop** in the Wireshark dialog box. Wireshark displays the captured packets.

32. In the Filter text box, type **ssh** and press **Enter**. The computer displays only those packets that have SSHv2 in the Protocol field. (You type *ssh* instead of *sftp* in the Filter text box because the SFTP program uses the SSH protocol.)

33. In the top pane, click the first packet. In the middle pane, click the plus next to SSH Protocol. Detailed information about the SSH portion of the packet appears. (You might need to scroll down to see it all.) Click any plus signs you see beneath SSH Protocol so that more information appears beneath them.

34. In the top frame, click the first packet again. Scroll down through the list of packets. As you scroll through the packets, click any plus signs you see beneath SSH Protocol. Do you see any of the text you typed when connected to *LINUX1*?

35. Log off all the computers.

Certification Objectives

Objectives for the CompTIA Network+ Exam:

- 3.2 Compare and contrast common network vulnerabilities and threats
- 4.2 Given a scenario, analyze and interpret the output of troubleshooting tools

Review Questions

1. True or False? Encrypted protocols such as SSH do not send passwords over the network.

2. If someone floods your gateway with so much traffic that it cannot respond to or accept valid traffic, what type of security breach has she caused?

   a. IP spoofing

   b. Social engineering

   c. Denial of service

   d. Trojan horse

3. In which of the following situations would it be most beneficial for a network administrator to restrict the time of day during which the users can log on to the network to improve security?

   a. A salesperson accesses a company's network via a dial-up connection to upload sales data every night.

   b. Groups of customer service representatives access customer financial data during regular business hours.

   c. A corporate executive frequently travels to a company's various locations and requires access to confidential information on the server.

   d. A group of engineers is establishing an international office in a country several time zones away from the server's location.

4. The practice of falsifying an IP address is known as _____.

   a. spoofing

   b. faking

   c. impersonating

   d. configuring a secondary IP address

5. Which of the following encryption methods is commonly used to secure transmissions over virtual private networks (VPNs)?

   a. Kerberos

   b. RAS

   c. PGP

   d. IPsec

NETWORK RISK MANAGEMENT

Labs included in this chapter

- Lab 8.1 Auditing
- Lab 8.2 Checking for Vulnerable Software
- Lab 8.3 Implementing Network Address Restrictions on a Linux Server
- Lab 8.4 Delegating Administrative Rights
- Lab 8.5 Understanding Malware
- Lab 8.6 Configuring a Firewall in Windows Server

CompTIA Network+ Exam Objectives

Objective	Lab
1.1 Explain the functions and applications of various network devices	8.6
2.5 Given a scenario, install and apply patches and updates	8.2
3.2 Compare and contrast common network vulnerabilities and threats	8.1, 8.3, 8.4, 8.5, 8.6
3.3 Given a scenario, implement network hardening techniques	8.3, 8.5
3.5 Given a scenario, install and configure a basic firewall	8.6

Lab 8.1 Auditing

Objectives

Although preventing security problems should be the first goal of network administrators, security problems cannot always be prevented. That makes auditing essential. It can help you identify both security vulnerabilities and potential security breaches.

Auditing is the gathering and analysis of large amounts of network-related information, including data about logons, access attempts, system events, and so on. For instance, auditing can indicate when someone is repeatedly attempting and failing to log on to your domain controller, which could in turn indicate that someone is attempting to compromise your network. Auditing can also help you troubleshoot server problems, such as an unexpected failure.

Auditing is not limited to a network operating system; in most cases, you can configure firewalls, routers, and switches to compile, or log, information (on their own disks or to an external server) as well. Often this information can be useful in determining whether intruders have attempted to access devices on your network.

In Windows Server (and in most other network operating systems), auditing is not enabled by default because it can affect performance and use a large amount of disk space. Thus, to view the failed logon attempts in a Windows Server 2012 R2 domain, you must first activate auditing for the domain. Then, you must activate auditing on the domain controller so that it will capture the logging.

After completing this lab, you will be able to:

- Enable auditing in Windows Server 2012 R2
- Review information on audited events

Materials Required

This lab will require the following:

- A computer running Windows Server 2012 R2 named *SERVER1*, with an IP address of 192.168.54.1 and a subnet mask of 255.255.255.0
- Access as the administrator to *SERVER1*
- A computer running Windows 8.1 or Windows 7 named *WORKSTATION1*, with an IP address of 192.168.54.3 and a subnet mask of 255.255.255.0
- Both computers connected to a switch with straight-through Cat 5 (or better) UTP cables

VIRTUAL LAB

Most of the steps in this lab can also be completed using virtualization software such as VMware.

Estimated completion time: **40 minutes**

Activity

1. Log on to *SERVER1* as the administrator. The Windows Server Manager opens.
2. Click **Manage**, and then click **Add Roles and Features**. The Add Roles and Features Wizard opens.

3. Click **Next**. The wizard asks you to select an installation type. Select **Role-based or feature-based installation**.

4. Click **Next**. The wizard asks you to select a server. Click **Next**.

5. Select **Active Directory Domain Services** and click **Next**.

6. Click **Add Features**, click **Next** several more times until the **Install** button is no longer grayed out, and then click **Install**.

7. The new roles will take a few minutes to install. When it's finished, click **Close** and then click on the alert that looks like a yellow triangle beside a flag.

8. Under Post-deployment Configuration, click **Promote this server to a domain controller**. The Active Directory Domain Services Configuration Wizard opens.

9. Select the **Add a new forest** option and type **Netpluslab.net** as the Root domain name. Click **Next**.

10. After several moments, the wizard asks you to select the forest and domain functional level. If necessary, select Windows Server 2012 R2.

11. The wizard asks you to select an administrator password for Directory Services Restore Mode. Enter the password **Passw0rd** in the Password and Confirm password text boxes and click **Next**.

12. Click **Next** three more times. The wizard summarizes the options you have selected. Click **Next** again.

13. Click **Install** and wait for the installation to proceed.

14. Log on to *WORKSTATION1* as an administrator. The Windows desktop appears.

15. Right-click **Start**, click **System**, and click **Change settings**.

16. Click **Network ID**.

17. The wizard asks what sort of network you use. Make sure the **This computer is part of a business network; I use it to connect to other computers at work** option is selected and click **Next**.

18. Click **Next**. The wizard asks for account information. Click **Next**.

19. In the User name text box, enter **Administrator**. In the Password text box, enter the password for the Administrator account of *SERVER1*. In the Domain name text box, enter **NETPLUSLAB.NET**. Click **Next**.

20. Click the **Do not add a domain user account** option and click **Next**.

21. Click **Finish** and then click **OK**.

22. Reboot the computer and then log on to the NETPLUSLAB domain as the domain administrator. The Windows desktop appears.

23. Log on to *SERVER1* as the administrator. The Windows Server desktop manager appears.

24. Click **Tools**, and click **Local Security Policy**. The Local Security Policy window opens.

25. Click **Local Policies** in the left pane. Icons for policies appear in the right pane.

26. In the right pane, double-click **Audit Policy**. Several icons whose names begin with "Audit" appear. As you'll see in the next few steps, you can double-click these icons to define and configure various policies.

27. Double-click **Audit account logon events**. The Audit account logon events Properties dialog box opens. This setting determines whether the computer will record every instance of a user logging on or off the domain.

28. If necessary, click to select the **Success** and **Failure** check boxes, and then click **OK**. Figure 8-1 shows the Audit account logon events Properties dialog box. You have now configured the computer to record every attempt by a user to log on, whether successful or unsuccessful.

29. Repeat Steps 27 and 28 for **Audit logon events**. (Note the distinction between "Audit account logon events" and "Audit logon events.") The Audit logon events settings determine whether the domain controller will record every instance of a user logging on or off a computer for which the domain controller performs authentication.

30. In the left pane, right-click **Security Settings** and click **Reload** from the shortcut menu. The computer updates the security policy for the domain with the changes that you have made.

31. For auditing events to be captured, you must specifically enable logging on the domain controller itself. Otherwise, the domain controller will discard audit events. Click **Tools**, and then click **Group Policy Management**. Double-click **Group Policy Management, Forest: netpluslab.net, Domains, netpluslab.net,** and **Domain Controllers**, and then right-click **Default Domain Controllers Policy** and click **Edit**. The Default Domain Controllers Policy window opens.

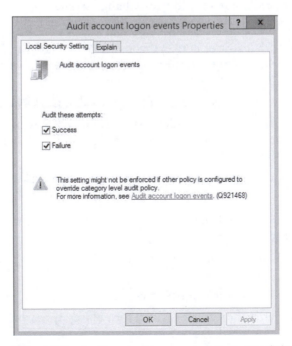

Figure 8-1   Audit account logon events Properties dialog box

32. In the tree in the left pane, expand **Computer Configuration, Policies,** then **Windows Settings,** then **Security Settings,** and then click **Local Policies.** A list of icons appears in the right pane. Double-click **Audit Policy.** Policies appear in the right pane.

33. Double-click **Audit account logon events.** The Audit account logon events Properties dialog box opens.

34. Make sure that the **Define these policy settings, Success,** and **Failure** check boxes are all checked, and then click **OK.**

35. Repeat Steps 33 and 34 for **Audit logon events.**

36. Right-click **Security Settings,** and then click **Reload.** The computer reloads security policies for the domain controller.

37. Attempt to log on to *WORKSTATION1* using an invalid password. An error message appears, indicating that the logon attempt failed.

38. Click **OK.**

39. Repeat Steps 37 and 38.

40. Log on as the netplus user with the correct password. The Windows desktop appears.

41. On *SERVER1,* click **Tools,** and click **Event Viewer.** The Event Viewer window opens.

42. In the left pane, expand **Windows Logs** (if necessary) and click **Security.** A list of security events appears in the middle pane, including all successful and failed logon attempts.

43. Double-click an **Audit Failure** icon. The Event Properties dialog box opens. The dialog box gives information about a failed logon attempt.

44. Repeat the previous step with an **Audit Success** icon.

45. Log off both computers.

Certification Objectives

Objectives for the CompTIA Network+ Exam:

- 3.2 Compare and contrast common network vulnerabilities and threats

Review Questions

1. As a network administrator, what should you do if you notice that a user account has experienced multiple failed logon attempts?

   a. Revoke the user's logon privileges.

   b. Change the user's password.

   c. Contact the user to find out whether she is having trouble logging on.

   d. Limit the times of day during which that user account may log on.

2. Which of the following best describes authentication?

   a. The process of verifying the precise spelling of a username

   b. The process of accepting and matching a username with unique account information, such as a password

   c. The process of replicating user logon information from one domain controller to the others on a network

   d. The process of tracking a user's logon habits and collecting that information in an audit log

3. How does knowing about failed logon attempts help a network administrator's security efforts?

   a. The information could help her determine whether stricter password requirements should be implemented.

   b. The information could help her refine the NOS schema.

   c. The information could help her determine whether an unauthorized user is attempting to log on with that username.

   d. The information could help her predict the likelihood of future security breaches.

4. Which of the following tools allows you to view security events that have occurred on a Windows Server 2012 R2 computer?

   a. Event Viewer

   b. Authentication Log

   c. Domain Security Policy

   d. Domain Controller Security Policy

5. In the context of Windows networking, why must failed logon attempts be recorded by a domain controller instead of by any random server on the network?

   a. Only a domain controller will have the resources necessary to record and hold the volume of information that auditing requires.

   b. Domain controllers contain a complete set of Windows Server 2012 R2 computer administrative tools, whereas other servers do not.

   c. Domain controllers typically provide Web and remote access, enabling a network administrator to remotely audit events on a network.

   d. Domain controllers authenticate users.

Lab 8.2 Checking for Vulnerable Software

Objectives

Software patches can reverse potentially dangerous vulnerabilities on a network. However, network administrators commonly compromise their networks' security by running unpatched software. Several worms, such as MyDoom and Sobig, have infected hundreds of thousands of computers even though software patches that could fix the vulnerabilities were available. Many administrators simply did not know that they needed to patch their software.

In this lab, you will run a utility that can determine which service packs or hot fixes you need to apply on a Windows Server 2012 R2 computer.

After completing this lab, you will be able to:

- Scan a Windows Server 2012 R2 computer to identify whether it is operating with vulnerable software

Materials Required

This lab will require the following:

- A computer running Windows Server 2012 R2 named *SERVER1* with Internet access and with Internet Information Services (IIS) installed

- Microsoft Baseline Security Analyzer 2.3 (currently available from *microsoft.com/technet /security/tools*) installed on the Windows Server 2012 R2 computer

- At least one missing security update for the computer; the missing security update should be minor or the computer should be protected by a firewall

- Access as the administrator to the Windows Server 2012 R2 computer

Estimated completion time: **30 minutes**

Activity

1. Log on to *SERVER1* as the administrator. Windows Server Manager opens.

2. Click **Start** type **Baseline,** and click **Microsoft Baseline Security Analyzer.** The Microsoft Baseline Security Analyzer opens, as shown in Figure 8-2.

3. Click **Scan a computer.** The computer asks you to choose a computer to scan for security vulnerabilities.

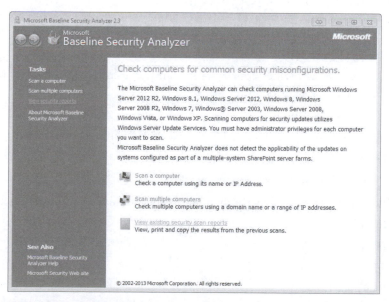

Figure 8-2   Microsoft Baseline Security Analyzer

4. Make sure that the name of the local computer is selected in the Computer name drop-down box, and that the **Check for Windows administrative vulnerabilities, Check for weak passwords, Check for IIS administrative vulnerabilities,** and **Check for security updates** check boxes are checked. Uncheck the **Check for SQL administrative vulnerabilities** check box. Click **Start Scan.** The computer downloads security information from Microsoft and checks for security vulnerabilities. This might take several minutes. The computer then displays the results.

5. At the top of the report is a summary of the security status of the computer. What is the security assessment for your computer?

6. Scroll down to the Security Update Scan Results section. The program displays a red shield with a white X for any items that present a serious security risk, a green shield with a white check mark for any items that do not present a security vulnerability, a white i in a blue circle for any informational items, a yellow ! (exclamation point) for any items that should be changed, and a blue star for any items that could be changed. Some types of items might not be present. Which critical security updates, if any, should you install on your computer?

7. Scroll down to the Administrative Vulnerabilities section under Windows Scan Results. What is the status of Automatic Updates on your computer? Do any items represent a serious security risk?

8. For one of the items with a red or yellow icon, click **Result details**. Internet Explorer opens to a page describing the security problem. Read the page and close Internet Explorer.

9. For the item you selected in the previous step, click **How to correct this**. Internet Explorer opens with instructions on how to correct the problem. Read the page and close Internet Explorer.

10. Log off the computer.

Certification Objectives

Objectives for the CompTIA Network+ Exam:

- 2.5 Given a scenario, install and apply patches and updates

Review Questions

1. Which of the following security risks can potentially be addressed by applying a new patch to a software program?

   a. Social engineering

   b. Insecure data transmissions between a Web client and Web server

   c. IP spoofing

   d. RF emission over a wireless network

2. Which of the following methods of accessing files over the Internet is the most secure?

   a. HTTP

   b. HTTPS

   c. TFTP

   d. FTP

3. Which of the following types of software can be patched to improve their security? (Choose all that apply.)

   a. Router OS

   b. Web browser

   c. Email client

   d. Workstation OS

4. Which of the following types of transmission media is the most secure?

   a. Fiber-optic cable

   b. Infrared wireless

   c. Shielded twisted-pair cable

   d. Coaxial cable

5. Which of the following network enhancements can introduce new security risks? (Choose all that apply.)

   a. Adding remote access for users who travel

   b. Adding time-of-day restrictions for logons

   c. Modifying a tape backup rotation scheme

   d. Providing Web access to a server's data files

Lab 8.3 Implementing Network Address Restrictions on a Linux Server

Objectives

Most NOSs have some mechanism that ensures that users can only log on from certain Network layer or Data Link layer addresses. The potential advantage to requiring users to log on from only certain machines is that you can prevent them from logging on to the network from any workstation but their own. This can help you keep a closer eye on users, as well as entirely prevent users from accessing certain networks. The disadvantage is that this requires more maintenance. If a user changes machines, you have to reconfigure the network address restrictions.

Additionally, some network devices can restrict access by Network layer or Data Link layer addresses. For instance, some switches allow you to configure ports so that only certain MAC addresses can pass traffic through those ports. If a user attempts to plug another machine with another MAC address into the same port, the switch will not allow it to pass traffic and the computer will be unable to use the network.

On a Linux or UNIX server, the most common mechanism for configuring network address restrictions is the use of TCP wrappers. TCP wrappers are used by a variety of programs to determine whether they should accept network traffic from a particular address. Firewall software, such as iptables for Linux, is also commonly used.

A careful intruder can circumvent this sort of protection. For instance, an intruder can manually configure both IP addresses and MAC addresses on a computer, or he can attack a computer with packets containing bogus IP addresses, in a type of attack called spoofing. However, good network security policies can make it difficult or impossible to use bogus addresses from outside a network. With sufficient network security, the only way an intruder can circumvent address restrictions would be to have a machine physically located on the network.

After completing this lab, you will be able to:

- Configure network address restrictions on a Linux server

Materials Required

This lab will require the following:

- A computer running a current version of Linux such as Ubuntu or Fedora named *LINUX1.NETPLUSLAB.NET*, configured with the firewall disabled, with SELinux disabled, and with the GNOME Desktop Environment
- *LINUX1.NETPLUSLAB.NET* configured with an IP address of 192.168.54.5 and a subnet mask of 255.255.255.0
- The default /etc/samba/smb.conf file in place
- A user named *netplus* on *LINUX1.NETPLUSLAB.NET* with a known password and a known password for the root account
- A computer running Windows 8.1 or Windows 7 named *WORKSTATION1*, configured with an IP address of 192.168.54.3 and a subnet mask of 255.255.255.0
- Cygwin 1.7.x (available at *cygwin.com*) installed on *WORKSTATION1*, with the openssh and openssl packages in the Net category installed in addition to the default packages
- Access to *WORKSTATION1* as an administrator
- Both computers connected to a switch with straight-through Cat 5 (or better) UTP cables

Estimated completion time: **35 minutes**

Activity

1. Log on to *LINUX1.NETPLUSLAB.NET* as the netplus user. The Linux desktop appears.

2. Open a terminal window. The `netplus@LINUX1:~` prompt appears.

3. Type `su -` and press **Enter**. The Password prompt appears.

4. Enter the password for the root account and press **Enter**. The prompt ends in a pound sign (#), indicating that you are logged on as the root user.

5. Type `echo "sshd: ALL" >>/etc/hosts.deny` and press **Enter**. The computer appends the text `sshd: ALL` to the file /etc/hosts.deny. This tells TCP wrappers to prohibit computers from any IP address from logging on to *LINUX1.NETPLUSLAB. NET*.

6. Type `cat /var/run/sshd.pid` and press **Enter**. The computer displays the PID for the running sshd daemon. Record this number.

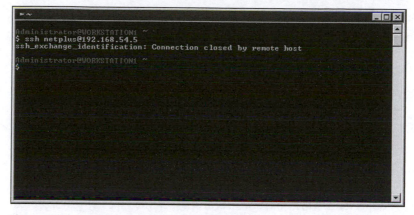

Figure 8-3   An SSH logon prevented by TCP wrappers

7. Type **kill -HUP** followed by the PID number you recorded in Step 6, and then press **Enter**. The computer restarts the sshd daemon.

8. Log on to *WORKSTATION1* as an administrator. The Windows desktop appears.

9. Click **Start**, then type **Cygwin**, and click **Cygwin Terminal**. A terminal window opens.

10. In the terminal window, type **ssh netplus@192.168.54.5** and press **Enter**. As shown in Figure 8-3, the computer displays the error message ssh_exchange_ identification: Connection closed by remote host.

11. Now you will configure *LINUX1.NETPLUSLAB.NET* to accept SSH connections from *WORKSTATION1*. In the terminal window on *LINUX1.NETPLUSLAB.NET*, type **echo "sshd: 192.168.54.3" >>/etc/hosts.allow** and press **Enter**. The computer appends the text sshd: 192.168.54.3 to the end of the file /etc/hosts.allow.

12. Repeat Steps 6 and 7 to restart the sshd daemon.

13. In the terminal window on *WORKSTATION1*, type **ssh netplus@192.168.54.5** and press **Enter**. If a message appears indicating that the authenticity of the connection cannot be confirmed, type **yes** and press **Enter**. The netplus@192.168.54.5's password: prompt appears.

14. Type the password for the netplus account and press **Enter**. The prompt changes, indicating that you have logged on to the remote server.

15. Log off both computers.

Certification Objectives

Objectives for the CompTIA Network+ Exam:

- 3.2 Compare and contrast common network vulnerabilities and threats
- 3.3 Given a scenario, implement network hardening techniques

Review Questions

1. In which of the following situations would it be most beneficial for a network administrator to employ network address restrictions on a TCP/IP-based network (that does not use DHCP) to improve security?

   a. A salesperson accesses a company's network via a dial-up connection to upload sales data every night.

   b. A corporate executive frequently travels to a company's various locations and requires access to confidential information on the server.

   c. A new employee is working on tutorials in temporary quarters until her office can be completely furnished.

   d. A contractor works on a project from a cubicle specially designated and furnished for use by consultants.

2. Which of the following is a potential weakness in using restrictions on either Network layer addresses or Data Link layer addresses to control access to a network or server?

   a. For a machine on the same network, both Network and Data Link layer addresses may be configured manually.

   b. For a machine on an external network, both Network and Data Link layer addresses may be configured manually.

   c. Network address restrictions typically require more maintenance.

   d. Network layer addresses may be configured manually, whereas Data Link layer addresses may not.

3. Which files on a Linux server are used to configure TCP wrappers? (Choose all that apply.)

   a. /etc/hosts

   b. /etc/hosts.allow

   c. /etc/hosts.deny

   d. /etc/tcpwrappers

4. Which of the following network security methods provides the greatest resistance to unauthorized external file access on a server?

   a. A central computer room that is accessible only to authorized personnel through hand scanning

   b. An NOS that is configured to allow logons only during the hours of 8:00 a.m. to 5:00 p.m.

   c. An NOS that requires a user's computer to have an address that matches one belonging to his LAN segment to log on to the server

   d. A proxy server that disguises transmissions issued from clients on a private LAN

5. What is the best defense against social engineering?

   a. A strong security policy and educating users

   b. Employing Kerberos authentication for all users

   c. Configuring a firewall to accept transmissions only from certain IP addresses

   d. Limiting the ports on a server through which client communication may take place

Lab 8.4 Delegating Administrative Rights

Objectives

One of the advantages of a directory service such as Microsoft Active Directory is that it allows the network administrator granular control over users and network resources. The administrator can make sure that users can access the network resources they need, while at the same time preventing them from accessing network resources they should not be able to access. This also allows the network administrator to delegate specific tasks to certain users without delegating any more authority than is needed.

For instance, in large organizations, resetting passwords, creating user accounts, and other relatively straightforward parts of network administration can take up a lot of time. This can prevent the network administrator from concentrating on larger issues of network design and maintenance. In some cases, it's more efficient to have a user in each department reset passwords and create user accounts specifically for that department, but only for that department. The network administrator is then free to spend time on more important issues. A department might also prefer to have control over its own resources. In large organizations, network administration might be divided between two or more groups.

One tool you can use to subdivide a domain is the organizational unit. An organizational unit is a group of users or network resources, such as printers. Organizational units can be used to enforce policies, including the delegation of administrative rights. For instance, a company might have a different organizational unit for each department. Dividing a domain into organizational units is simpler and usually more convenient than dividing a domain into multiple child domains.

Keep in mind that Active Directory can be quite complex, and it is often possible to find multiple ways to solve a particular problem. Although the simplest way to solve a problem might not be the best way, keeping your Active Directory installation as simple as possible will make it easier to administer over the long term.

After completing this lab, you will be able to:

- Create user accounts in Windows Server 2012 R2

- Create organizational units in Windows Server 2012 R2

- Delegate network administration roles as needed in Windows Server 2012 R2

Materials Required

This lab will require the following:

- The network configured at the end of Lab 8.1

- No organizational units named Accounting or Manufacturing in Active Directory

- Access to *SERVER1* as the administrator for the netpluslab.net domain

- Local logon for all users configured in the Domain Controller Security Policy (configured by an instructor, if necessary)

Estimated completion time: **40 minutes**

Activity

1. Log on to *SERVER1* as the administrator in the netpluslab.net domain. The Windows Server Manager appears.

2. Click **Tools**, click **Active Directory Users and Computers**. The Active Directory Users and Computers window opens. If necessary, click the **right arrow** next to netpluslab.net to expand the tree below it.

3. Right-click **netpluslab.net** in the tree in the left pane. In the shortcut menu, point to **New**, and then click **Organizational Unit**. The New Object – Organizational Unit dialog box opens.

4. Type **Accounting** in the Name text box and click **OK**. An Accounting icon appears below netpluslab.net in the tree.

5. Repeat Steps 3 and 4, creating an organizational unit named **Manufacturing**. Figure 8-4 shows the addition of a new organizational unit.

6. Right-click the icon for the **Accounting** object. In the shortcut menu, point to **New**, and then click **User**. The New Object – User dialog box opens.

7. In the Full name and User logon name text boxes, type **accounting-admin**. Click **Next**.

8. In both the Password and the Confirm password text boxes, type a password at least eight characters long that contains at least one number and a mixture of upper- and lowercase letters. Record or memorize this password.

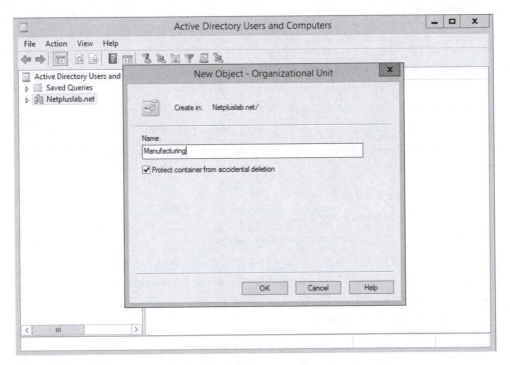

Figure 8-4 Adding an organizational unit

9. Click the **User must change password at next logon** check box to remove the check mark. Click **Next**. The dialog box summarizes the account information.

10. Click **Finish** to close the dialog box. Click **Accounting** in the left pane and note that an icon for the accounting-admin account appears in the right pane. (If an Active Directory dialog box opens indicating that Windows cannot set the password because it does not meet the minimum password policy requirements, click **OK**. Then click **Back**, change the password, click **Next**, and then click **Finish**.)

11. Right-click the **accounting-admin** object, and select **Add to a group** from the shortcut menu.

12. Now you will add the accounting-admin user to the Server Operators group. By default, users in the Server Operators group are able to log on to the domain controller, but ordinary users are not. In the "Enter the object names to select" text box, type **Server Operators**. Click **OK**. The Active Directory Domain Services dialog box opens, indicating that the addition was successful. Click **OK**.

13. Repeat Steps 6 through 12 to create a user named **accountant** and add it to the Server Operators group. Record the password for this account.

14. Right-click the **Manufacturing** object. In the shortcut menu, point to **New**, and then click **User**. The New Object – User dialog box opens. Repeat Steps 7 through 10, creating a user account named **manufacturer**.

15. Right-click the **Accounting** object and select **Delegate Control** from the shortcut menu. The Delegation of Control Wizard opens.

16. Click **Next**. The wizard offers you the option of selecting users or groups.

17. Click **Add**. The Select Users, Computers, or Groups window opens. In the "Enter the object names to select" text box, type **accounting-admin** and click **OK**. The name of the user appears in the Selected users and groups box.

18. Click **Next**. The wizard lists a series of tasks you could delegate.

19. Place a check in the **Create, delete, and manage user accounts** check box. Click **Next**. The wizard summarizes the options you have chosen.

20. Click **Finish**. The wizard closes. You have now delegated control over user accounts in the Accounting organizational unit to the accounting-admin user. This user will not have rights over other parts of Active Directory, including the Manufacturing organizational unit.

21. Log off *SERVER1*.

22. Log on to *SERVER1* as the **accounting-admin** user. The Windows Server Manager opens.

23. Click **Tools**, and then click **Active Directory Users and Computers**. The Active Directory Users and Computers window opens.

24. If the tree below netpluslab.net (in the left pane of the window) has not been expanded already, click the **right arrow** next to netpluslab.net. Then click the icon for the **Accounting** object. Icons for usernames appear in the right pane of the window.

25. Right-click the **accountant** user icon, and select **Reset Password**. The Reset Password dialog box opens.

26. Enter a new password in the New password and Confirm password text boxes. Click **OK**. A dialog box opens, indicating that the password for the accountant account has been changed.

27. Click **OK**.

28. Repeat Steps 6 through 10 for the Accounting object, creating a user named **bills**. Make sure to record the password.

29. Now you will verify that the accounting-admin account has no rights to other parts of Active Directory. Click the icon for the **Manufacturing** object. The icon for the manufacturer user appears.

30. Right-click the icon for the **manufacturer** user in the right pane of the window. In the shortcut menu, select **Reset Password**. The Reset Password dialog box opens.

31. Enter the new password in the New password and Confirm password text boxes. Click **OK**. A dialog box opens, indicating that Windows could not complete the password change and that access is denied. Click **OK**.

32. Right-click the **Manufacturing** icon in the left pane of the window. Select **Delegate Control**. A dialog box opens, indicating that you do not have permission to write security information for this object.

33. Click **OK**. The dialog box closes.

34. On *WORKSTATION1*, log on to the netpluslab.net domain as the **bills** user you created in Step 28. The Windows desktop appears.

35. Log off both computers.

Certification Objectives

Objectives for the CompTIA Network+ Exam:

- 3.2 Compare and contrast common network vulnerabilities and threats

Review Questions

1. In this lab, you grouped users in the same department into organizational units, and then used the organizational units to delegate permissions within them. What is another approach you could have used to perform the same task?

   a. Group each department into separate forests.

   b. Group each department into separate domains in the same tree.

   c. Create a new forest for each department.

   d. Group each department into separate workgroups within the same tree.

2. What is an organizational unit?

   a. A department or division within an organization

   b. A container used to group users with similar permissions and rights

   c. A container used to group similar objects such as users or groups

   d. An organization

3. If a user is assigned Read permissions to a folder, what may he do with the folder's contents? (Choose all that apply.)

   a. View the listing of files in the folder.

   b. Launch executable files in the folder.

   c. Delete files in the folder.

   d. View the contents of files in the folder.

4. If a user is assigned Modify permissions to a folder, what may she do with the folder's contents? (Choose all that apply.)

   a. View the list of files in the folder.

   b. Launch executable files in the folder.

   c. Delete files in the folder.

   d. View the contents of files in the folder.

5. Which of the following is a potential advantage of delegating user administration to another user? (Choose all that apply.)

   a. The network administrator can concentrate on more important network maintenance issues.

   b. One or more users in each department can handle user administration for their department.

   c. Large network administration departments can delegate tasks.

   d. Each user in a department can handle the administration of his own account.

6. By default, what permissions do users in the Everyone group have to a newly shared Windows Server folder?

   a. Read and Execute only

   b. List Folder Contents only

   c. Full Access

   d. By default, users have no rights to newly shared folders.

Lab 8.5 Understanding Malware

Objectives

Malware can infect computers in a variety of ways. For instance, the following can cause a malicious program to infect a client (or a server): running an infected executable file, reading email with an email client that has not been upgraded with the latest patches, browsing the Web with a Web browser that has not been upgraded with the latest patches, or even running certain services on the Internet. Keeping a file server free of viruses can be even more challenging, as your users might try to store infected files on its shared drives. Sometimes users save infected files to a shared drive, have their computers cleared of viruses, and then reinfect their computers from the files on the shared drive.

To complicate matters, virus scanners can't do their work if you fail to keep them up to date. Many virus scanners require that you periodically update the virus definition files they use to search for viruses. If you do not, the virus scanner will be unable to find newer viruses.

After completing this lab, you will be able to:

- Describe different types of malware
- Use malware-scanning software

Materials Required

This lab will require the following:

- A computer running Windows 8.1 or Windows 7 named *WORKSTATION1* with an Internet connection
- AVG FREE Edition 2015 Antivirus (available from *http://free.avg.com*), or the current version, installed on the computer

> Estimated completion time: **30 minutes or more depending on the size of the hard drive**

Activity

1. Log on to *WORKSTATION1* as an administrator. The Windows desktop appears. Connect to the Internet, if necessary.

2. Click **Start**, type **AVG 2015**, and then click **AVG 2015**.

3. Under the **Options** menu, click **Update**.

4. After AVG downloads and installs the updates, click **Close**.

5. Click the **Scan Options** button to the right of the **Scan now** button to open the Scan Options section shown in Figure 8-5.

6. Click **Scan Whole Computer**. The scan begins showing the progress of the virus scan. Do not click any buttons or press any keys until the scan is finished; this might take several minutes. The amount of time required for the scan depends on the power of the computer's CPU and the number of files on the computer. After the scan is finished, the computer shows a summary of the scan, including the number of files scanned, the number of viruses found, and the number of files repaired, quarantined, deleted, or excluded.

7. Click **Close** to return to the AVG AntiVirus FREE Edition 2015 main window.

8. Close AVG AntiVirus FREE Edition 2015.

9. To gain an understanding of virus-related terms, you will access the Webopedia Web site. Start Internet Explorer. In the address box, type **www.webopedia.com** and press **Enter**. The Webopedia home page opens.

10. Type **macro virus** in the search box and then click SEARCH. Scroll down and click the **macro virus** link. Record the definition in your own words.

11. Repeat Step 10 for the term **worm**.

12. Repeat Step 10 for the term **Trojan horse**.

13. Log off.

Figure 8-5   AVG AntiVirus FREE update manager
Source: AVG AntiVirus

Certification Objectives

Objectives for the Comp TIA Network+ Exam:

- 3.2 Compare and contrast common network vulnerabilities and threats
- 3.3 Given a scenario, implement network hardening techniques

Review Questions

1. A macro virus is most apt to affect which of the following programs?

   a. Microsoft Client for Networks

   b. Microsoft Outlook

   c. Microsoft Excel

   d. Microsoft SQL Server

2. If you receive an infected file as an executable program attached to an email message, which of the following is this program likely to be?

   a. A macro virus

   b. A Trojan

   c. A worm

   d. A boot sector virus

3. What is the difference between a Trojan and a true virus?

   a. A Trojan does not automatically replicate itself, whereas a true virus does.

   b. A Trojan causes harm by simply being on the computer's hard disk, whereas a true virus file must be executed by the user.

   c. A Trojan often can't be detected by a virus-scanning program, whereas a true virus can almost always be detected by such a program.

   d. A Trojan changes its binary characteristics to avoid detection, whereas a true virus's binary characteristics remain static.

4. Which of the following types of virus checking requires frequent database updates to remain effective?

   a. Signature scanning

   b. Heuristic scanning

   c. Rotation checking

   d. Integrity checking

5. If a virus is polymorphic, what is it able to do?

   a. Replicate itself over a network connection

   b. Change its binary characteristics each time it's transferred to a new system

   c. Modify the network properties of a client or server

   d. Remain inactive until a particular date

6. What is unique about a time-dependent virus?

   a. It changes its binary characteristics at regularly scheduled intervals.

   b. It can only be eradicated by applying a virus fix at certain times of the day.

   c. It is alternately detectable, then undetectable, by virus-scanning software, depending on the date.

   d. It remains dormant until a particular date or time.

Lab 8.6 Configuring a Firewall in Windows Server

Objectives

The Windows Firewall can be configured multiple ways in Windows Server 2012 R2. Although basic Firewall settings can be accessed through Control Panel, most configuration is done with either the Windows Firewall with Advanced Security interface or the `Netsh` command.

In this lab, the firewall will be configured to allow ICMP requests, such as ping, to reach the server.

After completing this lab, you will be able to:

- Configure the Windows Server 2012 R2 firewall using the Windows Firewall with Advanced Security

- Review information on audited events

Materials Required

This lab will require the following:

- A computer running Windows Server 2012 R2 named *SERVER1*, with an IP address of 192.168.54.1 and a subnet mask of 255.255.255.0

- Access as the administrator to *SERVER1*

- A computer running Windows 8.1 or Windows 7 named *WORKSTATION1*, with an IP address of 192.168.54.3 and a subnet mask of 255.255.255.0

- Both computers connected to a switch with straight-through Cat 5 (or better) UTP cables

> Estimated completion time: **20 minutes**

Activity

1. Log on to *SERVER1* as the administrator. The Windows Server Manager appears.

2. Click **Tools,** and then click **Windows Firewall with Advanced Security**. The Windows Firewall with Advanced Security interface opens.

3. Verify that Windows Firewall is on and click on **Inbound Rules**.

4. Right-click on **Active Directory Domain Controller – Echo Request (ICMPv4-In)**. If necessary, click **Disable Rule** so the circled check mark appears grayed out.

5. Scroll down and right-click on **File and Printer Sharing (Echo Request – ICMPv4-In)**. If necessary, click **Disable Rule**. The firewall should now block ICMP requests to the server.

6. Close the **Windows Firewall with Advanced Security** interface.

7. Log on to *WORKSTATION1* as an administrator. The Windows desktop appears.

8. Open a Command Prompt window and type `ping 192.168.54.1`.

9. The ping should fail, as shown in Figure 8-6.

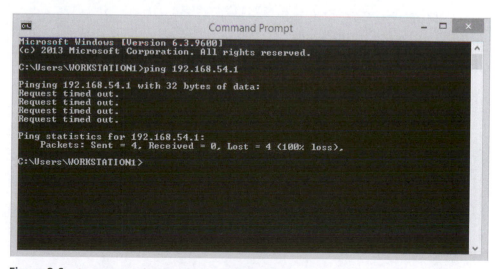

Figure 8-6 An unsuccessful attempt to ping *SERVER1*

10. Close the Command Prompt window.

11. Switch back to *SERVER1*, where you should still be logged in as the administrator. The Windows Server Manager appears.

12. Click **Tools**, and then click **Windows Firewall with Advanced Security**. The Windows Firewall with Advanced Security interface opens.

13. Enable the rules for both **Active Directory Domain Controller – Echo Request (ICMPv4-In)** and **File and Printer Sharing (Echo Request – ICMPv4-In)**.

14. Close the **Windows Firewall with Advanced Security** interface.

15. Switch back to *WORKSTATION1*, where you should still be logged in as an administrator. The Windows desktop appears.

16. Open a Command Prompt window and type `ping 192.168.54.1`.

17. This time the ping is successful because the firewall rules allow the ICMP request to pass.

18. Log off both computers.

Certification Objectives

Objectives for the CompTIA Network+ Exam:

- 1.1 Explain the functions and applications of various network devices
- 3.2 Compare and contrast common network vulnerabilities and threats
- 3.5 Given a scenario, install and configure a basic firewall

Review Questions

1. Which protocol is used by ping and traceroute?

   a. SMB

   b. FTP

   c. ICMP

   d. IMAP

2. A(n) _____ firewall is placed between a private and public network.

   a. host-based

   b. network-based

   c. content-based

   d. interface-based

3. The most common cause of a security issue with a firewall is _____.

   a. overheating

   b. network delay

   c. misconfiguration

   d. traffic jam

4. The Windows Server 2012 R2 firewall cannot be configured using the _____.

    a. event viewer

    b. Control Panel

    c. Windows Firewall with Advanced Security interface

    d. `Netsh` command

5. Simple packet-filtering firewalls operate at layer _____ of the OSI model.

    a. 2

    b. 4

    c. 6

    d. 3

NETWORK PERFORMANCE MANAGEMENT

Labs included in this chapter

- Lab 9.1 Establishing a Network Baseline
- Lab 9.2 Using Uninterruptible Power Supplies (UPSs)
- Lab 9.3 Configuring RAID
- Lab 9.4 Researching Open Source VoIP Solutions
- Lab 9.5 Backing Up a Windows Server
- Lab 9.6 Backing Up a Linux Server

CompTIA Network+ Exam Objectives

Objective	Lab
1.10 Identify the basic elements of unified communication technologies	9.4
2.1 Given a scenario, use appropriate monitoring tools	9.1
2.2 Given a scenario, analyze metrics and reports from monitoring and tracking performance tools	9.1
2.3 Given a scenario, use appropriate resources to support configuration management	9.5, 9.6
3.1 Compare and contrast risk related concepts	9.2, 9.3
5.7 Given a scenario, install and configure equipment in the appropriate location using best practices	9.2

Lab 9.1 Establishing a Network Baseline

Objectives

It's hard to know where you're going if you don't know where you are. Establishing a baseline allows you to measure the effect of any changes in your network by comparing new values with your baseline. Baseline measurements might include any number of relevant factors, such as network utilization, CPU activity, or packet loss. A baseline can be helpful in determining when an upgrade is necessary and in assessing its effectiveness afterward.

In this lab, you will establish a simple network baseline by taking a number of basic measurements using Windows Performance Monitor.

After completing this lab, you will be able to:

- Create a baseline of network and server performance

Materials Required

This lab will require the following:

- A computer running Windows Server 2012 R2 named *SERVER1*
- Administrative access to *SERVER1*

Most of the steps in this lab can also be completed using virtualization software such as VMware.

Estimated completion time: **30 minutes**

Activity

1. Log on to *SERVER1* as the administrator. The Windows Server Manager window opens.

2. Click **Tools**, and click **Resource Monitor**. Resource Monitor opens. This tool is useful for quickly gathering basic data about your server's performance.

3. If necessary, click the **Overview** tab and then use the graphical data to estimate the average CPU usage over the last minute. If this number is constantly over 50 percent, it might indicate that an upgrade is necessary.

4. Close Resource Monitor.

5. Next, you'll try Performance Monitor, which is a useful tool for gathering more detailed server information.

6. Click **Tools**, and click **Computer Management**. The Computer Management window opens.

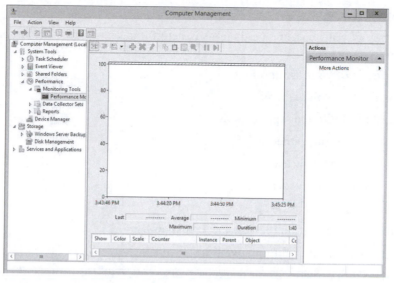

Figure 9-1   Performance Monitor

7. Click the right arrow next to Performance, expand **Monitoring Tools,** and then click **Performance Monitor**. The Performance Monitor window displays current activity, as shown in Figure 9-1.

8. Click the **Add** button (green plus sign), click the **Show description** check box, and take some time to explore the various counters that can be measured. If you were creating a baseline for a Web server, for example, you might choose to include the Web Service counters. In this case, we will select some counters that measure general server performance.

9. Select **% Processor Time** in the Processor section and click **Add**.

10. Using the same process, also add **Pages/sec** in the Memory section and **Bytes Total/sec** in the Network Adapter section.

11. Click **OK** to close the Add Counters dialog box.

12. Let Performance Manager run for a few minutes while you do some other tasks.

13. What did Performance Manager record as the average value for these three counters? The measurements were most likely quite low if your server is not part of a busy network.

14. Close the Computer Management Window and log off *SERVER1*.

Certification Objectives

Objectives for the CompTIA Network+ Exam:

- 2.1 Given a scenario, use appropriate monitoring tools
- 2.2 Given a scenario, analyze metrics and reports from monitoring and tracking performance tools

Review Questions

1. The accuracy of your baseline predictions is determined most by what factor? (Choose all that apply.)

    a. The accuracy of your assumptions

    b. How much data you gathered

    c. The number of different applications gathering data

    d. The relevance of the gathered data

2. What does the baseline measure?

    a. The current state of the network

    b. The minimal network traffic

    c. The maximum utilization the network can support

    d. The average amount of future downtime

3. Which system tool provides a quick summary of overall CPU, disk, network, and memory utilization?

    a. Performance Monitor

    b. Resource Monitor

    c. Task Manager

    d. Computer Management

4. The types of measurements recorded by Performance Monitor are called _____.

    a. metrics

    b. performance indicators

    c. monitoring tools

    d. counters

Lab 9.2 Using Uninterruptible Power Supplies (UPSs)

Objectives

A sudden power failure or outage can cause numerous computer problems. If power were interrupted while a computer's files were open, for instance, those files might be corrupted. An uninterruptible power supply (UPS) is a power supply that uses a battery to ensure that any device attached to it will be able to function for some length of time despite a power failure. If the power outage lasts only a few seconds, the UPS prevents the attached devices from losing power. If the power outage lasts more than a few seconds, the UPS affords you (or a software program) the opportunity to shut down the attached devices. Alternately, use of a UPS might allow a backup generator time to get up to full operating power.

Depending on the power requirements of your network devices and servers, and the amount of power produced by a UPS, you might be able to use one UPS with multiple devices.

However, you should check the power requirements of each device against the specifications of the UPS before attempting to do this. You should usually overestimate the power consumption to provide a healthy margin of error. A device's power consumption is commonly measured by its volt-amp (VA) rating. It can also be measured in amps. The VA rating can be found by multiplying the current consumed by the device (measured in amps) by the incoming voltage. For devices in the United States, this is 120 volts, but for international devices, this is usually 220 volts. In general, estimating the actual power consumption of a network device is difficult, as an individual device might use more or less power than its manufacturer indicates that it should.

Some servers come with multiple power supplies. If one power supply fails, the other power supply continues to power the computer. For truly critical servers or network devices, you might find that attaching multiple power supplies to a single UPS is insufficient. If the UPS fails, the device would also fail during a power outage. However, if you plugged each power supply into a separate UPS, the failure of a single UPS would not cause the computer to lose power in the event of an overall power failure. Some data centers might also plug each UPS into a different circuit and each circuit into a different generator. However, these fault-tolerance measures increase costs considerably.

In addition to the smaller UPSs you will investigate in this lab, you can also purchase large models designed to support many devices in large data centers.

After completing this lab, you will be able to:

- Perform a cost comparison of UPSs
- Discuss the characteristics of UPSs

Materials Required

This lab will require the following:

- A pencil or pen
- A computer with access to the Internet and online retailers who sell UPSs, such as *apc .com, tripplite.com,* or *emersonnetworkpower.com*

Estimated completion time: **60–90 minutes**

Activity

1. Suppose you are the network administrator for Hollisville Manufacturing. Table 9-1 shows the types of devices in your data center, the number of each device, and the VA rating for each device. Calculate and record the total VA rating of the devices in the data center.

2. Using the Internet to perform research, choose a model of UPS that exceeds the total power rating for all of the devices in the data center. Record the vendor name.

3. Record the model number.

4. Record the price.

Table 9-1 Power consumption of network devices in the Hollisville Manufacturing data center

Device	Number of devices	Volt-amp (VA) rating per device
Router	2	120
Server	8	285
Workstation	20	250
Switch	5	90

© 2016 Cengage Learning®

5. Record the amount of time that the UPS will keep a device running after a power failure.

6. Record whether the UPS comes with software that will automatically shut down a computer after a power failure.

7. Repeat Steps 2 through 6 with two other models of UPS.

Certification Objectives

Objectives for the CompTIA Network+ Exam:

- 3.1 Compare and contrast risk related concepts
- 5.7 Given a scenario, install and configure equipment in the appropriate location using best practices

Review Questions

1. What specification is necessary for you to determine the amount of electrical power that your computer devices require?

    a. Capacitance

    b. Impedance

    c. Resistance

    d. Wattage

2. What is line conditioning?

    a. Regular testing of the integrity of electrical systems

    b. Periodic application of a large amount of voltage to electrical systems to clean the lines

    c. Continuous filtering of an electrical circuit to protect against noise

    d. Intermittent fluctuation of voltage on a circuit, which over time will cause power flaws for connected devices

3. Which of the following devices, when used in conjunction with one or more UPSs, will allow other devices to continue running indefinitely after a power outage?

   a. Surge protector

   b. Circuit breaker

   c. Venerator

   d. Circuit mirror

4. Which of the following power conditions equates to a power failure?

   a. Sag

   b. Line noise

   c. Surge

   d. Blackout

5. Which of the following power conditions would not necessarily cause a power failure, but might adversely affect computer equipment? (Choose all that apply.)

   a. Sag

   b. Line noise

   c. Brownout

   d. Blackout

6. What is the difference between a standby UPS and an online UPS?

   a. A standby UPS engages when it detects a power failure, whereas an online UPS continuously provides power to its connected devices.

   b. A standby UPS requires that the network administrator connect it to key devices when a power failure is detected, whereas an online UPS can remain connected to devices indefinitely, even when not in use.

   c. A standby UPS continuously provides power to its connected devices, whereas an online UPS engages when it detects a power failure.

   d. A standby UPS can remain connected to devices indefinitely, even when not in use, whereas an online UPS requires that the network administrator connect it to the devices when a power failure is detected.

Lab 9.3 Configuring RAID

Objectives

If a hard drive on a computer fails, either the computer itself will fail or the computer will lose data. RAID (redundant array of independent disks) allows you to improve disk reliability by combining multiple disks. Depending on how RAID is configured, it can also help improve disk performance. In this lab, you will configure RAID in software. Keep in mind, however, that RAID is also commonly available in hardware. Hardware RAID has several advantages over software RAID, including greater reliability, better performance, and often the ability to swap out hard drives while the computer is still running. Most modern network operating systems (NOSs), including Windows, Linux, and UNIX, support software RAID. Windows server operating systems such as Windows Server 2012 R2 support all forms of software RAID, but workstation operating systems such as Windows 8.1 or Windows 7 only support some.

Each possible RAID configuration involves a different arrangement of disks and is called a level. RAID level 0 is called disk striping and requires at least two physical disks (almost always of the same size). Because the computer writes parts of each file to both physical disks at the same time, RAID level 0 results in higher performance. As in all levels of RAID, the disadvantage is that less disk space is available to the computer because it sees only one logical disk that is the size of just one of the physical disks. RAID level 0 does not provide any fault tolerance, and data on both disks will be lost if either of the physical disks fail.

RAID level 1, which you will configure in this lab, is known as disk mirroring. It requires at least two physical disks and provides 100 percent redundancy. Each time the computer writes data to its hard disks, the same data is written to each disk at the same time. If one disk fails, the computer can continue running normally because the other disk has precisely the same data. As in RAID level 0, the computer sees only one logical disk that is the size of one of the physical disks. In a variation of disk mirroring known as disk duplexing, the disks also have redundant disk controllers so that the failure of a single controller will not result in the loss of data.

RAID level 5 (commonly known as RAID 5) writes data to three or more physical disks. It also writes parity data to each disk. If one of the physical disks fails, the data and parity data written to the other disks can be used to recover any lost data. In RAID level 5, an amount of disk space equal to the space on one physical disk is unavailable. Although disks in a RAID level 5 configuration take longer to recover from the failure of a disk than disks in a RAID level 1 configuration, RAID level 5 allows the computer to have more disk space than RAID level 1.

To configure a RAID array in software in Windows Server 2012 R2, you must use two or more dynamic disks. The exact number of disks required depends on the level of RAID you want to use. A dynamic disk can be used in volumes that can be resized as needed without rebooting the server, or they can be included in RAID arrays. The disadvantage of using dynamic disks is that some operating systems cannot locally read these disks (although they can read data stored on them if it is shared over a network). In contrast, a basic disk can have primary and extended partitions and logical volumes, which can be read directly by other operating systems.

After completing this lab, you will be able to:

- Configure RAID level 1 on a Windows Server 2012 R2 computer

Materials Required

This lab will require the following:

- A computer running Windows Server 2012 R2 named *SERVER1* with two hard disks of equal size installed; one of the hard disks should contain the Windows Server 2012 R2 installation

- No partitions or logical volumes configured on the second hard disk
- Access as the administrator to the computer

Most of the steps in this lab can also be completed using virtualization software such as VMware.

Estimated completion time: **45 minutes**

Activity

1. Log on to *SERVER1* as the administrator. Windows Server Manager opens.

2. Click **Tools,** and then click **Computer Management**. The Computer Management window appears.

3. In the left pane, click **Disk Management**. Information about the disks installed in the computer appears in the right pane, as shown in Figure 9-2. If the Initialize Disk Wizard opens, ensure that the **Disk 1** check box is checked. Click **OK**.

4. In the middle pane, you see a list of the physical disks on the system. Right-click an area in the gray box around Disk 0, and then click **Convert to Dynamic Disk**. The Convert to Dynamic Disk dialog box opens.

5. Click the **Disk 1** check box so that both the Disk 0 and Disk 1 check boxes are checked. Click **OK**. The Disks to Convert dialog box opens, listing the disks to be converted to dynamic disks.

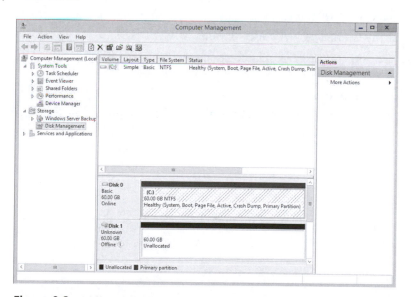

Figure 9-2   Disk Management

6. Click **Convert**. The Disk Management dialog box opens, indicating that after conversion you will be unable to start other operating systems installed on those disks. Click **Yes**.

7. If the Convert Disk to Dynamic dialog box opens, indicating that any file systems on these disks will need to be unmounted, complete the following steps. Otherwise, skip ahead to Step 13.

8. Click **Yes**. The Confirm dialog box opens, indicating that the computer will be rebooted to finish the conversion process.

9. Click **OK**. The computer reboots.

10. After the computer has rebooted, press **Ctrl+Alt+Del** to display the Log On to Windows dialog box. Log on as the administrator. Windows Server Manager opens. The System Settings Change dialog box opens, indicating that you must restart the computer before the changes you have made can take effect.

11. Click **Yes**. The computer reboots again.

12. After the computer has rebooted for a second time, repeat Steps 1 through 3. Both Disk 0 and Disk 1 now appear as dynamic disks.

13. Right-click the rectangle with the green bar at the top next to Disk 0, and click **Add Mirror** from the shortcut menu. The Add Mirror dialog box opens.

14. Click **Disk 1** to select it. Click **Add Mirror**. The bar at the top of the rectangles next to both Disk 0 and Disk 1 turns red, and text in each rectangle indicates that each disk is resyncing. After a few minutes, each disk is marked C: with a status of "healthy." You have successfully created a RAID level 1 set of disk mirrors.

15. Close the Computer Management dialog window and log off *SERVER1*.

Certification Objectives

Objectives for the CompTIA Network+ Exam:

- 3.1 Compare and contrast risk related concepts

Review Questions

1. What is the minimum number of physical hard disks required for disk mirroring?

   a. 1

   b. 2

   c. 4

   d. 5

2. Which of the following levels of RAID offers disk mirroring?

   a. 0

   b. 1

   c. 3

   d. 5

3. Why is RAID level 0 not considered fully fault tolerant?

   a. If a hard disk fails, its data will be inaccessible.

   b. It cannot stripe files whose size exceeds 64 MB.

   c. It is incompatible with modern NOSs.

   d. It cannot verify whether its fault-tolerance activities are successful.

4. RAID level 0 achieves performance benefits by simultaneously writing to multiple _____.

   a. NICs

   b. hard disks

   c. processors

   d. instances of RAID software

5. Which of the following RAID levels provides fault tolerance, while also making a large amount of disk space available?

   a. 0

   b. 1

   c. 3

   d. 5

6. What is one disadvantage of using RAID level 1 compared with using RAID level 5?

   a. RAID level 1 is not fault tolerant, whereas RAID level 5 offers at least some fault tolerance.

   b. RAID level 5 requires a third-party software program, whereas RAID level 1 is provided with every NOS.

   c. RAID level 1 requires more physical hard disks than RAID level 5.

   d. RAID level 1 makes a higher percentage of disk space unavailable when compared with RAID level 5.

Lab 9.4 Researching Open Source VoIP Solutions

Objectives

VoIP (Voice over IP) is quickly becoming common in the workplace because of its lower cost, enhanced features, and centralized management. The infrastructure for voice and data is often integrated to avoid the redundancy of having separate networks and private branch exchange (PBX) systems.

To access VoIP, users can run client applications called soft phones and place calls through their computers or, with specialized hardware, place calls through either analog or digital telephone handsets. These devices are often connected through an IP PBX, which may be a hardware system, an application running on a server, or a remote hosted or virtual service offered by an Internet provider.

One of the more common open source IP PBX applications is called Asterisk. In this lab, you will investigate some of the features available for a Windows version of Asterisk called AsteriskWin32.

After completing this lab, you will be able to:

- Identify some of the features available on an open source IP PBX

Materials Required

This lab will require the following:

- Pencil and paper
- A computer running Windows 8.1 or Windows 7 with Internet access
- An ordinary user account on the computer

Most of the steps in this lab can also be completed using virtualization software such as VMware.

Estimated completion time: **20 minutes**

Activity

1. Press **Ctrl+Alt+Del** to display the Log On to Windows dialog box. Log on as an ordinary user. The Windows desktop appears.

2. Perform whatever steps are necessary for the computer to access the Internet.

3. Start Internet Explorer.

4. Go to **www.asterisk.org** and click the **Wiki** link at the top. Use the wiki to do the following:
   a. Record some of the protocols supported by Asterisk.
   b. Explain the four key applications of Asterisk.
   c. Record some of the operating systems that can run Asterisk.

5. There is also a Windows-based version of Asterisk called AsteriskWin32. Go to **http://asteriskwin32.com/** and click the **About** tab. Does Asterisk require any additional hardware to connect soft phones?

6. Click the **Install & Notes** tab.

7. Under "1-Installation," click **View a demo of AsteriskWin32 PBX installation** and watch the video.

8. Under "2-Configuration," click **View a demo of PBX Manager & Console application** and watch the video.

9. Under "3-Run it," click **View a demo of AsteriskWin32 PBX running** and watch the video.

10. Under "4-Setup your SoftPhones," click **View a demo of firefly softphone configuration** and watch the video.

11. Close any open windows and log off.

Certification Objectives

Objectives for the CompTIA Network+ Exam:

- 1.10 Identify the basic elements of unified communication technologies

Review Questions

1. Why is the infrastructure for voice and data often integrated into a single system?

   a. To improve security

   b. To adhere to local regulations

   c. To filter outgoing communications

   d. To avoid redundancy

2. Client applications for placing VoIP calls are called _____.

   a. soft phones

   b. digital phones

   c. analog phones

   d. IP phones

3. True or False? Analog telephones require additional hardware to be used with VoIP.

4. Which of the following is *not* a benefit of using VoIP?

   a. Lower potential costs

   b. Existing phone system can be used with no new hardware

   c. Readily incorporates new features

   d. Centralized management

5. True or False? VoIP can only be used on private networks.

Lab 9.5 Backing Up a Windows Server

Objectives

In this lab, you will use the Backup utility on a Windows Server 2012 R2 computer to back up files to a shared network folder or a second hard drive. Then you will restore the files from the backup media. Many companies supply software for backing up data. Examples include Symantec Backup Exec and Tivoli Storage Manager. The capabilities (and the cost) of these programs vary widely. Some software allows you to back up a single machine, while other software allows you to back up an entire data center. Almost all backup software allows you to schedule a backup for a time when activity on the machine is low.

The usefulness of backups is limited if they are not performed regularly. If you need to restore a user's file and you have not backed that file up in six months, the file will not contain any changes the user has made in the last six months. This might be as unhelpful to the user as no backup at all.

Backups should be stored in a safe, off-site location because they are useless if the backup media have been destroyed. For instance, if backup media are kept near the servers that store the original data, a fire in the data center could destroy both the server and the backup tapes. For this reason, many organizations regularly rotate copies of their backups to off-site locations or back up to remote drives over the Internet so that at least one good copy will be available even after a disaster. Your backup location should also be secure, as your backup tapes will contain any sensitive information on your servers.

After completing this lab, you will be able to:

- Back up data
- Restore data

Materials Required

This lab will require the following:

- A computer running Windows Server 2012 R2 named *SERVER1* with Windows Server Backup installed
- Access as the administrator to the computer
- Access to a remote shared folder or a second local drive large enough to back up the local volume

 Most of the steps in this lab can also be completed using virtualization software such as VMware.

Estimated completion time: **30 minutes**

Activity

1. Log on to *SERVER1* as the administrator. Windows Server Manager opens.
2. Click **Tools**, and then click **Windows Server Backup**. The Windows Server Backup window opens, as shown in Figure 9-3.
3. Click **Local Backup** in the left pane and then click **Backup Once** in the Actions pane. The Backup Once Wizard opens.
4. Make sure that the **Different options** button is selected, and click **Next**. The wizard asks what you want to back up.

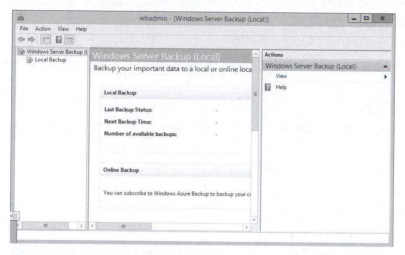

Figure 9-3   Windows Server Backup

5. Click the **Custom** option button, and then click **Next**. Click the **Add Items** button.

6. The wizard asks you what volumes you want to back up. Select only the **Local disk (C:)** check box and click **OK**. Click **Next**.

7. The wizard asks you to specify the destination media. Choose the backup media appropriate to your system and click **Next**.

8. Choose the destination volume and click **Next**. If a message appears noting that the selected volume is also included in the list of items to back up, click **Yes** to exclude the volume.

9. Click **Backup**. The Backup progress window opens and the status box indicates the various backup states being completed.

10. After a few minutes, the Backup progress window indicates that the backup is complete. Click **Close**. The Backup progress window closes.

11. Now you will test the backup by restoring some of the files you have just backed up. Click **Recover** in the Actions pane. The Recovery Wizard opens.

12. Choose the server you are logged on to and click **Next**.

13. Select the date and time that the backup was made and click **Next**.

14. Click the **Files and folders** option and click **Next**. In the Select Items to Recover window, expand the **SERVER1** node, click the **Local disk** node, select the **inetpub** folder, and then click **Next**.

15. Click **Next** again to accept the recovery options and click **Recover**.

16. When the recovery has completed, click **Close**.

17. Log off *SERVER1*.

Certification Objectives

Objectives for the CompTIA Network+ Exam:

- 2.3 Given a scenario, use appropriate resources to support configuration management

Review Questions

1. Which of the following methods will back up only data that has been changed since the last backup?

   a. Full

   b. Incremental

   c. Differential

   d. Interval

2. Assume that a company has 50 users (at a single location), a limited budget, and significant security concerns. What method would it most likely use to back up its server data?

   a. Online backup

   b. DASD

   c. RAID level 5

   d. DVD

3. Which of the following types of backup requires the most attention to the security of data while the backup is taking place?

   a. Online backup

   b. DASD

   c. RAID level 5

   d. DVD

4. Why do network administrators prefer not to back up every file on their servers every day? (Choose all that apply.)

   a. It would take too much time.

   b. It would be less accurate than periodic backups.

   c. It would be more costly.

   d. It's hard to configure backup software to perform daily backups.

5. Which backup method will back up data regardless of whether the data has been changed?

   a. Full

   b. Incremental

   c. Differential

   d. Interval

Lab 9.6 Backing Up a Linux Server

Objectives

As with Windows, you can back up a Linux server with either commercial software or built-in commands. The `tar` command, short for *tape archiver*, is one of the most common methods for making a backup. In addition to making backups of files on tape, the `tar` command (like the Zip program) is also commonly used to package software for distribution. A file created with the tar program is often called a tar file. A tar file can be updated incrementally with any files that have changed since the tar file was created.

The `tar` command is commonly used with one of two compression programs, gzip and bzip2. Each program uses a different algorithm to compress files. The bzip2 program creates smaller compressed files, but the gzip program is faster. A compressed tar file made with the gzip program usually ends with the suffix .tar.gz or .tgz, whereas a compressed tar file made with the bzip2 program usually ends with the suffix .tar.bz2 or .bz2.

Another useful command for backing up files on a Linux server is the `rsync` command. The name `rsync` is short for *remote synchronization*. This command can be used to copy files from one machine to another and to copy files incrementally. An incremental backup copies only the files that have changed since the last backup. To copy files remotely, the `rsync` command typically uses the capabilities of another command. In this lab, the `rsync` command will use the `ssh` command to copy files to the remote server.

After completing this lab, you will be able to:

- Back up files on a Linux server with the `tar` command
- Back up files on a Linux server with the `rsync` command
- Compress files on a Linux server with the `gzip` and `bzip2` commands

Materials Required

This lab will require the following:

- A computer running a current version of Linux named *LINUX1.NETPLUSLAB.NET*, configured with no firewall
- *LINUX1.NETPLUSLAB.NET* configured with an IP address of 192.168.54.5 and a subnet mask of 255.255.255.0
- A second computer running a current version of Linux named *LINUX2.NETPLUSLAB .NET*, configured with no firewall
- *LINUX2.NETPLUSLAB.NET* configured with an IP address of 192.168.54.6 and a subnet mask of 255.255.255.0
- Access as the netplus user and as root to both *LINUX1.NETPLUSLAB.NET* and *LINUX2.NETPLUSLAB.NET*
- Both computers connected to a switch or hub with straight-through Cat 5 (or better) UTP cables
- No firewall software enabled on either computer

Most of the steps in this lab can also be completed using virtualization software such as VMware.

Estimated completion time: **35 minutes**

Activity

1. Log on to *LINUX1.NETPLUSLAB.NET* as the netplus user.

2. Open a terminal window, type **su -**, and press **Enter**. The Password prompt appears.

3. Enter the password for the root account and press **Enter**. The prompt now ends in a pound sign (#), indicating that you are logged on as the root user.

4. Type **echo "*Your name*" >/usr/local/netplus.txt**, replacing *"Your name"* with your name, and press **Enter**. The computer creates a text file named netplus.txt containing your name.

5. Type **ls /usr/local** and press **Enter**. The computer displays a list of the files in the /usr/local directory, including the file netplus.txt.

6. In the terminal window, type **tar -zcvf backup.tar.gz /usr/local** and press **Enter**. As shown in Figure 9-4, the computer creates a tar file named backup.tar.gz, backs up all the files in the /usr/local directory, and compresses the files with the gzip program. It displays a list of files as it backs them up. Note that all the files and directories located within the /usr/local directory are included in the archive.

```
                              root@localhost:~                          ×

 File  Edit  View  Search  Terminal  Help
[root@localhost ~]# tar -zcvf backup.tar.gz /usr/local
tar: Removing leading `/' from member names
/usr/local/
/usr/local/lib64/
/usr/local/netplus.txt
/usr/local/share/
/usr/local/share/applications/
/usr/local/share/applications/mimeinfo.cache
/usr/local/share/man/
/usr/local/share/man/man4/
/usr/local/share/man/man7/
/usr/local/share/man/man4x/
/usr/local/share/man/man9/
/usr/local/share/man/man9x/
/usr/local/share/man/man7x/
/usr/local/share/man/man3/
/usr/local/share/man/man8x/
/usr/local/share/man/man1/
/usr/local/share/man/man1x/
/usr/local/share/man/mann/
/usr/local/share/man/man2x/
/usr/local/share/man/man5x/
/usr/local/share/man/man6x/
/usr/local/share/man/man8/
```

Figure 9-4 Creation of a tar file

7. Type **mv backup.tar.gz /tmp** and press **Enter**. The computer moves the file backup.tar.gz to the /tmp directory.

8. Type **cd /tmp** and press **Enter**. The computer changes your directory to /tmp.

9. Type **tar -zxvf backup.tar.gz** and press **Enter**. The computer unarchives and uncompresses all the files contained in backup.tar.gz.

10. Type **ls /tmp/usr/local** and press **Enter**. The computer displays a list of the files that you have just extracted from the tar archive. Note that the tar command has preserved the directory structure of all the files it has archived.

11. Type **cd usr** and press **Enter**. The computer changes your current directory to the /tmp/usr directory.

12. Type **cd local** and press **Enter**. The computer changes your current directory to the /tmp/usr/local directory that was created when backup.tar.gz was untarred. (Do not type cd /local, as that will change your current directory to the /local directory instead.)

13. Type **cat netplus.txt** and press **Enter**. The computer displays the contents of the netplus.txt file.

14. Type **tar -jcvf backup.tar.bz2 /usr/local** and press **Enter**. The computer creates an archive as it did in Step 6 with a name of backup.tar.bz2 and using the bzip2 program.

15. Now you will back up files to a remote machine. Type **rsync -zav -e ssh /usr /local 192.168.54.6:/tmp** and press **Enter**. The -z option tells the rsync command to compress the files like the gzip command, the -a option tells the rsync command to archive all the files, and the -v option tells it to be verbose, or display detailed messages explaining what the command is doing. The -e option tells the rsync command to use the ssh command. The last two options tell it to copy the /usr/local directory to the /tmp directory on 192.168.54.6. If the "Are you sure you want to continue connecting (yes/no):" prompt appears, type **yes** and press **Enter**. The password prompt appears.

16. Enter the password for the root account and press **Enter**. The rsync command indicates that it is building a list of files to transfer to the remote computer, lists the files it transfers, and then summarizes the size and speed of the transfer.

17. Type **echo "New file" >/usr/local/newfile.txt** and press **Enter**. The computer creates a text file containing the text "New file."

18. Repeat Steps 15 and 16. The rsync command indicates that it is building a list of files to be copied and displays the names of the files and directories that have changed. (A directory in Linux changes when files are added to or removed from it.)

19. Log on to *LINUX2.NETPLUSLAB.NET* as the netplus user. Open a terminal window, type **su -** and press **Enter**. Enter the password for the root account and press **Enter**.

20. In the terminal window on *LINUX2.NETPLUSLAB.NET*, type **cd /tmp** and press **Enter**. This is the directory to which the rsync command copied files from *LINUX1 .NETPLUSLAB.NET*.

21. Type **cd local** and press **Enter**. The computer changes the current directory to /tmp/local.

22. Type **ls** and press **Enter**. The computer displays a list of all the files and directories copied from *LINUX1.NETPLUSLAB.NET*.

23. Type **cat netplus.txt** and press **Enter**. The computer displays the contents of the netplus.txt file.

24. Type **cat newfile.txt** and press **Enter**. The computer displays the contents of the newfile.txt file.

25. Log off both computers.

Certification Objectives

Objectives for the CompTIA Network+ Exam:

- 2.3 Given a scenario, use appropriate resources to support configuration management

Review Questions

1. Which of the following programs would be used to back up data to a tape drive on a Linux computer?

    a. tar

    b. gzip

    c. rsync

    d. cat

2. Which of the following commands could *not* be used in the process of creating backups on a Linux computer?

    a. tar

    b. rsync

    c. bzip2

    d. cat

3. Which of the following commands would create an archive file named march13.tar.gz containing the directory /usr and all of the files and directories within it and compressed by the gzip command?

    a. tar -jzvf march13.tar.gz /usr

    b. tar -zxvf march13.tar.gz /usr

    c. tar -jcvf march13.tar.gz /usr

    d. tar -zcf march13.tar.gz /usr

4. Which programs are likely to have made a file named `foo.tar.bz2`?

   a. rsync and bz2

   b. ssh and bz2

   c. tar and gzip

   d. tar and bzip2

5. You are a network administrator working for Red Rectangle Manufacturing. Red Rectangle has 12 servers, which it would like to back up to a single server attached to a tape library capable of backing up many computers. How would you use the tools in this lab to accomplish this task?

   a. Use the `tar` command every night to back up each server individually, then transfer the tar files to the backup server with floppies.

   b. Use the `tar` command every night to back up each server individually, then transfer the files using the `ssh` command.

   c. Use the `rsync` command each night to back up each server to the backup server, then use the `tar` command to create an archive file for each server.

   d. Use the `rsync` command each night to back up each server to the backup server, then use the `tar` command to write each backup to a separate tape.

CHAPTER TEN

NETWORK SEGMENTATION AND VIRTUALIZATION

Labs included in this chapter

- Lab 10.1 Subnetting a Network
- Lab 10.2 Understanding the Purpose of the Default Gateway
- Lab 10.3 Understanding the TCP/IP Hosts File
- Lab 10.4 Setting Up a Virtual FTP Server
- Lab 10.5 Configuring a Virtual Mail Server
- Lab 10.6 Investigating Server Virtualization Options

CompTIA Network+ Exam Objectives

Objective	Lab
1.3 Install and configure the following networking services/applications	10.3
1.8 Given a scenario, implement and configure the appropriate addressing schema	10.1
1.9 Explain the basics of routing concepts and protocols	10.2
1.11 Compare and contrast technologies that support cloud and virtualization	10.4, 10.5, 10.6
4.2 Given a scenario, analyze and interpret the output of troubleshooting tools	10.2
4.6 Given a scenario, troubleshoot and resolve common network issues	10.2

Lab 10.1 Subnetting a Network

Objectives

Subnetting allows you to divide a single network into several smaller, separate networks. This might be done to enhance security, improve performance, or simplify network trouble-shooting. Subnetting is accomplished by changing the subnet mask on each of the computers in a network. Because subnet masks are used to determine which part of an IP address corresponds to the network address, changing the subnet mask can also change the network address. In this lab, you will subnet a network by changing the subnet mask on the host computers.

After completing this lab, you will be able to:

- Subnet a network into several smaller networks

Materials Required

This lab will require the following:

- A computer running Windows 8.1 or Windows 7 named *WORKSTATION1* and configured with an IP address of 192.168.54.3, a subnet mask of 255.255.255.0, no default gateway, and Windows Firewall disabled
- A computer running Windows 8.1 or Windows 7 named *WORKSTATION2* and configured with an IP address of 192.168.54.132, a subnet mask of 255.255.255.0, no default gateway, and the Windows firewall disabled
- Administrative access to both computers
- Both computers connected to an Ethernet switch (not a router) with straight-through Cat 5 (or better) UTP cables
- Pencil and paper

Most of the steps in this lab can also be completed using virtualization software such as VMware.

Estimated completion time: **30 minutes**

Activity

1. Log on to *WORKSTATION1* as an administrator. The Windows desktop appears.

2. Open a Command Prompt window.

3. At the command prompt, type **ping 192.168.54.132** and press **Enter**. The computer indicates that it has received four replies from the remote computer and is, therefore, on the same network.

4. On *WORKSTATION1*, right-click **Start**, click **Control Panel**, click **Network and Internet**, click **Network and Sharing Center**, and then click **Change adapter settings**.

5. Right-click **Ethernet0** (or the name of your NIC), and then click **Properties** from the shortcut menu. The Ethernet0 Properties window opens.

6. Double-click **Internet Protocol Version 4 (TCP/IPv4)**.

7. Change the subnet mask from 255.255.255.0 to **255.255.255.240**. This creates 16 new networks from your original Class C network.

8. Repeat Steps 4 through 7 on *WORKSTATION2* to change its subnet mask as well.

9. Use ping to test the connection between *WORKSTATION1* and *WORKSTATION2* (see Steps 2 and 3). The ping test is not successful because the computers are now on separate networks. *WORKSTATION1* is still on network 192.168.54.0, whereas *WORKSTATION2* has been moved to network 192.168.54.128.

10. On a separate piece of paper, create a chart containing the network addresses, broadcast addresses, and assignable ranges for all 16 new networks.

11. Test your chart by assigning both *WORKSTATION1* and *WORKSTATION2* new IP addresses from the third new network created.

12. Use ping to test the connection between *WORKSTATION1* and *WORKSTATION2*. Because they're now on the same network, they should again be able to ping.

13. Log off both computers.

Certification Objectives

Objectives for the CompTIA Network+ Exam:

- 1.8 Given a scenario, implement and configure the appropriate addressing schema

Review Questions

1. What Boolean function is used to derive the network address by combining the IP address with the subnet mask?

   a. NAND

   b. AND

   c. OR

   d. NOT

2. Why are *WORKSTATION1* and *WORKSTATION2* no longer able to communicate?

   a. They have different IP addresses.

   b. They are on different networks.

   c. TCP/IP was uninstalled on *WORKSTATION2*.

   d. The ping command can be used only once.

3. Which of the following is *not* an advantage of subnetting?

   a. Enhanced network security

   b. More hosts per network

   c. Improved network performance

   d. Simplified network troubleshooting

4. How is subnetting accomplished?

   a. By changing the subnet mask on the host computers

   b. By changing the IP address on the host computers

   c. By installing the subnet protocol

   d. By installing a router running DHCP

5. What is the default subnet mask for a Class C network?

   a. 255.0.0.0

   b. 255.255.0.0

   c. 255.255.255.0

   d. 255.255.255.255

Lab 10.2 Understanding the Purpose of the Default Gateway

Objectives

To ensure that a computer knows where to send packets outside its own network, you can configure a default gateway. The default gateway is a computer or router that knows where to send packets so that they reach their destination. Often, the default gateway appears in a computer's routing table as a route to 0.0.0.0 with a subnet mask of 0.0.0.0. The IP address 0.0.0.0 is a generic way to refer to all possible IP addresses.

For instance, suppose a small network has a single router that is attached to the Internet. Suppose also that each computer on the network has this Internet router configured as its default gateway. Each computer has a route in its routing table for the local network so it can send packets bound for local network resources to the appropriate computer. If the address of a network resource is not on the local network, each computer sends the packet to the Internet router. The Internet router knows where to send the packet so that it reaches its destination.

Often, the Internet router's routing table specifies just a few local routes and a default route to an ISP router. It sends any packet with a destination address that is not in its routing table to the ISP router. The ISP router usually has a large routing table containing information about destination networks on the Internet.

After completing this lab, you will be able to:

- Identify the purpose of a default gateway
- Configure a default gateway

Materials Required

This lab will require the following:

- A computer running Windows 8.1 or Windows 7 named *WORKSTATION1* and configured with an IP address of 192.168.54.3, a subnet mask of 255.255.255.0, no default gateway, and the Windows firewall disabled

- A computer running Windows 8.1 or Windows 7 named *WORKSTATION2* and configured with an IP address of 192.168.54.4, a subnet mask of 255.255.255.0, no default gateway, and the Windows firewall disabled

- Administrative access to both computers

- Both computers connected to an Ethernet switch with straight-through Cat 5 (or better) UTP cables

Most of the steps in this lab can also be completed using virtualization software such as VMware.

Estimated completion time: **30 minutes**

Activity

1. Log on to *WORKSTATION1* as an administrator. The Windows desktop appears.

2. Open a Command Prompt window.

3. At the command prompt, type **ping 192.168.54.4** and press **Enter**. The computer indicates that it has received four replies from the remote computer.

4. Repeat Steps 1 through 3 on *WORKSTATION2*, but this time ping the address **192.168.54.3** instead.

5. Now you will add a secondary IP address to one of the computers. On *WORKSTATION1*, right-click **Start**, click **Control Panel**, click **Network and Internet**, click **Network and Sharing Center**, and then click **Change adapter settings**. The Network Connections window opens.

6. Right-click **Ethernet0** and then click **Properties** from the shortcut menu. The Ethernet0 Properties window opens.

7. Double-click **Internet Protocol Version 4 (TCP/IPv4)**. The Internet Protocol Version 4 (TCP/IPv4) Properties window opens.

8. Click **Advanced**. The Advanced TCP/IP Settings window opens, as shown in Figure 10-1.

9. Below the IP addresses box, click **Add**. The TCP/IP Address window opens. In the IP address text box, type **172.16.1.1**. In the Subnet mask text box, type **255.255.255.0**.

10. Click **Add**, and then click **OK** three times to finish configuring the secondary IP address.

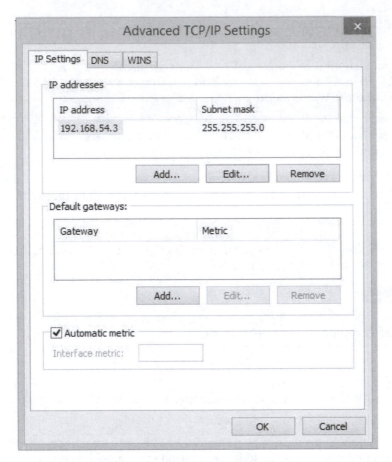

Figure 10-1 The Advanced TCP/IP Settings window

11. In the Command Prompt window on *WORKSTATION2*, type **ping 172.16.1.1** and press **Enter**. The computer indicates that it is unable to reach the remote computer. *WORKSTATION2* does not know where to send packets destined for 172.16.1.1.

12. Type **netstat -r** and press **Enter** to display the routing table on *WORKSTATION2*. Record the destination addresses listed in the routing table.

13. You now add a default gateway to *WORKSTATION2*. Repeat Steps 5 through 7 on *WORKSTATION2* to open the Internet Protocol Version 4 (TCP/IPv4) Properties window.

14. In the Default gateway text box, type **192.168.54.3**. This tells *WORKSTATION2* to send packets to 192.168.54.3 whenever it does not have another route for them. Click **OK**, and then click **Close**.

15. At the command prompt on *WORKSTATION2*, type **ping 172.16.1.1**. The computer indicates that it has received four replies from *WORKSTATION1*.

16. Type **netstat –r** and press **Enter** to show the routing table again on *WORKSTATION2*. Compare this routing table with the one you saw in Step 12. Record the new destination addresses.

17. Log off both computers.

Certification Objectives

Objectives for the CompTIA Network+ Exam:

- 1.9 Explain the basics of routing concepts and protocols
- 4.2 Given a scenario, analyze and interpret the output of troubleshooting tools
- 4.6 Given a scenario, troubleshoot and resolve common network issues

Review Questions

1. What is the purpose of the default gateway?

   a. To assign IP addresses to clients as soon as they log on to the network

   b. To ensure that no two nodes on the same subnet have identical TCP/IP addresses

   c. To accept and relay packets from nodes on one network destined for nodes on another network

   d. To advertise the best, current routing paths between networks from one router to another

2. Which of the following is most likely to act as a default gateway?

   a. Modem

   b. Hub

   c. Switch

   d. Router

3. What type of information would the netstat –r command yield when typed at the command prompt of a networked client?

   a. A list of all routers to which that client might connect

   b. A list of the client's NIC adapter IP addresses

   c. The client's routing table

   d. The client's TCP/IP settings

4. What is the default subnet mask for a Class B network in the IP version 4 addressing scheme?

   a. 255.255.0.0

   b. 255.255.255.0

   c. 255.255.255.255

   d. 0.0.0.0

5. Which of the following utilities can show the route a packet traverses between its source node and destination node on a network?

a. Ping

b. Nbtstat

c. Netstat

d. Tracert

Lab 10.3 Understanding the TCP/IP Hosts File

Objectives

To use host names instead of IP addresses to reach remote computers, a computer must have some way to find the IP address that corresponds to each remote computer. One of the simplest ways to do this is to use the hosts file. The hosts file contains a list of IP addresses and the names of the computers at those addresses. When the computer recognizes the name of another computer in its hosts file, it uses the associated IP address when it tries to communicate with that computer.

Because it would be impossible to distribute hosts files to all the computers on the Internet, computers typically use the Domain Name System (DNS) to associate host names with IP addresses rather than use a copy of the hosts file. However, the hosts file is often useful as a temporary measure or when you cannot make a DNS entry. The hosts file can be useful, for example, when you want to make a DNS entry in a domain you do not control or when you are using Network Address Translation (NAT). An IP address translated by NAT might not match the actual IP address of a computer, but a hosts entry forces the computer to use the appropriate IP address.

After completing this lab, you will be able to:

- Identify the purpose of the hosts file
- Modify a computer's hosts file
- Connect to another computer using its host name

Materials Required

This lab will require the following:

- A computer running Windows 8.1 or Windows 7 named *WORKSTATION1* with an IP address of 192.168.54.3 and a subnet mask of 255.255.255.0
- Administrative access to the Windows computer
- A computer running a current version of Linux such as Ubuntu or Fedora named *LINUX1.NETPLUSLAB.NET*, installed as a server with no firewall
- *LINUX1.NETPLUSLAB.NET* configured with an IP address of 192.168.54.5 and a subnet mask of 255.255.255.0

- A user named *netplus* on *LINUX1.NETPLUSLAB.NET* and the root password for *LINUX1.NETPLUSLAB.NET*
- Each computer connected to a switch with straight-through Cat 5 (or better) UTP cables

Most of the steps in this lab can also be completed using virtualization software such as VMware.

Estimated completion time: **25 minutes**

Activity

1. Log on to *WORKSTATION1* as an administrator. The Windows desktop appears.

2. Open a Command Prompt window.

3. In the Command Prompt window, type **cd C:\windows\system32\drivers\etc** and press **Enter**. On a Windows computer, this directory contains the hosts file.

4. To modify the hosts file, type **notepad hosts** and press **Enter**. Notepad opens with the text of the hosts file. Note that many lines begin with a pound sign (#). These lines are comments and are ignored by the computer when it uses the hosts file.

5. At the bottom of the file, on a line by itself, type **192.168.54.5 linux1 .netpluslab.net**. Click **File** on the menu bar, and then click **Save**. Figure 10-2 shows the Windows 8.1 hosts file.

Figure 10-2   Windows 8.1 hosts file

6. Click **File** on the menu bar, and then click **Exit**. Notepad closes.

7. At the command prompt, type **ping linux1.netpluslab.net** and press **Enter**. The computer indicates that it has received four replies from *LINUX1.NETPLUSLAB.NET*.

8. Log on to *LINUX1.NETPLUSLAB.NET* as the netplus user. The desktop appears.

9. Open a terminal window. At the prompt, type **su –** and press **Enter**. The Password prompt appears.

10. Type the root password for *LINUX1.NETPLUSLAB.NET*, and press **Enter**. The prompt changes to end in #, indicating that you are now logged on as the root user.

11. Type **cd /etc** and press **Enter**.

12. Type **echo "192.168.54.3 workstation1.netpluslab.net" >> hosts** and press **Enter**. The computer appends the IP address and the host name between the quotation marks into the hosts file.

13. To see what the hosts file contains, type **cat hosts** and press **Enter**. The computer displays the contents of the hosts file.

14. Type **ping workstation1.netpluslab.net** and press **Enter**. The computer indicates that it is receiving replies from *WORKSTATION1*. Press **Ctrl+C** to stop the ping utility.

15. Log off both computers.

Certification Objectives

Objectives for the CompTIA Network+ Exam:

• 1.3 Install and configure the following networking services/applications

Review Questions

1. What is the purpose of a host name?

   a. To uniquely identify a node on a network

   b. To associate a node with a particular domain

   c. To indicate which domain a node belongs to

   d. To identify the IP address of a host

2. What is the purpose of a hosts file?

   a. To help determine the best route for packets between gateways

   b. To make it easier for network administrators to remember a computer's IP address

   c. To map IP addresses to host names

   d. To indicate which hosts on a network are available to a client

3. What file on a Linux system holds information about host names and their IP addresses?

   a. /etc/hosts

   b. /bin/hosts

   c. /lib/users/hostfile

   d. /root/hostfile

4. Which of the following symbols indicates a comment in the hosts file?

   a. >

   b. >>

   c. :

   d. #

5. What is the alias of the computer whose host name is C2 in the following hosts file?

160.12.122.13	C1C2.gameco.com	canasta
156.11.21.145	Comp2.gameco.com	chess
123.14.11.214	C2.gameco.com	checkers
44.112.133.15	CIC2.gameco.com	backgammon

   a. canasta

   b. chess

   c. checkers

   d. backgammon

Lab 10.4 Setting Up a Virtual FTP Server

Objectives

With virtualization software, one physical machine can host more than one virtual machine. This software can range from products that only emulate a couple of desktop workstations up to more complex (and expensive) software that can virtualize a large number of servers. In this lab, you will install Microsoft Server 2012 R2 in a virtual environment using VMware Workstation 10 and then configure it as an FTP server. In Lab 10.5, you will add a second virtual machine acting as a mail server.

File Transfer Protocol (FTP) is an Application layer protocol used to send and receive files. The process requires both server and client software. In Lab 2.6, you learned how to use an FTP client to download files from an FTP server running on a remote host. In this lab, you will learn how to install and configure the FTP service on Windows Server running in a virtual environment.

After completing this lab, you will be able to:

- Install the FTP service in IIS on a virtual server

- Set permissions so that certain users can connect to the FTP server and download files

Materials Required

This lab will require the following:

- A computer running Windows 8.1 or Windows 7 running VMware Workstation 10 from Lab 1.2 with an IP address of 192.168.54.1 and a subnet mask of 255.255.255.0
- A Windows Server 2012 R2 DVD or ISO file
- Access to *SERVER1* as the administrator
- A second computer running Windows 8.1 or Windows 7, configured with an IP address of 192.168.54.3 and a subnet mask of 255.255.255.0
- Both computers connected to a switch with Cat 5 (or better) UTP cables

Estimated completion time: **30–60 minutes**

Activity

1. Log on to your physical machine as an administrator and launch VMware Workstation 10.
2. Click the **Create a New Virtual Machine** icon in the File menu. The New Virtual Machine Wizard opens.
3. Select **Custom (advanced)** and click **Next**.
4. Click **Next** to accept the default hardware compatibility.
5. Select the location of your Windows Server installation DVD or ISO file and click **Next**.
6. Enter the Windows product key and select Windows Server 2012 R2 Standard as the Version of Windows to install.
7. Enter a password, record it so you don't forget it later, and click **Next**.
8. Change the Virtual machine name to *SERVER1*.
9. Record the location of the virtual machine and click **Next**.
10. Accept the default Processor Configuration unless your instructor suggests otherwise, and then click **Next**.
11. If your physical machine has 8 GB of RAM or more, allocate 2 GB of RAM to the virtual server. Otherwise, set the memory for the virtual server to 1 GB. Click **Next**.
12. Choose **Use bridged networking** as the network type and click **Next**.
13. Continue to click **Next** to accept the default selections for I/O controller types, disk type, and disk selection.
14. Accept the default maximum disk size and click **Next**.
15. Click **Next** again to use the default disk filename.
16. Review your virtual machine selections and click **Finish**. VMware Workstation will take a few minutes to create the virtual machine, power it on, and begin installing Windows Server.
17. Windows Setup will handle most of the installation process and may restart the virtual machine several times.

18. VMware Workstation now has a tab for your virtual server.

19. Log on to *SERVER1* as the administrator. Windows Server Manager opens.

20. Click **Manage**, and then click **Add Roles and Features**. The Add Roles and Features Wizard opens.

21. Click **Next** to continue, click **Role-based or feature-based installation** if necessary, and click **Next** twice.

22. Select the **Web Server (IIS)** check box, and click the right arrow to expand the list of associated roles. Click **Add Features** and click **Next** three times.

23. Select **FTP Server**, and click **Next**.

24. Click **Install** to confirm your installation selections, and click **Close** after the installation is complete.

25. Click **Tools**, click **Internet Information Services (IIS) Manager**, and click **Start** (if necessary).

26. Double-click *SERVER1*, and then double-click **Sites**. If the Microsoft Web Platform opens, click Cancel.

27. Click **Add FTP Site** in the right pane.

28. Name the site **FTP** and choose **C:\inetpub\ftproot** for the physical path. Click **Next**.

29. Choose the IP address of your server and select **No SSL**. Click **Next**.

30. Select **Anonymous** authentication and allow access for **Anonymous users**. Give users Read and Write permissions and click **Finish**.

31. Click **FTP** in the left pane. The Internet Information Services (IIS) Manager displays information about the FTP site, as shown in Figure 10-3.

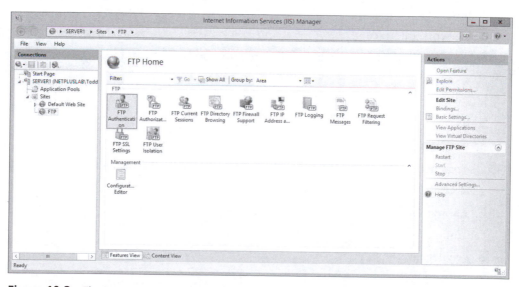

Figure 10-3   The Internet Information Services (IIS) Manager

32. Open a Command Prompt window.

33. In the Command Prompt window, type `echo` *your name* `>` `C:\Inetpub\ftproot` `\netplus.txt` and press **Enter**. (Substitute your name for *your name*.) This creates a file named *netplus.txt* containing your name in the C:\Inetpub\ftproot directory.

34. Use the skills you learned in Lab 2.6 to connect to the FTP server from the Windows client.

35. When you're finished, close any open windows and log off both computers.

Certification Objectives

Objectives for the CompTIA Network+ Exam:

- 1.11 Compare and contrast technologies that support cloud and virtualization

Review Questions

1. What is the default FTP directory in Windows Server 2012 R2?

   a. C:\ftp\root

   b. C:\root\dir\ftp

   c. C:\ftproot\ftproot

   d. C:\Inetpub\ftproot

2. The FTP protocol functions at which layer?

   a. Application

   b. Transport

   c. Internetwork

   d. Network Interface

3. Using FTP to upload or download data requires both server and _____ software.

   a. session

   b. client

   c. IIS

   d. remote host

4. General access to an FTP server is referred to as what kind of access?

   a. Root

   b. Anonymous

   c. Limited

   d. Privileged

Lab 10.5 Configuring a Virtual Mail Server

Objectives

Email is one of the most important applications on the majority of business networks. Email is sent from a user's computer to its destination using the Simple Mail Transfer Protocol (SMTP). A wide variety of programs run SMTP. In this lab, you will configure one such program, Sendmail, which is used primarily on Linux and UNIX computers.

A computer running SMTP looks at the domain name in the email address and performs a DNS lookup to find the mail exchanger, or MX, record for the domain. The MX record is the domain name of the email server where email for that domain must be sent. For instance, the netpluslab.net domain might have an MX record of linux1.netpluslab.net. This tells other computers running SMTP that any email sent to email addresses in the netpluslab.net domain (such as netplus@netpluslab.net) should be sent to the server linux1.netpluslab.net. As you might expect, DNS must be properly configured for SMTP to work correctly and for email to be delivered. A domain might have multiple MX records with different priorities, which allows for load balancing or for a backup server to collect email in case the primary server fails.

After an email has been delivered to its final destination, the user must collect it. Email programs employ a variety of methods to collect email. Some popular protocols used for collecting email include POP3 and IMAP. In this lab, you will configure the Windows Live Mail program to use POP3 to collect email. Typically, settings for receiving mail are given to users by their network administrators.

After completing this lab, you will be able to:

- Configure an email server

Materials Required

This lab will require the following:

- A computer running Windows 8.1 or Windows 7 running VMware Workstation 10 from Lab 1.2 or 10.4

- A virtual computer image running Windows Server 2012 R2 named *SERVER1*, configured as a domain controller for the netpluslab.net domain and with an IP address of 192.168.54.1 and a subnet mask of 255.255.255.0

- A user named *netplus* configured in the netpluslab.net domain

- A second virtual computer image running Windows 8.1 or Windows 7 named *WORKSTATION1* configured with an IP address of 192.168.54.3 and a subnet mask of 255.255.255.0

- A Windows Mail client installed on *WORKSTATION1* such as Windows Live Mail

- A third virtual computer running a current version of Linux such as Ubuntu or Fedora named *LINUX1.NETPLUSLAB.NET*, installed as a server with no firewall; in addition to the Mail Server package, Dovecot IMAP needs to be installed

- *LINUX1.NETPLUSLAB.NET* configured with an IP address of 192.168.54.5 and a subnet mask of 255.255.255.0
- A user named *netplus* on *LINUX1.NETPLUSLAB.NET*
- *LINUX1.NETPLUSLAB.NET* configured to use 192.168.54.1 as its DNS server; the file /etc/resolv.conf should contain the line `nameserver 192.168.54.1`
- The DNS server on *SERVER1* configured and running, with a domain named *net-pluslab.net*
- Forward and reverse DNS entries for *LINUX1.NETPLUSLAB.NET* at 192.168.54.5 and for *WORKSTATION1.NETPLUSLAB.NET* at 192.168.54.3
- All three virtual computers configured to use 192.168.54.1 for DNS resolution
- A line in the /etc/hosts file on *LINUX1.NETPLUSLAB.NET* for 192.168.54.5 containing the text `192.168.54.5 linux1.netpluslab.net`
- No email accounts already configured on *WORKSTATION1*
- The default /etc/mail/sendmail.mc and /etc/dovecot.conf or /etc/dovecot/dovecot.conf files on *LINUX1.NETPLUSLAB.NET*

 Filenames and paths may vary with different Linux distributions.

NOTE

Estimated completion time: **90–120 minutes**

Activity

1. Log on to *LINUX1.NETPLUSLAB.NET* as the netplus user. The Linux desktop appears.
2. Open a terminal window, and, at the prompt, type **su –** and press **Enter**. The Password prompt appears. Type the root password, and press **Enter**. The prompt now ends in a pound sign (#), indicating that you are logged on as the root user.
3. Next, you configure the dovecot daemon to allow users to check for email from this computer. Dovecot is one of a variety of programs that delivers email to users using POP3, IMAP3, and other protocols. Type **vi /etc/dovecot.conf** and press **Enter**. The vi editor opens the file /etc/dovecot.conf in normal mode.
4. Press **G** to move the cursor to the last line of the file and press **O** to insert a new line.
5. Press **i**. The vi editor enters insert mode.
6. Type **protocols = pop3** and press **Esc**. The vi editor enters normal mode.
7. Type **:wq** and press **Enter**. The vi editor saves the file and exits.
8. Type **sudo service dovecot restart** and press **Enter**. The computer starts the Dovecot mail server.

9. Now you configure the Sendmail program so that this computer can be used to send email. Type **vi /etc/mail/sendmail.mc** and press **Enter**. The /etc/mail/sendmail.mc file opens.

10. Type **/127.0.0.1** and press **Enter**. The vi editor searches for the text 127.0.0.1. Type **/** and press **Enter**. The vi editor searches for the text from the previous search (127.0.0.1). Repeat until the vi editor places the cursor at the beginning of the IP address 127.0.0.1 in the line DAEMON OPTIONS('Port=smtp,Addr=127.0.0.1, Name=MTA') dnl.

11. Press 0. The cursor moves to the beginning of the line.

12. Press i. The vi editor goes into insert mode.

13. Type **dnl #** at the beginning of the line. This command tells the computer to ignore this line when the file is processed later in the lab. Press **Esc** to put the vi editor back into normal mode.

14. Type **/LOCAL_DOMAIN** and press **Enter**. The cursor moves to the start of a line containing the text LOCAL_DOMAIN.

15. Press **w** twice. The cursor moves to the beginning of the word localhost. localdomain.

16. Type **d3w**. The computer deletes the text localhost.localdomain.

17. Press i. The vi editor goes into insert mode. Type **netpluslab.net** and press **Esc**.

18. Type **:wq** and press **Enter**. The vi editor saves the file and then closes.

19. Type **cd /etc/mail** and press **Enter**. The computer changes your current working directory to /etc/mail.

20. Type **make** and press **Enter**. The computer processes the changes you made in the sendmail.mc file and places them in the sendmail.cf file.

21. Type **sudo service sendmail restart** and press **Enter**. The computer restarts the Sendmail daemon with the configuration changes you have made.

22. Now you will configure DNS so that each computer on the network knows where to send email. Log on to *SERVER1* as the administrator. Windows Server Manager opens.

23. Click **Tools**, and then click **DNS**. The DNS Manager window opens.

24. In the left pane of the window, click **SERVER1**. Icons appear in the right pane.

25. Double-click the **Forward Lookup Zones** icon in the right pane of the window. A list of domains appears. Double-click the **netpluslab.net** icon in the right pane.

26. Right-click **netpluslab.net** in the left pane, and click **New Mail Exchanger (MX)**. The New Resource Record dialog box opens.

27. In the "Fully qualified domain name (FQDN) of mail server" text box, enter **linux1 .netpluslab.net**. See Figure 10-4.

28. Click **OK**. The New Resource Record dialog box closes. Right-click the **netpluslab.net** icon, and click **Reload**. The DNS dialog box opens, asking if you want to reload the domain.

29. Click **Yes**. The computer reloads the netpluslab.net domain.

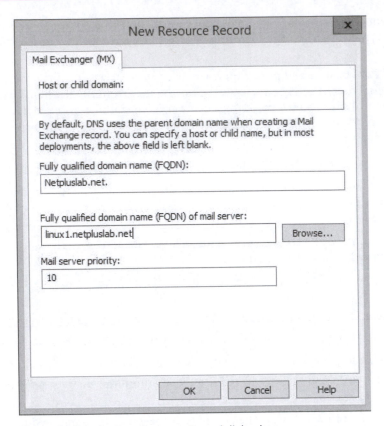

Figure 10-4 The New Resource Record dialog box

30. Log on to *WORKSTATION1* as the netplus user. The Windows desktop appears.

31. Click **Start**, type **windows live mail** in the Start Search text box, and then press **Enter**. The Windows Live Mail program opens. If necessary, accept the service agreement.

32. In the Email address text box, enter **netplus@netpluslab.net**.

33. In the Password text box, enter the password for the netplus account on *LINUX1. NETPLUSLAB.NET*.

34. Click the **Manually configure server settings** check box, and click **Next**.

35. In the Incoming Server address text box, enter **linux1.netpluslab.net**. In the Outgoing Server address text box, enter **linux1.netpluslab.net**. Click **Next**.

36. A window indicates that your email account was added. Click **Finish**.

37. In the Windows Live Mail window, click **Email message**. The New Message window opens.

38. In the To… text box, enter **netplus@netpluslab.net**. In the Subject text box, enter **Test Message**. In the bottom window, enter your name. Click **Send**. Windows Mail sends the message.

39. Click **Send/Receive**. The Windows Live Mail dialog box opens briefly as the program checks for email.

40. In the tree in the left pane, click **Inbox**. In the upper-right pane, a message with the subject "Test Message" appears.

41. Double-click the message with the subject "Test Message" to open it in a new window.

42. Click the **Windows Live Mail** tab on the Ribbon, and then click **Close** to close the Test Message window.

43. Click the **Windows Live Mail** tab on the Ribbon, and then click **Exit**. Windows Live Mail closes.

44. Log off all three virtual computers.

Certification Objectives

Objectives for the CompTIA Network+ Exam:

- 1.11 Compare and contrast technologies that support cloud and virtualization

Review Questions

1. Which of the following protocols is used to send email?

   a. POP3

   b. SMTP

   c. IMAP

   d. SNMP

2. You are sending email to your friend Bob, whose email address is bob@otherdomain.com. What information does your SMTP server need to deliver this email to Bob?

   a. It needs to look up the IP address of otherdomain.com.

   b. It needs to look up the IP address of the otherdomain.com POP3 server.

   c. It needs to use the MX record for the otherdomain.com domain to find the IP address of the appropriate IMAP server.

   d. It needs to use the MX record for the otherdomain.com domain to find the IP address of the appropriate SMTP server.

3. The DNS server on your network is not functioning properly. Which of the following is *not* a possible consequence of this?

   a. User email programs inside your network are unable to find the IP address of your SMTP server.

   b. SMTP servers outside your network are unable to make TCP connections to your mail server.

   c. Your SMTP server is unable to find the IP addresses of remote mail servers.

   d. User email programs inside your network are unable to find the IP address of your IMAP server.

4. Why is it important to secure and configure a mail server properly?

   a. A misconfigured or improperly secured mail server might not be able to deliver email.

   b. A misconfigured or improperly secured mail server might be hijacked to send large amounts of unsolicited commercial email.

   c. A misconfigured or improperly secured mail server might not be able to run SMTP.

   d. A misconfigured or improperly secured mail server might not allow clients to download their email.

5. A user has been given an email address of sally@otherorg.net. How is this user most likely to determine the settings she needs to receive email?

   a. From the MX record for the otherorg.net domain

   b. By finding the IP address of the otherorg.net domain

   c. From the network administrator

   d. From other SMTP servers on the Internet

Lab 10.6 Investigating Server Virtualization Options

Objectives

The difference between hosting a single virtual workstation and hosting a large number of virtual servers is mostly one of scale. Most software providers offer a range of products to meet your specific needs. Some are intended to give a user access to a number of different operating systems on a single desktop computer, while others will virtualize multiple servers on a single machine. In this lab, you will compare several virtualization programs in terms of price and features.

After completing this lab, you will be able to:

- Compare virtualization software in terms of price and features

Materials Required

This lab will require the following:

- Pencil and paper
- A computer running Windows 8.1 or Windows 7 with Internet access
- An ordinary user account on the computer

Estimated completion time: **30 minutes**

Activity

1. Log on to the computer as an ordinary user. The Windows desktop appears.

2. Open your browser and browse the Web sites of the following distributors of virtualization software:

   - *vmware.com*
   - *virtualbox.org*
   - *microsoft.com*
   - *citrix.com*
   - *linux-kvm.org*

3. Do any of these distributors offer a solution for virtualizing a Windows desktop? If so, list the distributor, product names, latest versions, system requirements, and cost.

4. Do any of these distributors offer a solution for virtualizing multiple Windows servers? If so, list the distributor, product names, latest versions, system requirements, and cost.

5. Compare the most popular server virtualization solutions. What are the key advantages and disadvantages of each? Please cite your sources.

6. Imagine that you've been asked to select a product to virtualize 16 Web servers on a single physical server. What kinds of information would you need to ask before making a choice?

7. When you're finished, log off the computer.

Certification Objectives

Objectives for the CompTIA Network+ Exam:

- 1.11 Compare and contrast technologies that support cloud and virtualization

Review Questions

1. Which is not emulated by virtualization?

   a. Hardware

   b. Applications

   c. Operating system

   d. Users

2. The physical machine running the virtualization software is called a _____.

   a. host

   b. client

   c. hypervisor

   d. guest

3. The most widely used virtualization software in use today is made by _____.

   a. Microsoft

   b. Oracle

   c. Citrix

   d. VMware

4. A virtual network adapter operates at which layer of the OSI model?

   a. Data Link

   b. Transport

   c. Session

   d. Network

5. In _____ mode the virtualization software acts as a DHCP server.

   a. NAT

   b. host-only

   c. server-only

   d. bridged

CHAPTER ELEVEN

WIDE AREA NETWORKS

Labs included in this chapter

- Lab 11.1 Pricing WAN Services
- Lab 11.2 Connecting to the Internet with a Modem
- Lab 11.3 Connecting to a Cisco Router with Telnet
- Lab 11.4 Connecting to a Cisco Router with a Terminal Emulator
- Lab 11.5 Configuring a Cisco Router at the Command Line

CompTIA Network+ Exam Objectives

Objective	Lab
1.1 Explain the functions and applications of various network devices	11.2, 11.3, 11.4, 11.5
1.4 Explain the characteristics and benefits of various WAN technologies	11.1, 11.2
1.6 Differentiate between common network topologies	11.1
4.8 Given a scenario, troubleshoot and resolve common WAN issues	11.4, 11.5

Lab 11.1 Pricing WAN Services

Objectives

In this lab, you will price several options for WAN services. Many organizations use multiple types of WAN links for redundancy and to eliminate single points of failure on the network. For example, an organization might use T-1s to connect its two largest remote offices to its central office, and it might use ISDN lines as backups in case either T-1 fails. To connect its smaller offices to the central office, an organization might use ISDN lines as the primary link and a dial-up modem as the backup link. Many organizations will also have a backup link for their Internet connection.

You can use these services to connect an organization to the Internet, as well as to connect offices in one location to offices in another. The pricing of Internet services is often more complicated, as you must purchase both a WAN link and Internet access itself. Depending on the type of WAN link, however, many WAN service providers offer both the WAN connection and the Internet access. Many telephone companies, for example, install a T-1 and then provide Internet access along with the T-1 service.

WAN topologies can also have a huge impact on price. The star, partial-mesh, and full-mesh WAN topologies are used most commonly. Independent of the cost of the actual WAN, the star topology is the cheapest. A star topology consists of one link from a central office to each satellite office. For each new office you add, you need to add only one new link. However, a star topology offers no redundancy in case of a link failure. In a partial-mesh topology, some (but not all) of the satellite offices are interconnected. If one link fails, there is often (but not always) a backup link. The price of adding an office rises depending on the number of satellite offices and on the degree to which they are linked. In a full-mesh topology, all offices are connected to each other. The price of adding an office increases with the number of offices. With a large number of offices, a full-mesh WAN topology costs many times what a star topology for the same number of offices would cost. Other WAN topologies, such as bus and ring topologies, do not scale well and are rarely used for WANs with more than a handful of locations.

In this lab, you will have the choice of calling a local company for information or doing research on the Web. You will record information in Figure 11-1. If you choose to call a company, take time to review Figure 11-1 and the lab steps before calling, so you can speak knowledgeably and efficiently with the customer representative. In some cases, your instructor might want to minimize the disruption to local companies by making arrangements ahead of time. Take care to be polite and work as quickly as possible so as not to waste the representative's time. Remember to say "Thank you" when you are finished. Follow up with a thank-you email or letter after the call.

After completing this lab, you will be able to:

- Compare WAN links in terms of cost and speed
- Compare WAN topologies in terms of price and redundancy
- Identify WAN hardware components

Company name	
Phone call or Web research?	
Types of connections offered	
T-1	
Is service available in your area?	
Geographic restrictions	
Bandwidth	
Does the company charge a monthly fee, or does the cost vary with usage?	
Monthly fee/usage charges	
Additional equipment required?	
If additional equipment is required, does the company provide it?	
If additional equipment is required, is the hardware charge a single flat fee or a monthly charge?	
Typical hardware cost	
Setup fees	
Cable or DSL	
Is service available in your area?	
Geographic restrictions	
Bandwidth	
Does the company charge a monthly fee, or does the cost vary with usage?	
Monthly fee/usage charges	
Additional equipment required?	
If additional equipment is required, does the company provide it?	
If additional equipment is required, is the hardware charge a single flat fee or a monthly charge?	
Typical hardware cost	
Setup fees	
128-Kbps Partial T-1 or ISDN	
Is service available in your area?	
Geographic restrictions	
Bandwidth	
Does the company charge a monthly fee, or does the cost vary with usage?	

Figure 11-1 Table for recording answers to Lab 11.1 (*continues*)

Monthly fee/usage charges	
Additional equipment required?	
If additional equipment is required, does the company provide it?	
If additional equipment is required, is the hardware charge a single flat fee or a monthly charge?	
Typical hardware cost	
Setup fees	

Public Switched Telephone Network (PSTN) Connection

Is service available in your area?	
Geographic restrictions	
Bandwidth	
Does the company charge a monthly fee, or does the cost vary with usage?	
Monthly fee/usage charges	
Additional equipment required?	
If additional equipment is required, does the company provide it?	
If additional equipment is required, is the hardware charge a single flat fee or a monthly charge?	
Typical hardware cost	
Setup fees	

Totals

Total setup, installation, and equipment costs	T-1: DSL: 128-Kbps partial T-1 or ISDN: PSTN: Other:
Two years of service, excluding hardware	T-1: DSL: 128-Kbps partial T-1 or ISDN: PSTN: Other:
Two years of service for star topology shown in Figure 11-2, excluding hardware	T-1: DSL: 128-Kbps partial T-1 or ISDN: PSTN: Other:

Figure 11-1 Table for recording answers to Lab 11.1 (*continues*)

Two years of service for the partial mesh topology shown in Figure 11-3, excluding hardware	T-1: DSL: 128-Kbps partial T-1 or ISDN: PSTN: Other:
Two years of service for the full-mesh topology shown in Figure 11-4, excluding hardware	T-1: DSL: 128-Kbps partial T-1 or ISDN: PSTN: Other:

© Cengage Learning.

Figure 11-1   Table for recording answers to Lab 11.1 (*continued*)

Materials Required

This lab will require the following:

- Pencil and paper
- If some of the services discussed in this lab are not offered in your area, use representative pricing provided by your instructor for those services

Estimated completion time: **60–90 minutes**

Activity

1. Go to the Web site of a local Internet service provider or telephone company and look for information about the cost and availability of high-speed Internet links for businesses. Alternatively, call and speak to a representative. Explain that you are doing research for a school project on the pricing of Internet links. Give your name, the name of the networking class you are taking, and the name of your school.

2. In Figure 11-1, write the name of the company, and indicate whether you did your research on the Web or called directly.

3. What types of WAN services do they offer? (i.e., T-carrier, DSL, SONET, etc.) Record the answer in Figure 11-1.

4. Is T-1 service available in your area? Record the answer in Figure 11-1. If the service is available, are there any geographic restrictions on the service? For instance, some services might not be available in all areas because the necessary infrastructure has not yet been built. Record the geographic availability of the service in Figure 11-1.

5. If the service is available, find out the bandwidth of the service and record it in Figure 11-1.

6. Does the company charge a monthly fee for T-1 service, or does the charge vary depending on usage? Record this information in Figure 11-1.

7. If the company charges a monthly fee, record the amount in Figure 11-1; otherwise, record the usage charges.

8. Is any additional equipment required for the service and, if so, does the company provide it?

9. Is the hardware charge a onetime fee or a monthly charge? If necessary, ask for the typical price of the additional equipment. In Figure 11-1, record the typical hardware charge.

10. What are the typical setup fees, such as fees for the installation of the T-1 line itself? Record any setup fees in Figure 11-1.

11. Repeat Step 3 through Step 7, this time referencing DSL.

12. Repeat Step 3 through Step 7, this time referencing 128-Kbps partial T-1 or ISDN.

13. Repeat Step 3 through Step 7, this time referencing a Public Switched Telephone Network (PSTN) connection with a modem.

14. If you want, repeat Step 3 through Step 7, for any other WAN services offered by the carrier.

15. For each service, calculate the total setup and installation fees and the cost of equipment required (excluding monthly charges for hardware) and record this information in Figure 11-1.

16. For each service, calculate the cost of two years of service, including any monthly charges for hardware. If the service is billed based on usage, estimate the cost based on medium usage. Record the cost of two years of service.

17. For each service, compare the costs calculated in Step 15 and Step 16.

18. Now you will examine the effects of different WAN topologies on WAN pricing. Calculate the cost of T-1 service connecting each office in Figure 11-2 in the star WAN topology shown. Use the two-year monthly service fees you calculated in Step 16.

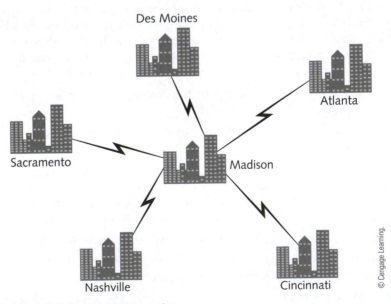

Figure 11-2 Star WAN topology

© Cengage Learning.

19. Calculate the cost of T-1 service connecting each office in the partial-mesh WAN topology shown in Figure 11-3. Use the two-year monthly service fees you calculated in Step 16.

20. Calculate the cost of T-1 service connecting each office in the full-mesh WAN topology shown in Figure 11-4. Use the two-year monthly service fees you calculated in Step 16.

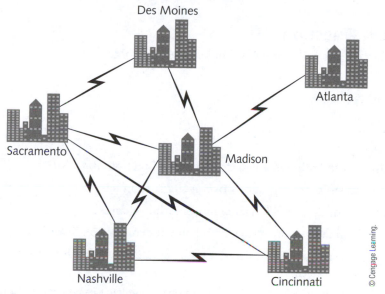

Figure 11-3   Partial-mesh WAN topology

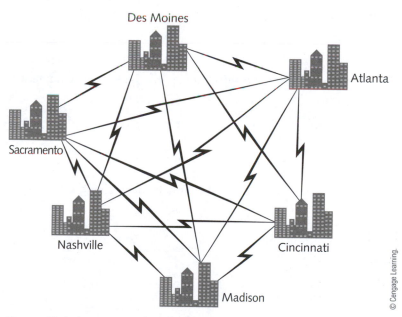

Figure 11-4   Full-mesh WAN topology

Certification Objectives

Objectives for the CompTIA Network+ Exam:

- 1.4 Explain the characteristics and benefits of various WAN technologies
- 1.6 Differentiate between common network topologies

Review Questions

1. Which of the following WAN links is most reliable?

   a. DSL

   b. PSTN

   c. ISDN

   d. SONET

2. Which of the following best describes the function of a CSU?

   a. It transmits several signals over a single channel.

   b. It separates a single channel into multiple channels.

   c. It terminates a digital signal and ensures connection integrity.

   d. It converts the digital signal used by connectivity devices into the digital signal sent through the cabling.

3. Which of the following WAN topologies is the least expensive to build?

   a. Star-wired ring

   b. Full-mesh

   c. Partial-mesh

   d. Star

4. Which of the following WAN topologies gives the most redundancy?

   a. Bus

   b. Partial-mesh

   c. Full-mesh

   d. Star

5. What is the maximum number of channels that a single T-1 can contain?

   a. 12

   b. 24

   c. 48

   d. 64

6. What is the maximum throughput of a T-3 line?

   a. 1.544 Mbps

   b. 45 Mbps

   c. 672 Mbps

   d. 275 Mbps

7. What does DSL use to achieve higher throughput than PSTN over the same lines?

   a. Full duplexing

   b. Data modulation

   c. Message switching

   d. Framing

8. Which of the following is the most expensive type of connection to install and lease?

   a. DSL

   b. ISDN

   c. T-1

   d. T-3

Lab 11.2 Connecting to the Internet with a Modem

Objectives

In this lab, you will make a connection to an ISP through a modem. Although higher-speed connections such as DSL or cable allow many people to connect more quickly to the Internet, dial-up connections to the Internet are still used in some areas and are often used as a backup method of remotely connecting to a server. Dial-up access using the Public Switched Telephone Network (PSTN), also known as the plain old telephone service (POTS), is still essential in many rural areas that do not yet have access to high-speed alternatives. In your work as a networking professional, you will find it valuable to understand how to configure and troubleshoot dial-up connections because some of your rural clients will rely on such connections for network access.

In many small networks, many or all users need at least occasional access to the Internet. Sharing a single Internet connection is cheaper and easier to configure than giving users their own modems and ISP accounts. Using Internet Connection Sharing (ICS), you can configure one modem on one computer and the rest of the office can connect through that computer. ICS will automatically configure the server to give DHCP addresses to workstations. Furthermore, you can configure the ICS server to dial the ISP connection whenever a workstation requests information on the Internet. However, a dial-up connection can quickly become congested as you add users so, if possible, most businesses will choose a high-speed connection option.

Additionally, ICS will automatically configure Network Address Translation (NAT) for the ISP connection. NAT allows an ICS server and any workstation using the ICS server to connect to the Internet to appear to the ISP as one IP address. Otherwise, you would need to arrange with the ISP for each workstation to have its own IP address. This would require additional configuration, as well as additional expense in many cases.

After completing this lab, you will be able to:

- Configure a dial-up connection to an ISP
- Share a dial-up Internet connection with a workstation

Materials Required

This lab will require the following:

- A computer running Windows 8.1 or Windows 7 named *WORKSTATION1* with a NIC configured with an IP address of 192.168.54.2 and a subnet mask of 255.255.255.0; no secondary IP addresses must be configured for this NIC
- A modem installed and configured on *WORKSTATION1*, without any location or Internet connection information configured
- Access to an analog outside phone line, or a digital-to-analog converter (to prevent the digital phone lines from ruining the modems)
- Knowledge of any additional number, such as 9, required to access the outside line
- The phone number of an ISP's dial-up pool, and a username and password for a valid account that does not require any advanced settings
- A computer running Windows 8.1 or Windows 7 named *WORKSTATION2* with a NIC, and configured with an IP address of 192.168.54.3 and a subnet mask of 255.255.255.0
- Administrative access to both computers
- Both computers connected to an Ethernet hub with straight-through Cat 5 (or better) UTP cables

Estimated completion time: **30 minutes**

Activity

1. Plug the RJ-11 connector on one end of the phone cable into the modem attached to *WORKSTATION1*. Plug the other end into the wall jack for the phone line.

2. Log on to *WORKSTATION1* as the administrator. The Windows desktop appears.

3. Open Control Panel, click **Network and Internet,** click **Network and Sharing Center,** and click **Set up a new connection or network**. The Set Up a Connection or Network window opens.

4. When you're asked to select a connection or network, make sure that the **Connect to the Internet** option is selected, and click **Next**.

5. Next, you are asked how you want to connect to the Internet. If necessary, click the **Dial-up** option.

6. Enter **Netplus Lab** in the Connection name text box.

7. Enter the phone number of the ISP in the Dial-up phone number text box. Include any additional digits needed, such as a 1, the area code, or any numbers (often a 9) required to use an outside phone line.

8. If necessary, select the **Allow other people to use this connection** option.

9. Enter the username in the User name text box, and enter the account's password in the Password text box.

10. Click **Create**, and then click **Close**.

11. If necessary, open Control Panel, click **Network and Internet**, and then click **Network and Sharing Center**.

12. Click **Change adapter settings**, click **Netplus Lab**, and then click **Change settings of this connection**. The Netplus Lab Properties dialog box opens.

13. Click the **Sharing** tab. The Sharing tab of the Netplus Lab Properties dialog box opens.

14. Click the **Allow other network users to connect through this computer's Internet connection** check box to place a checkmark in it, as shown in Figure 11-5.

15. Click **OK**. A dialog box might open, indicating that when Internet Connection Sharing is enabled, the NIC will be automatically configured with an IP address of 192.168.137.1 and that it might lose contact with other devices on the network.

16. Click **Yes**. If necessary, close the Netplus Lab Properties dialog box.

17. On *WORKSTATION2*, log on as an administrator. The Windows desktop appears.

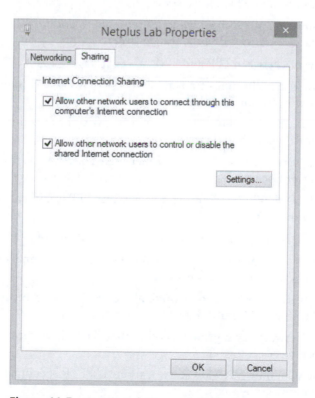

Figure 11-5   Netplus Lab Properties dialog box

18. Open Internet Explorer.

19. In the address box, type **www.microsoft.com** and press **Enter**. The modem attached to *WORKSTATION1* dials the ISP connection, and the Microsoft home page opens.

20. Log off both computers.

Certification Objectives

Objectives for the CompTIA Network+ Exam:

- 1.1 Explain the functions and applications of various network devices
- 1.4 Explain the characteristics and benefits of various WAN technologies

Review Questions

1. Which of the following best describes the asynchronous communications method?

   a. Data that is transmitted and received by nodes must conform to a timing scheme.

   b. Data that is transmitted and received by nodes does not have to conform to any timing scheme.

   c. Data that is transmitted and received by nodes is subject to resequencing by each connectivity device through which it passes.

   d. Data that is transmitted and received by nodes requires an additional sequencing bit to ensure that data is reassembled in the proper order.

2. What are two differences between PPP and SLIP?

   a. SLIP can handle only asynchronous transmission, whereas PPP can handle both asynchronous and synchronous transmission.

   b. SLIP encapsulates traffic according to its original Network layer protocol, whereas PPP masks SLIP traffic as IP-based data.

   c. SLIP cannot carry Network layer protocols other than TCP/IP, whereas PPP can carry any Network layer protocol.

   d. SLIP is compatible with only NetWare servers, whereas PPP is compatible with both NetWare and Windows computers.

3. Which of the following is one primary difference between PPP and PPTP?

   a. PPP can handle only asynchronous transmission, whereas PPTP can handle both asynchronous and synchronous transmission.

   b. PPP encapsulates traffic according to its original Network layer protocol, whereas PPTP masks PPP traffic as IP-based data.

   c. PPP cannot carry Network layer protocols other than TCP/IP, whereas PPTP can carry any Network layer protocol.

   d. PPP is compatible with only NetWare servers, whereas PPTP is compatible with both NetWare and Windows computers.

4. Which of the following is the most secure remote access protocol?

   a. SLIP

   b. PPP

   c. RAS

   d. PPTP

5. If your ISP uses DHCP to assign TCP/IP information to a dial-up connection, which of the following must you still specify in your connection parameters?

   a. The type of server into which you are dialing

   b. Your workstation's IP address

   c. The network's DHCP server address

   d. The network's subnet mask

Lab 11.3 Connecting to a Cisco Router with Telnet

Objectives

Most small home and office routers can be set up through a network using a Web-based browser like Internet Explorer. Commercial routers and switches, on the other hand, are usually configured using a command-line interface (CLI). The CLI is typically accessed through a network using a virtual terminal program such as Telnet or SSH or through a direct serial connection called the console port.

After completing this lab, you will be able to:

- Connect to a Cisco router using Telnet

Materials Required

This lab will require the following:

- An Ethernet switch or hub
- Two straight-through Cat 5 (or better) UTP cables
- A Cisco business-class router such as the Catalyst 2600 series with a password set for Telnet
- Administrative access to a computer running Windows 8.1 or Windows 7 on the same network as the router with the Telnet client installed

This lab could also be adapted to a virtual environment using network virtualization software, such as GNS3 or Cisco's Packet Tracer.

Estimated completion time: **20 minutes**

Activity

1. Connect one end of the straight-through cable to the Windows computer and connect the other end to the hub or switch.

2. Connect the other cable between the hub or switch and the first Ethernet port on the router.

3. Log on to the computer as the administrator. The Windows desktop appears.

4. Open a Command Prompt window.

5. At the command prompt, type **telnet**. The Telnet client opens, as pictured in Figure 11-6.

6. To connect to the router, type **open *x.x.x.x*** (where *x.x.x.x* is your router's IP address) and press **Enter**. A password prompt appears. Enter the router's password and press **Enter**.

7. To enter privileged mode, which allows you to carry out administrative tasks, type **enable** and press **Enter**.

8. Type **show version** to display the IOS version running on the router. Examine the output to determine what types of interfaces are available on your router.

9. You can gather additional information on the router's interfaces by typing **show interfaces**. What is the Internet address of your first Ethernet port?

10. Type **show running-config** to examine the router's current running configuration file. This command can be used to determine information such as the IP addresses of the Ethernet ports or the DHCP configuration. How is the duplex and speed configured on your router's first Ethernet port?

11. Many networking commands are also available in the IOS. You can test a connection between the router and another device with the ping command. Type **ping *x.x.x.x*** (where *x.x.x.x* is your computer's IP address) and press **Enter**. What was the average round-trip time (in milliseconds) between your router and your computer?

12. Type **quit** and press **Enter** to log off the router.

13. Type **exit** to close the Command Prompt window and log off the computer.

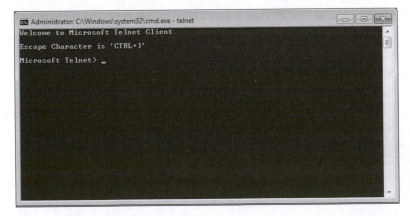

Figure 11-6 The Microsoft Telnet Client

Certification Objectives

Objectives for the CompTIA Network+ Exam:

- 1.1 Explain the functions and applications of various network devices

Review Questions

1. Routers operate at Layer _____ of the OSI model.

    a. 2

    b. 3

    c. 4

    d. 5

2. What CLI command would you use to test a connection between a router and another device on the network?

    a. `enable`

    b. `ping`

    c. `show interfaces`

    d. `show version`

3. What direct serial connection can be used to access routers that are not already part of a network?

    a. Console port

    b. Telnet

    c. SSH

    d. Ethernet port

4. A router determines logical addressing information by interpreting the contents of an incoming _____.

    a. datagram

    b. segment

    c. packet

    d. frame

5. Routers can perform all of the following tasks except:

    a. Connect dissimilar networks

    b. Determine the best path to send data

    c. Reroute traffic if the primary path is not available

    d. Interpret MAC address information

Lab 11.4 Connecting to a Cisco Router with a Terminal Emulator

Objectives

If a router is not already a member of your network, it can't be accessed through Telnet. In that case, you have to connect a computer directly to the console port of the router with a special cable and then use terminal emulation software such as Windows HyperTerminal or PuTTY. This is often required to initially configure a router as part of your local network.

In this lab, you will configure the router so it can be accessed through Telnet as in Lab 11.3.

After completing this lab, you will be able to:

- Connect directly to a router through the console port
- Configure a router using the command-line interface

Materials Required

This lab will require the following:

- A Cisco business-class router such as the Catalyst 2600 series
- A console management cable to connect a PC to the console port; the specifics of this cable may vary depending on your computer's configuration and may involve combining several devices such as a rollover cable, an RJ-45 to DB-9 adapter, and a serial to USB adapter
- Administrative access to a computer running Windows 8.1 or Windows 7
- Access to terminal emulation software such as HyperTerminal or PuTTY (free to download from *putty.org*)

Estimated completion time: **20 minutes**

Activity

1. Attach the console management cable to the console port of the router and the serial or USB port of the computer.
2. Log on to the computer as the administrator. The Windows desktop appears.
3. Open the terminal emulation client with the appropriate port settings for your router. For example, Figure 11-7 shows PuTTY configured to COM1, 9600bps, 8 data bits, no parity, 1 stop bit, and no flow control.
4. Press **Enter**. The router's prompt appears.
5. To examine a list of available CLI commands, type ? and press **Enter**.
6. To enter privileged mode, type **enable** and press **Enter**. How does the prompt change to let you know that you've enabled privileged mode?

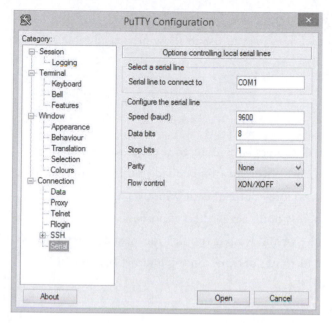

Figure 11-7   The PuTTY client

7. To enter global configuration mode, type **configure terminal** and press **Enter**. How does the prompt change to let you know that you're in global configuration mode?

8. Type **interface fastethernet0/0** and press **Enter** to enter the configuration mode for the first Ethernet port.

9. Type **ip address 192.168.54.254 255.255.255.0** to set the IP address of the first Ethernet port.

10. Type **exit** and press **Enter** to move back into the global configuration mode.

11. Type **line vty 0 4** and press **Enter** to enter configuration mode for the virtual terminal on the router.

12. Type **login local** and press **Enter** to allow users to log on through Telnet like in Lab 11.3.

13. Type **end** and press **Enter** to exit privileged mode.

14. Close the terminal emulation software and log off the computer.

Certification Objectives

Objectives for the CompTIA Network+ Exam:

- 1.1 Explain the functions and applications of various network devices
- 4.8 Given a scenario, troubleshoot and resolve common WAN issues

Review Questions

1. What symbol does the CLI use to show privileged mode?

    a. >

    b. <

    c. #

    d. %

2. Why can't all routers be configured through an Ethernet port?

    a. The Ethernet port must first be made a member of a local network.

    b. Telnet is no longer available in Windows 7.

    c. Most routers don't have Ethernet ports.

    d. The router's bandwidth is too fast for most computer NICs to handle.

3. What kind of router operates on the Internet backbone?

    a. Interior

    b. Exterior

    c. Border

    d. Gateway

4. What CLI command is used to enter privileged mode?

    a. `configure`

    b. `configure terminal`

    c. `reload`

    d. `enable`

5. Which CLI command shows a list of available commands?

    a. `?`

    b. `list`

    c. `line`

    d. `h`

Lab 11.5 Configuring a Cisco Router at the Command Line

Objectives

You need to configure an enterprise-level router before it can function in your network. Among other things, you need to name the router, assign passwords, and assign IP addresses to ports. This configuration is usually done at the command-line interface and then saved to nvram.

After completing this lab, you will be able to:

- Perform some basic router configuration using the command-line interface

Materials Required

This lab will require the following:

- An Ethernet switch
- Two straight-through Cat 5 (or better) UTP cables
- A Cisco business-class router such as the Catalyst 2600 series with a password set for Telnet
- Administrative access to a computer running Windows 8.1 or Windows 7 on the same network as the router

This lab could also be adapted to a virtual environment using network virtualization software, such as GNS3 or Cisco's Packet Tracer.

Estimated completion time: **20 minutes**

Activity

1. Connect one end of the straight-through cable to the Windows computer and connect the other end to the hub or switch.
2. Use the other cable to connect the hub or switch to the first Ethernet port on the router.
3. Log on to the computer as the administrator. The Windows desktop appears.
4. Open a Command Prompt window.
5. Use Telnet to connect to the router as you did in Lab 11.3. Then, to enter privileged mode, type **enable** and press **Enter**.
6. You can perform basic router configuration with the setup command. Type **setup** and press **Enter**.
7. The router's command-line interface (CLI) asks if you want to continue with the configuration. Type **yes** and press **Enter**.
8. The CLI asks if you would like to enter basic management setup. Type **no** and press **Enter**.
9. The CLI asks if you would first like to see the current interface summary. Type **yes** and press **Enter**.
10. The CLI displays the current status of the interfaces.
11. Type **ROUTER1** as the host name and press **Enter**.
12. Type **Password1** as the enable secret password, or choose a password of your own, and press **Enter**.
13. Type **Password2** as the enable password, or choose a password of your own, and press **Enter**.

14. Type **Password3** as the virtual terminal password, or choose a password of your own, and press **Enter**.

15. Type **FastEthernet0/0** and press **Enter**.

16. Type **yes** to configure IP on this interface and press **Enter**.

17. Type **192.168.54.254** as the IP address and press **Enter**.

18. To accept the default subnet mask of 255.255.255.0, press **Enter**.

19. The IOS creates a configuration script. Does it look like the Enable Password and Virtual Terminal Password are encrypted?

20. You do not want to save this configuration file, so press **0** and press **Enter**.

21. To examine the running-config file, type **show running-config** and press **Enter**. Note that the changes you made were not saved.

22. Type **quit** and press **Enter** to log off the router.

23. Type **exit** to close the Command Prompt window and log off the computer.

Certification Objectives

Objectives for the CompTIA Network+ Exam:

- 1.1 Explain the functions and applications of various network devices
- 4.8 Given a scenario, troubleshoot and resolve common WAN issues

Review Questions

1. Which CLI password is used to protect access to privileged executive mode?

   a. enable

   b. secret

   c. virtual terminal

   d. hidden

2. Where is the startup-config file saved on a router?

   a. nvram

   b. BIOS

   c. Hard drive

   d. Floppy drive

3. Why is it considered more secure to only use the enable secret password?

   a. Fewer passwords are easier to remember.

   b. It's the only password that can use complex characters.

   c. It's encrypted.

   d. It's disabled by default.

4. A router must be properly _____ to ensure it will work correctly in your network.

   a. shut down

   b. configured

   c. mounted

   d. throttled

5. What CLI command is used to exit privileged mode?

   a. `no mode`

   b. `demote`

   c. `demode`

   d. `exit`

Industrial and Enterprise Networking

Labs included in this chapter

- Lab 12.1 Creating a Project Plan
- Lab 12.2 Planning an Upgrade
- Lab 12.3 Observing a Network Upgrade
- Lab 12.4 Installing and Removing Updates on Windows Server
- Lab 12.5 Researching Network Solutions
- Lab 12.6 Managing Network Inventory

CompTIA Network+ Exam Objectives

Objective	Lab
2.5 Given a scenario, install and apply patches and updates	12.4
4.1 Given a scenario, implement the following network troubleshooting methodology	12.5
5.7 Given a scenario, install and configure equipment in the appropriate location using best practices	12.2
5.8 Explain the basics of change management procedures	12.1, 12.2, 12.3,12.6

Lab 12.1 Creating a Project Plan

Objectives

When planning a project—particularly a large, technical project—you must keep track of details pertaining not only to the hardware and software involved, but also to the people responsible for tasks, the time each task might take, and which tasks rely on other tasks. To track all these details, it's helpful to use project planning software.

Microsoft Office Project Professional 2013 is one of several project planning software packages available. An advantage of using such software is that it allows you to create charts and timelines easily. For example, you could create a Gantt chart that displays the timelines of all project tasks and illustrates relationships between the project tasks.

After completing this lab, you will be able to:

- Create a project plan using project planning software such as Microsoft Office Project Professional 2013

Materials Required

This lab will require the following:

- A Windows 8.1 or Windows 7 computer with Microsoft Office Project Professional 2013 installed

- Microsoft Office Project Professional 2013

If you don't have access to Microsoft Office Project Professional 2013, you could use an earlier version, such as the 60-day free trial of Project Professional 2010, which is available for download from Microsoft.com. You could also use an open source alternative such as ProjectLibre from *www.projectlibre.org*.

- Access to the Windows computer as an ordinary user

Estimated completion time: **20 minutes**

Activity

1. In this lab, you will use Microsoft Office Project Professional 2013 to create a Gantt chart, which provides a graphical diagram of a project. Review the task list in Table 12-1.

2. Log on to the Windows computer. The Windows desktop appears.

3. Launch Microsoft Office Project Professional 2013.

Table 12-1   Project task list

Number	Task description	Predecessors	Duration
1	Order and ship server hardware	None	7 days
2	Order and ship server software	None	7 days
3	Install server hardware	1	1 day
4	Install server software	2, 3	1 day
5	Add server to LAN	4	1 day

© Cengage Learning.

4. If a new project does not open, click the **File** tab, click **New**, and then click **Blank project**. Under Available Template, click **Create**. A new project opens.

5. On the left side of the window, look for the Task Name column. You can enter task information in this column. On the right side of the window, a chart will appear after tasks have been entered, marking the tasks on the calendar with boxes and showing precedence information.

6. In the Task Name column, enter the first task description given in Table 12-1 and press **Tab**.

7. If necessary, click the cell in the Duration column next to the first entry you've made. Up and down arrows appear in the cell. Click the up arrow until the duration matches the number of days given for that task in Table 12-1.

8. In the Predecessors column, enter the appropriate numbers from the Predecessors column in Table 12-1. (Leave the column blank if Table 12-1 indicates that the task has no predecessors.)

9. Right-click the first task and click **Information** from the shortcut menu. The Task Information dialog box opens.

10. Click the **Resources** tab. In the top line of the Resources text box, enter your name or the name of your lab partner and then click the **green check mark**.

11. Click **OK**. The name you entered in Step 10 appears in the chart in the right pane of the Microsoft Project window.

12. Repeat Steps 6 through 11 with the remaining tasks. When repeating Step 8, be sure to enter the appropriate information in the Predecessors column.

13. Click the **File** tab, and then click **Save As**. The Save As dialog box opens.

14. Enter a unique filename in the File name text box. Click **Save**. The computer saves your project.

15. Close Microsoft Project and log off the computer.

Certification Objectives

Objectives for the CompTIA Network+ Exam:

- 5.8 Explain the basics of change management procedures

Review Questions

1. You are a network administrator managing a network backbone upgrade. Your supervisor has scheduled a meeting to discuss the project's status with you. What is the advantage of taking a Gantt chart to the meeting?

   a. A Gantt chart will help the supervisor better understand the project's costs.

   b. A Gantt chart will determine the maximum possible amount of each employee's time to be spent on each task.

   c. A Gantt chart will allow the supervisor to see timelines of each task in addition to the project as a whole.

   d. A Gantt chart will demonstrate why some tasks have taken longer to complete than first anticipated.

2. The task that must be completed before another task is begun is called a(n) _____.

   a. successor

   b. predecessor

   c. antecedent

   d. dependent

3. In a significant network upgrade project, which of the following tasks takes place first?

   a. Identify which tasks are dependent on other tasks.

   b. Complete a needs assessment survey.

   c. Test the proposed solution on a pilot network.

   d. Assign tasks to the most qualified or appropriate people on the project team.

4. Which of the following best describes contingency planning?

   a. Obtaining support from high-level project sponsors before committing resources to the project

   b. Installing identical software and hardware, on a smaller scale, as the project's proposed solution will require, to test the feasibility of the solution

   c. Identifying a team and assigning roles to that team in case of disaster

   d. Identifying steps that will minimize the impact of unforeseen obstacles

5. True or False? One way of predicting how long a task might take is by examining the time taken to complete previous similar tasks.

Lab 12.2 Planning an Upgrade

Objectives

Even when you make relatively minor changes, a project plan can be helpful. The potential benefits include minimizing downtime, creating an efficient implementation, and planning for when something goes wrong. For instance, a project plan for changing the NIC on a server might include contingency plans in case the new NIC is defective, the NIC is accidentally damaged during installation, or the server does not boot after installation. Alternately, a configuration change made on a remote router might cut you off from the router. By including contingency plans in your project plan, you prepare yourself to solve problems quickly and efficiently.

In environments in which downtime must be minimized at all costs, contingency planning is even more important. Although the odds of a problem occurring might be low, you must be prepared just in case. During a server upgrade, for example, you might have a spare server ready in case the server fails. (Note that you can also use network design to minimize potential downtime. For instance, you might use redundant servers.)

In this lab, you will create a project plan for replacing the NIC in a Windows Server 2012 R2 computer. Your project plan should include a task breakdown, which divides the project into smaller parts, and a list of dependencies—that is, a list of tasks that depend on the completion of previous tasks. Your contingency planning should cover situations such as a defective NIC, drivers that are not available for the NIC, a NIC or server that is damaged during installation, and a server that cannot boot after installation of the NIC. Also include a testing plan, in which you outline your plans for determining whether the project or change was successful and whether the results of the project include any unforeseen side effects. Finally, your plan should contain a timeline, the resources required, and the project milestones.

After completing this lab, you will be able to:

- Make a project for a network upgrade
- Perform a network upgrade

Materials Required

This lab will require the following:

- Pencil and paper, or planning software such as Microsoft Office Project Professional 2013

 **NOTE** If you don't have access to Microsoft Office Project Professional 2013, you could use an earlier version, such as the 60-day free trial of Project Professional 2010, which is available for download from Microsoft.com. You could also use an open source alternative such as ProjectLibre from *www.projectlibre.org*.

- A computer running Windows Server 2012 R2 named *SERVER1*, configured as a domain controller for the netpluslab.net domain with an IP address of 192.168.54.1 and a subnet mask of 255.255.255.0
- A shared folder on *SERVER1* named *NETPLUS*
- Access as the administrator to *SERVER1*
- An extra NIC or USB network adapter (with a driver disk, if necessary)
- A computer running Windows 8 or Windows 7.1 named *WORKSTATION1*, configured as a member of the netpluslab.net domain, with an IP address of 192.168.54.3 and a subnet mask of 255.255.255.0
- An ordinary user account in the Domain Users group in the netpluslab.net domain
- Both computers connected to a hub with straight-through Cat 5 (or better) UTP cables
- A toolkit with a Phillips screwdriver, a ground mat, and a ground strap

Estimated completion time: **60 minutes**

12

Activity

1. First, you will verify that the network works properly. Log on to *WORKSTATION1* with an ordinary user account. The Windows desktop appears.

2. Click the **File Explorer** icon on the task bar. The This PC window opens. (In Windows 7, click **Start** and click **Computer**. The Computer window opens.)

3. Click the **Computer** tab, and then click **Map network drive** on the toolbar. The Map Network Drive dialog box opens.

4. If necessary, select **Z:** (or another available drive letter) from the Drive drop-down menu. In the Folder text box, type **\\192.168.54.1\netplus** and click **Finish**. The computer maps the NETPLUS shared folder.

5. If necessary, return to This PC (or Computer). The netplus on '192.168.54.1' (Z:) icon now appears below *Network Drives*.

6. Right-click the **netplus on '192.168.54.1' (Z:)** icon and click **Disconnect** from the shortcut menu. The drive mapping disappears as the computer disconnects the network drive.

7. On a separate piece of paper, or in project planning software such as Microsoft Office Project Professional 2013 or ProjectLibre, write the project plan that will cover the activities in Steps 8 through 17. Use Steps 2 through 5 as your testing plan.

8. Power down *SERVER1* and remove the power cable. Place the computer on the ground mat.

9. Place the ground strap on your wrist and attach the strap to the ground mat underneath the computer.

10. Remove any screws, as necessary, to open the cover of the computer case.

11. Remove the computer case cover.

12. Unscrew the NIC from its slot in the computer, and carefully remove it.

13. Place the new NIC in the slot.

14. Attach the NIC to the system unit using the Phillips screwdriver to secure the NIC in place.

15. Replace the computer case and reinsert any screws you removed in Step 10. Remove the ground strap and the ground mat.

16. Plug in the computer and turn it on.

17. To verify that the network is working properly, perform the steps in your testing plan.

18. Review your project plan and note anything that did not work according to the plan.

Certification Objectives

Objectives for the CompTIA Network+ Exam:

- 5.7 Given a scenario, install and configure equipment in the appropriate location using best practices
- 5.8 Explain the basics of change management procedures

Review Questions

1. Which of the following tools might you use to assess the success of a project whose purpose is to upgrade an entire network from 100 Mbps to 1000 Mbps?

    a. Network Monitor

    b. Sniffer or packet analyzer

    c. Microsoft SQL Server

    d. System Monitor

2. What is the purpose of identifying milestones in a project plan?

    a. They indicate when project staff changes must occur.

    b. They mark significant events of the project's progress.

    c. They offer a quick assessment of how successfully the project is staying within budget.

    d. They help predict the result of a project.

3. Which of the following are examples of resources related to a project plan that proposes to upgrade the network cards inside each workstation on a network from 100 Mbps to 1000 Mbps? (Choose all that apply.)

    a. NIC device drivers

    b. A team member's time

    c. IP addresses

    d. NICs

    e. Switches

4. Which of the following are examples of stakeholders of a project whose purpose is to upgrade an entire network from 100 Mbps to 1000 Mbps? (Choose all that apply.)

    a. Network users

    b. Software vendors of applications running on the client machines

    c. High-level managers who approved the project

    d. IT staff who helped implement the change

    e. Network cabling vendors

5. Which of the following obstacles could halt or seriously impair the progress of a project whose purpose is to upgrade the NICs in all workstations on a network from 100 Mbps to 1000 Mbps?

    a. The use of two different NIC models

    b. The use of different installation personnel on different shifts

    c. Management's requirement that the cost of each NIC remain under $75

    d. A large group of defective NICs

Lab 12.3 Observing a Network Upgrade

Objectives

Observing a network upgrade will help you appreciate the complexities that can arise in a real-world situation. Depending on the project, you might be able to observe only a small part of an upgrade at any one time. For larger projects, the networking professional is more likely to have a formal project plan; for smaller projects, the plan might be very informal.

After completing this lab, you will be able to:

- Explain how a network upgrade is performed

Materials Required

This lab will require the following:

- Pencil and paper
- A person (such as a network professional) willing to allow you to observe a network upgrade
- If you are unable to visit another location, an instructor can play the role of a network administrator and demonstrate a network upgrade in the classroom environment
- Alternatively, you can search "network upgrade" on YouTube and watch a suitable video

Estimated completion time: **2 hours**

Activity

1. Visit the site where the network upgrade will be performed.
2. Ask the network engineer who is allowing you to observe the upgrade to discuss any project plans that might be used during the upgrade.
3. Ask the network engineer to discuss any contingency planning that might have been done as part of the upgrade.
4. Record any changes occurring at the site. For example, the upgrade might involve replacing Cat 5 cable with Cat 6 cable. Another change might involve altering the IP addressing scheme.
5. Record the time required for the network upgrade.
6. Write a letter or email thanking the network engineer who allowed you to observe the upgrade.

Certification Objectives

Objectives for the CompTIA Network+ Exam:

- 5.8 Explain the basics of change management procedures

Review Questions

1. In a very large company (for example, one with over 10,000 employees), which of the following staff is most likely to decide whether a project such as an entire network upgrade will be funded?

    a. Network administrator

    b. Personnel director

    c. Chief information officer

    d. Accountant

2. Which of the following best describes project management?

    a. Recording and analyzing the time and resources required for each task in a project

    b. Assessing network statistics before and after a project is completed

    c. Monitoring the needs of users prior to the beginning of a project, then later assessing how the project's completion met their needs

    d. Planning for and handling the steps required to accomplish a goal in a systematic way

3. Which of the following projects is most likely to be driven by a company's security needs?

    a. Doubling the RAM in a key file server

    b. Installing a firewall on a connection to the Internet

    c. Upgrading the version of client software on each workstation

    d. Changing from the use of static IP addressing to DHCP on an entire network

4. What is one good technique for assessing the feasibility of a suggested project deadline before the project begins?

    a. Begin calculating task timelines from the deadline, working back to the start of a project.

    b. Issue a survey to key staff asking their opinion of the suggested deadline.

    c. Use the Web to research similar projects completed by other companies.

    d. Calculate the ratio of the number of project milestones to the proposed project duration, in months, to check that it does not exceed 2:1.

5. Which of the following situations might necessitate changing all the IP addresses on a company's networked workstations?

    a. The company has divided its network into several smaller subnets.

    b. The company has hired 50 new employees.

    c. The company has decided to use Network Address Translation (NAT) for all connections to public networks.

    d. The company has decided to establish a Web server with e-commerce capability.

Lab 12.4 Installing and Removing Updates on Windows Server

Objectives

Keeping software up to date on both servers and network devices is an important part of maintaining and upgrading a network. Usually software updates consist of patches or other fixes to problems that users and administrators have encountered when using the software. In other cases, a software update might solve a potential security problem, or it might even add a new feature.

Microsoft typically releases its software updates in one of two forms. The first form is a hot fix, which is an update to a specific piece of software, often used to correct a specific problem. For instance, a hot fix might solve a problem with Internet Information Services (IIS), which is the Web server sold by Microsoft. The second form is a service pack, which is a group of numerous software updates. You might install a service pack as part of a server's regular maintenance.

Both forms of updates are accessible through the Microsoft Windows Update service. Additionally, you can automate the installation of hot fixes so that no administrator intervention is required. Automatic updates can often prevent security problems from occurring because they fix security vulnerabilities as soon as they are discovered. However, a software update might cause problems. For instance, you might run a certain application on your Windows Server. If this application relies on a piece of software that has been changed in a service pack or hot fix, the application might no longer work after the update has been applied. As a result, you might have to backlevel, or revert to the previous version of the software, after the upgrade. Thus, if at all possible, you should verify that a software upgrade will work in a test environment prior to applying it to production machines. Additionally, you should carefully consider the implications before scheduling automatic updates on important servers. Automatic updates are more safely scheduled for workstations, but it is also possible that an update installed automatically could cause problems on all workstations in your organization. You should carefully weigh the benefits of scheduling automatic updates before you implement them.

After completing this lab, you will be able to:

- Install updates to a computer running Windows Server
- Remove updates from a computer running Windows Server

Materials Required

This lab will require the following:

- A computer running Windows Server 2012 R2 with access to the Internet
- At least one update or hot fix that needs to be installed on the computer
- Administrator access to the computer

Most of the steps in this lab can also be completed in a virtual environment using virtualization software such as VMware.

Estimated completion time: **30 minutes**

Activity

1. Log on to the server as the administrator. The Windows Server Manager opens.

2. Open Control Panel, click **System and Security**, and then click **Windows Update** to open the Windows Update window shown in Figure 12-1.

3. Click **Check for updates** in the left pane. The Windows Update dialog box indicates that it is checking for updates.

4. When Windows has finished checking for updates, you're presented with the number of important and optional updates that are available.

5. Choose the update you want to install by clicking on the check box and then click the **Install** button.

6. If necessary, select **I accept the license terms** and click **Finish**.

NOTE Depending on the updates required, the installation process might vary somewhat from this step. Often not all of the required updates can be installed at the same time. Some of the updates might require other updates to be installed first and the computer rebooted before they can be installed. As a result, you might have to update your computer in stages.

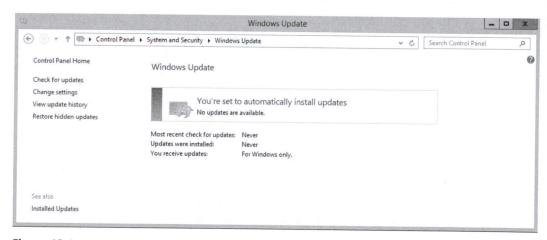

Figure 12-1   Microsoft Windows Update

7. If Windows indicates that you need to restart the computer to finish installing the updates, click **OK**. After the computer reboots, log back on as the administrator.

8. Now you will remove an update added earlier. Open Control Panel, click **Programs**, and then click **Programs and Features**.

9. Click **View installed updates** in the left pane. A list of installed updates appears, as shown in Figure 12-2.

10. A number of hot fixes are listed, followed by the number of a Microsoft Knowledge Base article describing the problem solved by the hot fix. Select a hot fix chosen by your instructor or pick one at random.

11. Search the Microsoft Knowledge Base at http://support.microsoft.com for the hot fix you've chosen. Try to determine what issues are resolved with this update.

12. Click **Uninstall** for the selected hot fix and then click **Yes**. Windows begins to remove the hot fix. Depending on the hot fix to be removed, additional steps might be required.

13. If a dialog box opens, indicating that some programs might not function properly after the removal of the hot fix, click **Yes**. The wizard finishes.

14. Click **Finish**. The wizard closes.

15. Repeat Steps 2 through 7 to reapply any necessary hot fixes.

Certification Objectives

Objectives for the CompTIA Network+ Exam:

- 2.5 Given a scenario, install and apply patches and updates

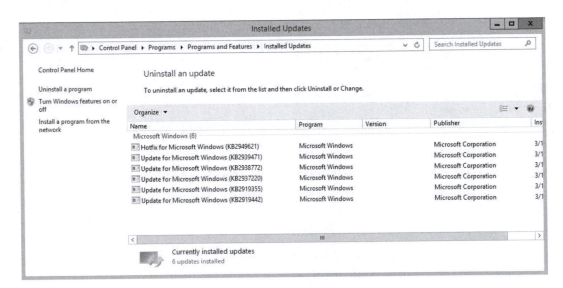

Figure 12-2 Installed Updates window

Review Questions

1. In Microsoft terminology, what is a hot fix?

    a. A patch that replaces all or a portion of the NOS

    b. A patch that requires that the server be connected to the Microsoft Web site as it is installed

    c. A patch that updates a specific type of software, often the operating system

    d. A patch that can be installed while users are logged on without causing adverse effects

2. In which of the following situations would it be wise to backlevel?

    a. You have just performed a complete backup of your server's data directories, and you cannot confirm that the backup was successful.

    b. You have just applied a fix to your network operating system (NOS) and have discovered that the fix resulted in a lack of network access for half of your users.

    c. You have just installed a database program on one of your servers and have discovered that you neglected to install an optional component that your users will need.

    d. You have just installed Windows Server 2012 R2 on a new computer and you cannot get the operating system to recognize the NIC.

3. Which two of the following can typically be accomplished by applying a patch to an NOS?

    a. Replacing all the NOS's program files

    b. Modifying an existing feature

    c. Removing an old feature

    d. Fixing a known bug

4. Before installing a major NOS patch, you should _____.

    a. remove all protocols installed on the server

    b. prevent users from logging on

    c. disable Internet services

    d. disable network connectivity

5. What is the primary difference between a software upgrade and a patch?

    a. The software manufacturer issues a patch, whereas an upgrade may be issued by any organization that has the software's source code.

    b. A patch fixes a specific part of a software program, whereas an upgrade typically replaces much or all of a software program.

    c. A patch typically does not require that the network administrator test its changes before applying it to a server; an upgrade does.

    d. A patch typically is not supported by the software manufacturer; an upgrade is.

Lab 12.5 Researching Network Solutions

Objectives

In this lab, you will research network solutions by examining business case studies on vendor Web sites. By examining these case studies, you can get an idea of how each vendor uses its product line to help customers solve problems or fulfill business needs. It is important to keep in mind, however, that few vendors are objective about their products. When considering a solution, you should look for information from multiple sources. Additionally, you might find it helpful to talk to someone who has attempted to implement a solution such as the one you are considering.

When looking at case studies, you will often find it helpful to look for organizations that are similar to your own. For instance, a large bank with thousands of employees and a high-security network environment is likely to have different needs than a small, nonprofit organization. Seeing how an organization similar to your own has solved certain problems might help you solve similar problems in your organization.

It is also important to try to anticipate future network trends when researching network solutions. A solution that might help you solve future problems will tend to be more cost effective in the long run than a solution that only addresses an immediate problem. For instance, suppose you are researching software packages that diagnose potential problems in business productivity software on user workstations. If you have noticed a trend toward greater user support of personal digital assistant (PDA) applications, then software packages that also diagnose potential problems in PDA software might prove more useful than ones that do not.

After completing this lab, you will be able to:

- Review case studies of networking companies
- Identify the needs of the customer in a case study
- Identify the solutions provided by the networking companies

Materials Required

This lab will require the following:

- Pencil and paper
- A computer with Internet access
- An ordinary user account on the computer

Estimated completion time: **20 minutes**

Activity

1. Log on to Windows as an ordinary user. The Windows desktop appears.
2. Perform whatever steps are necessary for the computer to access the Internet.
3. Open your Web browser.

4. Go to microsoft.com.

5. In the Search text box, type **case study**, and then press **Enter**. A list of links for this search term appears.

6. Select a case study from the search results by clicking the case study's title. The case study's page appears. Scroll through the page and read the details of the study. Record the name of the customer and the type of business you reviewed.

7. Record background information on the company in the case study. This information might include the type of business, its size, and the networking hardware or software used.

8. Record the business need or challenge for the company (that is, the customer) in the case study.

9. Record the Microsoft solution. Be sure to identify the software or hardware solution used.

10. Record the results of the solution.

11. Do you agree with this solution? Is there anything you would add or do differently?

12. Close your Web browser.

Certification Objectives

Objectives for the CompTIA Network+ Exam:

- 4.1 Given a scenario, implement the following network troubleshooting methodology

Review Questions

1. You work for the Best Roast Coffee Company, which has 100 employees in nine retail stores. You are looking at case studies for a product you are researching. Which of the following case studies is most likely to be helpful?

   a. A case study for an automobile manufacturer with hundreds of thousands of employees

   b. A candy maker with 200 employees that sells candy in 13 malls across the country

   c. An insurance company with thousands of employees in three locations, plus hundreds of agents all over the country

   d. A small school district with 300 employees and 10,000 students

2. You are trying to decide whether to purchase a software package from a vendor. Who among the following is most likely to provide objective information about the software package?

   a. The vendor's sales staff

   b. A business partner of the vendor

   c. A current customer of the vendor

   d. A vendor who makes a competing product

3. You are researching a new Internet access router for your company's network. You have also noticed a trend toward greater use of your company's network resources from home. Given this, which of the following features would you expect to be most valuable in a new Internet access router?

   a. Support for additional routing protocols

   b. Support for virtual private networks

   c. Support for additional security features

   d. Support for multiple protocols

4. When implementing a network solution, why is it important to anticipate future trends as much as possible?

   a. So that the solutions you implement meet the future needs of your users

   b. So that the solutions you implement meet the current needs of your users

   c. So that the solutions you implement are more scalable

   d. So that you can justify the purchase of the solution to management

5. When investigating a network solution, which two of the following should you do?

   a. Get information about possible solutions from only one source.

   b. Get information about possible solutions from multiple sources.

   c. Look at the product lines from only one vendor.

   d. Talk to someone who has implemented a similar solution.

Lab 12.6 Managing Network Inventory

Objectives

Managing network assets is an important role of a network manager. This includes taking an inventory of all of the network's physical components as well as network software and configuration. This information can be recorded in a document or, more often, managed with specialized software. In this lab, you will use a network asset management system to inventory part of a network. To complete this lab, you will inventory the components of your classroom or home network.

After completing this lab, you will be able to:

- Identify hardware and software components of a network
- Use an asset management system to track network inventory

Materials Required

This lab will require the following:

- A computer running Windows 8.1 or Windows 7 with Internet access
- An administrative account on the computer

Estimated completion time: **30 minutes**

Activity

1. Log on to Windows as an administrator. The Windows desktop appears.

2. Download and install the free version of Network Inventory Advisor 4.3 from **network-inventory-advisor.com**.

3. Run the Network Inventory Advisor and click **Continue trial** and preconfigure the software for your network.

4. If necessary, click **Network summary** in the left pane. The Network Inventory Advisor displays a network summary, as shown in Figure 12-3.

5. In the left pane, select your computer. The Network Inventory Advisor displays an asset snapshot of your computer.

6. Ensure that Node summary is selected in the right pane and scroll down in the center pane to the software section. What antivirus did it record for your system?

7. Now click **License audit** in the right pane. Were there any product keys that could not be determined?

8. Click on the **Reports** tab at the top. Select **Inventory** from the predefined reports and click **OK**. How many assets does your inventory include?

9. Close Network Inventory Advisor and log off your computer.

Certification Objectives

Objectives for the CompTIA Network+ Exam:

- 5.8 Explain the basics of change management procedures

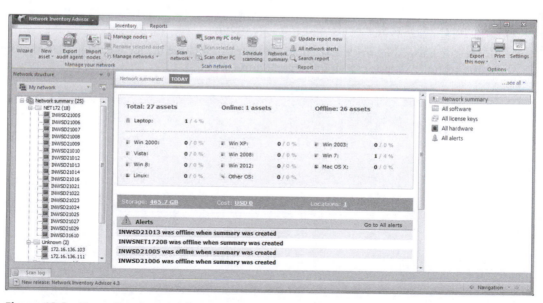

Figure 12-3   Network Inventory Advisor

Review Questions

1. The hardware devices attached to a network such as computers and printers are also called _____.

   a. communication endpoints

   b. nodes

   c. connection points

   d. contacts

2. Asset management records should be available to _____.

   a. all personnel involved in maintaining the network

   b. only the system administrator

   c. everyone in the organization

   d. anyone

3. Who is protected by documenting hardware and software changes?

   a. Users

   b. Managers

   c. The organization

   d. All of the above

4. When should changes be made to the asset management database?

   a. Monthly

   b. Weekly

   c. Daily

   d. As changes to hardware and software occur

5. True or False? Network asset management can include device locations, serial numbers, and technical support contact information.

Notes

Notes

Notes

Notes